This book has built hope in my own heart as I read and prayed. We all face a paradoxical choice: Either we live in our own strength or die to self and taste the divine. With the divine life, we begin to love the way Jesus loves. Read and grow.

—**GARY HARPST,** AUTHOR OF *EXECUTION REVOLUTION*, A
NEW YORK TIMES BESTSELLER

If there ever was an opportunity for the global church to respond, it's now. To do that, God's people must be real disciples—in love with Jesus and sharing his story. This book cuts to the heart of this challenge. May you be blessed as you read, reflect, and take personal action.

—**PHILL BUTLER,** FOUNDER AND SENIOR STRATEGIC ADVISOR OF
VISIONSYNERGY; PREVIOUS FOUNDER AND DIRECTOR OF INTERDEV AND
INTERCRISTO; AUTHOR OF *WELL CONNECTED*

This book shows us what it takes to be a true disciple of Jesus. It is my prayer that the stories of this book will not only inspire you but also challenge you to multiply your influence by making more disciple-makers for the Great Commission.

—**BEKELE SHANKO,** VICE PRESIDENT FOR GLOBAL CHURCH
MOVEMENTS, CRU; PRESIDENT, GLOBAL ALLIANCE FOR CHURCH
MULTIPLICATION (GACX); AUTHOR OF *NEVER ALONE: FROM ETHIOPIA VILLAGE
TO GLOBAL LEADER*

Ordinary Disciples, Extraordinary Influence recounts inspiring stories of men and women around the world who are transforming their communities with God's love, evidenced in relationships restored, bodies healed, and bonds broken. God is at work through ordinary disciples, and this book will encourage and prepare you to become one of them: a disciple-making disciple who brings God's hope to a hurting world.

—**PETER GREER,** PRESIDENT AND CEO, HOPE INTERNATIONAL;
COAUTHOR OF *MISSION DRIFT*

Galen and Tefera take us on a remarkable journey across Africa, Asia, and Latin America where we meet a new generation of disciples who are multiplying the church like modern-day Acts. As American Christians, we have so much to learn from these ordinary men and women whom God is using to do extraordinary things as they sacrificially follow Christ. Through powerful stories, discipleship principles, and thoughtful questions, you'll be challenged to re-think what it means to be a disciple who makes disciples.

—**KÄRIN BUTLER PRIMUTH,** CEO OF VISIONSYNERGY, DEDICATED TO
EQUIPPING MISSION LEADERS FOR COLLABORATION TO ACCELERATE THE
GREAT COMMISSION

What an encouraging and challenging book! I love the work of Global Disciples in Africa, but this is for North America. Here are stories of miraculous church growth flowing out of costly discipleship. This is evidence of what Jesus does with people who are completely sold out to him. Galen and Tefera ask: "Might the same happen in North America?" Here is a call to renewed discipleship, a closer walk with Jesus, a seeking after the Lord's heart. I highly recommend it.

—**LUKE HERRIN,** INTERNATIONAL DIRECTOR, AIM (AFRICA INLAND
MISSION INTERNATIONAL); MISSIONARY DOCTOR AND DISCIPLE-MAKER IN
MUSLIM COUNTRIES OF AFRICA

I love this book! Galen and Tefera have crafted this amazing resource that helps us refocus on our kingdom identity in Christ. The global God-stories are eye-opening, riveting, and convicting. Reading this book made me want to be more like Jesus. *Ordinary Disciples, Extraordinary Influence* is a must-read for every believer who desires to make a difference in this world.

—**LARRY KREIDER,** INTERNATIONAL DIRECTOR OF DOVE
INTERNATIONAL, LITITZ, PENNSYLVANIA; AUTHOR OF *HOUSE TO HOUSE; THE
CRY FOR SPIRITUAL FATHERS AND MOTHERS*; AND OTHER TITLES

Of the many ideas that Jesus introduced in the first century, discipleship is among the most important. This book will give you fuel to continue an ever-deepening relationship with the Author and Perfector of our faith.

—**TED ESLER,** PHD; PRESIDENT, MISSIONEXUS, ORLANDO, FLORIDA;
AUTHOR OF *THE INNOVATION CRISIS* AND *OVERWHELMING MINORITY*

Galen and Tefera give every earnest Christ-follower an urgent, raw, deeply moving, and utterly practical resource for disciple-making. Their storytelling is emotional, gripping, and thrilling to experience. Their teaching is compelling, simple, and immensely practical. And their purpose is to winsomely invite us to become more effectual in reaching those who are spiritually lost. This is easily the best book I've read in several years, and I urge you to read it, share it broadly, and take it deeply to heart!

—**DR. JOHN STAHL-WERT,** FOUNDER OF CENTER FOR SERVING LEADERSHIP, A GLOBAL LEADERSHIP DEVELOPMENT COMPANY; AUTHOR AND COAUTHOR, INCLUDING THE INTERNATIONAL BESTSELLER, *THE SERVING LEADER*

When the two key strands of discipleship DNA are the trustful submission of all of life to Christ and an eagerness to share good news with those who haven't heard, the church becomes a dynamic engine of God's mission. Galen and Tefera lived and learned the effectiveness of Jesus' vision for disciple-making among peoples of the world otherwise little reached with the gospel. Now they're passing it on to us.

—**TIM CROUCH,** VICE PRESIDENT FOR ALLIANCE MISSIONS, CHRISTIAN & MISSIONARY ALLIANCE, USA

Unprecedented times call for unconventional strategies in maintaining the biblical mandate of disciple-making. These impacting stories of persons taking quantum leaps of faith to follow Jesus represent a fresh wind and fresh fire sometimes lacking in our North American church and theological institutions. This book is a clarion call for the church to revisit its roots by building God's kingdom through disciple-making.

—**DR. LAWRENCE F. CHILES,** ADJUNCT PROFESSOR, PRACTICAL THEOLOGY, LANCASTER BIBLE COLLEGE PHILADELPHIA CAMPUS; OVERSEER OF KOINONIA FELLOWSHIP OF CHURCHES

This book provides answers to the five Ws—Who, What, Where, When, and Why of being a global disciple of Jesus Christ. It is filled with kingdom principles illustrated with real-life stories from around the world. Galen and

Tefera have a keen understanding of global missions as they lovingly serve strategic leaders having significant impact on the frontlines. Although the stories are from everywhere, the book has a deeply personal message with practical tips on being a true disciple of our Master.

—**JOSEPH VIJAYAM,** CEO, OLIVE TECHNOLOGY;
LAUSANNE CATALYST FOR WORKPLACE MINISTRY;
EDITOR, *THE SCROLL: A COMPENDIUM OF INDIA INQUIRY*

Building on a solid biblical foundation, Galen and Tefera provide an engaging roadmap for discipleship. The local and global church needs this book and its gentle yet compelling reminder to be Jesus-centered, kingdom focused, self-sacrificing and Word-anchored if we are going to impact the world around us with the gospel and help fulfill the Great Commission in our lifetime.

—**RICK FRANKLIN,** PHD; VICE PRESIDENT, ARROW LEADERSHIP,
DEVELOPING JESUS-CENTERED LEADERS FOR GREATER KINGDOM IMPACT

If we in the North American church will live the principles and practices described in *Ordinary Disciples, Extraordinary Influence,* we will no doubt experience similar stories of multiplication and miracles. Simple, reproducible, "off-stage" disciple-making works as well today as it did when Jesus first introduced it.

—**JOE SHOWALTER,** PRESIDENT, ROSEDALE INTERNATIONAL;
COORDINATOR OF THE COLUMBUS NETWORK
OF MICROCHURCHES, COLUMBUS, OHIO

Galen and Tefera recount the dynamic and compelling stories of surrendered and Holy Spirit-empowered believers around the world. But be forewarned, *Ordinary Disciples, Extraordinary Influence* isn't a book about others. Rather, it's an invitation for each of us to experience extraordinary influence through a willingness to follow Christ, no matter the cost.

—**DR. CRAIG SIDER,** CEO, MOVEMENT.ORG, BRINGING TOGETHER
CHRISTIAN BUSINESS, NON-PROFIT AND CHURCH LEADERS TO ADDRESS
ACUTE SPIRITUAL AND SOCIAL NEEDS OF OVER 900
CITIES AROUND THE WORLD

ORDINARY DISCIPLES

Stories to **Fuel** a **Life** of **Unshakable** Faith

EXTRAORDINARY INFLUENCE

Galen Burkholder & Brother Tefera

100 MOVEMENTS PUBLISHING

First published in 2022 by 100 Movements Publishing
www.100Mpublishing.com

ISBN (Print) 978-1-955142-10-6
ISBN (ebook) 978-1-955142-11-3

100 Movements Publishing
An imprint of Movement Leaders Collective
Cody, Wyoming

www.movementleaderscollective.com
www.catalysechange.org

To the ordinary disciples who are living out the hard stories and whose examples of faith and obedience soften our hearts and inspire us to be more like Jesus.

CONTENTS

FOREWORD
Alan Hirsch

Most of us are familiar with the adage, "Out of sight, out of mind." We tend to give little thought to events and circumstances that are not part of our immediate world. Yet sometimes it's important to draw our attention to what is out of sight, and that's exactly what this book does. Galen and Tefera share what God is doing through the work of Global Disciples in the southern hemisphere, work that is normally beyond our frame of reference. These are not just statistics we can neatly compartmentalize and forget about. These are real stories from real disciples; people with names, faces, and narratives that have the potential to wake us from our somewhat anaesthetized forms of Western Christianity.

Educator, activist, and writer Terry Tempest Williams once said, "Stories have the power to create social change and inspire community."[1] In my book *Reframation*, I explore the idea that if we are to effectively share the gospel in a Western context, we need to be prepared to tell a bigger gospel story, and to not only *tell* a bigger story but to *demonstrate* a credible expression of the gospel with our lives:

It is *love* that is the final defense of the faith. Jesus himself actually expected

---

[1] Michael Austin, ed., *A Voice in the Wilderness: Conversations with Terry Tempest Williams* (Utah: Utah State University Press, 2006), 173.

no other kind of apologetic when he said that it is by our love that the world will know we are his disciples (John 13:34–35). Love is therefore the defining mark of authenticity.

It is not the theological manuals (full as these may be of unquestionable truths) that can plausibly express to the world the truth of the gospel, but rather, the existence of the authentic, faithful, heroic disciples who have been grasped by Christ and his gospel.[2]

Ordinary Disciples, Extraordinary Influence is packed with such "authentic, faithful, heroic disciples who have been grasped by Christ and his gospel." And the challenge that Galen and Tefera bring to the reader is to not simply remain inspired but to allow the stories contained in this book to prompt us to walk in faith and obedience to Christ's invitation. Obedience is the evidence that our knowledge of God has been received and understood. The real test of what we know is how we live.

The adventures of Gabriel or of Desta or of Kofi—and all the other individuals featured in these pages—share in common at least two key components. First, each and every one is an ordinary disciple. It is Christ alone who has brought extraordinary influence in and through their lives. Second, each of these ordinary disciples has chosen to surrender their own agendas and instead make Jesus their Lord. And herein lies the fundamental challenge for the North American Christian. We are so absorbed by the competing idols of our time—whether they be middle-class consumerism, family, relationships, careers, or anything else that captivates our hearts—that Jesus is simply viewed as one of the many things that can bring us fulfillment, happiness, and satisfaction. The idea of true and full surrender to Christ is perhaps something we might declare with our tongues but rarely live with our lives. Yet, any genuine encounter with Jesus inevitably produces a radical transformation of every area of life, as we embark on a lifelong journey to become like him. Conformity to Jesus is the disciple's highest calling, and this book

---

[2]   Alan Hirsch and Mark Nelson, *Reframation: Seeing God, People, and Mission Through Reenchanted Frames* (Wyoming: 100 Movements Publishing, 2019), 181.

not only tells the stories of those who are living this way but also unpacks key principles to help each of us do the same.

To make Jesus the Lord of our life will no doubt require some un-learning—our minds are ingrained in a Western mindset that is not always compatible with the ultimate call to lay down our lives and follow Christ. The futurist Alvin Toffler once suggested that, "The illiterate of the 21st century will not be those who cannot read and write, but those who cannot learn, unlearn and relearn."[3] This has a twofold application for us as readers of this book. First, we must be willing to unlearn our Western ways (the main thrust of Toffler's quote); and second, it will be the radical disciples of the global south (many of whom are unable to read and write) from whom we must learn. The questions we, as North American Christians, must all wrestle with are therefore twofold: "Are we prepared to unlearn?"; and "Are we prepared to relearn from those in the global south?"

There is a beautiful simplicity to the confessional and incarnational ex-pression of faith we see in the global south—an affront to our over-educated, over-stimulated, over-complicated Western church. But it is precisely this trusting simplicity that we need at this moment in history. We are educated beyond our ability to obey. And our over-reliance on budgets, diplomas, staff, and property means that we are producing and pursuing an unscalable and unsustainable form of church. We watch as the celebrities of the North American church are applauded on their pedestals, while the rest of us are left on the sidelines, cheering the star player.

When something is scalable, however, every member of a church com-munity owns the vision for multiplication, and each person is actively engaged in doing their part to realize the vision. Each person functions as a disciple-making disciple. And disciple-making disciples are the essence of movements. The churches that Global Disciples serve around the world are experiencing accelerated growth because they consist of disciples who are making disciples—who are then equipped and motivated to make other disciple-making disciples.

---

[3]   Associated Press and staff, "Alvin Toffler, author of Future Shock, dies aged 87," *The Guardian*, June 30, 2016, https://www.theguardian.com/books/2016/jun/30/alvin-toffler-author-of-future-shock-dies-aged-87.

We have much to learn from them.

If we are wise and humble enough, we will allow the stories in this book to unlock our imagination for what is possible in our own spheres of influence. Marcel Proust once noted, "The only true voyage of discovery … would be not to visit strange lands but to possess other eyes."[4] This aptly describes the journey Global Disciples are inviting the reader to take. We must see with "other eyes," not only to see where we have fallen captive to the idolatries of our Western world, but also to see where God is at work right where we are. The North American Christian does not have to go abroad to be a missionary. If only we might surrender to Jesus as Lord and open our eyes and our hearts to the opportunities around us, we, too might become ordinary disciples with extraordinary influence.

---

[4]   Marcel Proust, *Complete Works of Marcel Proust* (East Sussex: Delphi Classics, 2012) ebook, 9504.

Authors' Note

This is a collaboration between Galen Burkholder and Brother Tefera. We have developed this material over the course of twenty-five years, in numerous countries and through hundreds of hours in conversation, planning, and prayer. Most first-person stories are shared by Galen; if a story is shared by Tefera, his name will appear in parentheses after the first use of the word *I*. The stories we share are real. Some names are used with permission, but most names, locations, and identifying details have been changed to protect the identity of individuals serving in areas where it is risky or dangerous to be a Christ-follower.

Introduction

When my son was fifteen years old, I took him along on a visit to Nepal. He was six feet tall and built like a football lineman, so the Nepalis would see him and ask how old he was. When he told them his age, they would shake their heads in disbelief and say he was bigger than three of their fifteen-year-old kids put together!

The day before we arrived at our destination, two of the Nepali pastors had been shot point blank in front of their church door by Marxists. Even amid their turmoil and grief, this faithful church community gave us a warm welcome. We sat with them one evening, huddled under blankets in a room lit by lanterns, as they shared story after story after story of their persecution.

During our flight home, I looked over at my son—he had my computer and was sending emails to his friends. Tears ran down his cheeks.

"What's wrong?" I asked him.

"I don't know, Dad. There are people risking their lives to follow Jesus, and yet back home, so many of us think being a Christian is just a *nice* thing to do."

He was right.

In North America, we have domesticated Jesus. We have created a Savior whose primary role is to make our lives comfortable. We equate being a Christian with being a good person and living a good life. And we have confused being a disciple with acquiring the right head knowledge ... something we can look up, and master, on the Internet.

But following Jesus is so much more.

[Extra]Ordinary Discipleship

When we began Global Disciples in 1996, our primary goal was to help clusters of churches equip and send out their people as disciple-makers. Soon we were partnering with clusters of churches around the world, helping them to make disciples and disciple-makers. Our small partnership initiatives began gaining momentum. Since those early days, Global Disciples has helped to launch over 2,000 training programs in sixty-two countries. Out of these programs, between 200 to 300 new fellowships of believers are planted each month. And between 1,200 and 1,600 new believers are coming to faith in Christ and worshipping in these new fellowships or related churches *each week*.

In our early meetings with church leaders, one of their first questions was, "Can we see your curriculum?" They had seen the fruit of the ministry, which was the blessing of the Holy Spirit, and they were curious about what we were doing, how we were leading churches and leaders in making disciples. They assumed we were following a complex system.

When we explained that our only text was the Bible, the leaders smiled or nodded understandingly. Then they asked to see the workbook or lesson outlines. We explained we had simply identified nine essential components of equipping disciples who are prepared to make disciples—and we can fit the outline of these principles onto a single page. You can see these at the back of the book (Appendix A).

Although many were turned off by the simplicity of our approach, others were interested. We were not trying to sell them a program. Apparently, we had discovered a strategy that was transforming lives and equipping effective disciple-makers. What God had led us into was simple, adaptable, easily contextualized, and effective. It's a pattern Jesus used in making disciples—based on relationships, practical experience, biblical truths, and the empowering of the Holy Spirit.

This book is the fruit of that learning. It shares what we believe are the essential ingredients and effective patterns for multiplying disciples—methods that will work anywhere from Kathmandu to the heartland of the United States.

Where Disciples Begin

Jesus' first disciples were ordinary people, working hard and going about their normal lives, when he approached them and made it clear he wanted them to be his disciples.

"Follow me."

Jesus didn't pick a bunch of superstars to follow him. Peter and Andrew, two of Jesus' disciples, were the blue-collar workers of their day, striving to run a successful business. Yet they were transformed by their encounter with Jesus, and these ordinary disciples went on to accomplish extraordinary things for God.

In our Global Disciples training, we talk about discipling the way Jesus did, including three specific aspects: Teaching, Applying, and Reflecting. We emphasize that these three, though interchangeable in order, must be surrounded by and immersed in prayer. And central to this discipleship experience is an attentiveness to the Holy Spirit, absorbing the truth of Scripture, and the iron-sharpening-iron accountability and influence of authentic relationships with other wholehearted disciples in the body of Christ.

This is what we see in the relationships Jesus had with his disciples—and the relationships among the disciples.

Discipleship is a team sport. Although we each have a personal relationship with Jesus, and we're individually accountable for our actions, we are at our strongest and most effective as disciples of Christ when we are in healthy relationships with other fully surrendered disciples. It's why we encourage you to read this book with other Christ-followers and work together at putting these components into practice. Working together in a community environment helps our knowledge of the gospel make its way from our head to our heart.

Many of us focus on learning, studying, and gaining knowledge—but then we do nothing with it. And we wonder why our lives stay the same.

Jesus' first instructions to his disciples were not about understanding a particular Scripture passage or knowing facts. He didn't even give them a list of things they needed to believe before they could become his disciples.

Again, his initial instructions were simple and unambiguous.

"Follow me."

When Jesus called Peter and Andrew, we are told that "at once they left their nets and followed him" (Matthew 4:20). This straightforward exchange is what lies at the heart of what it means to be an ordinary disciple with extraordinary influence: Jesus' simple call, and our unwavering response to step away from familiar ways, risk obedience, and follow him.

As the disciples obeyed and followed Jesus, he taught them along the way. Much of their learning came through observing him as he carried out his ministry and taught the crowds.

This approach is significantly different from how many of us have been taught discipleship in our churches. Much of the discipleship teaching you've likely encountered is through sermons, in a classroom setting, and maybe with a workbook or video series. It probably included teaching on spiritual disciplines and other good and important things. It's less likely that it included lessons in multiplication, teaching you to make disciples of others—who will then disciple still others.

The problem with so much good teaching is that the eighteen inches between our heads and our hearts can be a long journey. We are called not only to understanding, but also to a deep love attachment with Jesus. It's a heart attachment so strong that the thought of not pleasing and honoring Jesus is unbearable. It's the same heart attachment that compelled Jesus to bring glory to his Heavenly Father even as he faced the cross.[5] Becoming the voice, hands, and feet of Jesus in our world, even in hard times, is born of love and relationship, not an automatic outcome of cognitive understanding.

The solution is simple: follow him.

It really is that straightforward.

Ordinary Disciples

This is your invitation to be an ordinary disciple—with extraordinary influence—right where you are.

Throughout this book, you will find stories of ordinary disciples who

---

[5] John 17:1–5.

love, obey, and follow Jesus in extraordinary ways. Out of their relationship with him, remarkable things are taking place in the kingdom of God. Their influence for Christ reaches far and wide.

Many people are intrigued and amazed when we enthusiastically share these stories from Global Disciples of how God is at work around the world. North American Christians often recognize that such stories are far from their own experience, yet they are eager to be part of what God is doing in their own contexts and to see similar things happen in their day-to-day lives.

What's the secret to being disciples and making disciples like that?

"Follow me."

We see ordinary disciples every day in our work with Global Disciples across Africa, Asia, and Latin America. Most of the people we serve are not highly educated or sophisticated intellectuals. Rarely are they famous in their country, and they are not normally wealthy CEOs of important businesses. When they walk the streets of their communities, they're not hounded by paparazzi, and you probably won't find them on television or on YouTube.

Yet, like Peter and John before the Sanhedrin in Acts 4:13, it is evident that these men and women have been with Jesus, as demonstrated by their unshakable faith. Whatever life throws at them, they show remarkable wisdom, courage, and boldness—and they walk closely with other Christ-followers. This book is filled with their stories because we believe the North American church has much to learn from them. The challenges you face will be different, but there is no one better than you to respond to the prompting of the Holy Spirit and invest in the kingdom of God, right where you are.

As you read, we invite you to discover the vibrant, faith-filled life Jesus calls us into as his disciples. God is miraculously bringing people from Muslim communities in North Africa, Hindu and Buddhist families from South Asia, and even middle-of-the-road North Americans into a living, dynamic relationship with Jesus Christ. And this same God is eager to transform you and those in your community into disciples of extraordinary influence.

PART ONE
DEEPER

Take a deep dive below the surface: discover the risks and reasons to lay it all down for a fresh, God-breathed perspective on your life and future.

"So then, just as you received Christ Jesus as Lord, continue to live in him, rooted and built up in him, strengthened in the faith as you were taught, and overflowing with thankfulness."

Colossians 2:6–7

1

Risking it All for the Treasure

The man on the phone identified himself as Ahmed. Just his name and the sound of his voice made Kofi anxious and unsettled. Ahmed was an imam[1] and renowned for inciting violence and brutality against Christ-followers and churches in the region.

"Is this Pastor Kofi?" Ahmed demanded.

Pastor Kofi was suspicious. What could Ahmed possibly want from a Christian pastor other than to expose him and create trouble?

"Yes, this is Kofi," he replied hesitantly.

The imam explained that he'd had an encounter with Jesus and needed to talk to a pastor. He had questions, things he didn't understand. Would Kofi meet with him and answer his questions about Christianity and Jesus?

Kofi paused. The stories he'd heard about Ahmed filled his mind with doubts. *Imam Ahmed … experiencing Jesus? Wanting direction from a pastor? Curious about Christianity?*

---

[1] An Arabic word for a leader of a mosque who provides leadership for worship and prayers.

Kofi knew what was going on. This was a setup. There was no other explanation. He had heard about pastors lured into dangerous situations by people claiming to want to know more. Then, when the pastor arrived, he was beaten, imprisoned, or even killed. But Kofi sensed something different in the voice on the phone. It was not threatening but pleading. And after his initial fear and suspicion dwindled, Kofi heard the still small voice of the Spirit asking him a question, one that he could not simply ignore.

What if he's not lying? What if Ahmed was looking for the truth? Yes, Kofi knew he could be killed. But what if Ahmed really did have an encounter with Jesus Christ?

"Yes, I will meet with you," Kofi heard himself responding. "Where shall we meet?" His hands were shaking as he disconnected the call.

Was he walking into a trap? Or was he about to experience the most amazing miracle of his life?

A few hours later, Kofi was waiting at the designated location, an out-of-the-way spot at the back of a business that was closed for the day. *The perfect place if they want to kill me,* he thought, but something else also entered his mind. *Or the ideal place for a persecutor of Christians to secretly confess he was surrendering his life to Jesus Christ.*

Kofi looked around nervously. Then he saw the silhouette of a man in long robes, the imam's traditional clerical garb, walking down the alley toward him. He was alone. That was a good sign … at least for now. As the man approached, he glanced around quickly. Kofi didn't know what to expect. They were alone. Ahmed took a few steps closer, revealed the empty palms of his hands, then stepped into the shadows, motioning for Kofi to join him.

Imam Ahmed greeted Pastor Kofi by name.

"Thank you for meeting with me." Ahmed spoke in hushed tones, "I called two other pastors before you, but they refused to meet."

He was kinder and warmer in his approach than Kofi anticipated. "Let me tell you what happened," Ahmed continued. He laid his trembling hand on Kofi's arm as he told his story.

He and his small group of imams, who had been stirring up violence and trouble against the followers of Jesus, were walking from one town to another. Suddenly, a bright light shone down from heaven, and Ahmed fell to his knees. He heard a voice from heaven that said, "Stop persecuting my people." Then the voice gave him a verse from the Qur'an, and the light faded. The others saw the light, but only Ahmed heard a voice he could understand.

When he returned to his house, he grabbed his Qur'an to look for the verse the voice had given him. It said, "Honor the People of the Book."[2]

As he met with Kofi in that dark alley, Ahmed pleaded, "I met Isa al-Masih[3] on the road. Can you help me?"

Pastor Kofi took Imam Ahmed to a secret place for a week of instruction on what it means to be a born-again disciple of Jesus Christ. It was an intense time of prayer, deliverance, and study of God's Word. When Ahmed returned to his mosque, he was a new man. He began to teach from the Ingil,[4] which the Qur'an instructs faithful Muslims to read. Those in the mosque were curious about these new teachings and began to visit Ahmed to ask questions. Ahmed led one family after another into relationship with Jesus Christ.

Eventually, the imams, who had been with Ahmed when he had his first encounter with Jesus, heard his story. They thought he was crazy. But one by one, they too came to know Jesus as their Savior and Lord. In the meantime, Ahmed began to secretly attend a gathering of pastors with the churches that Kofi represented. One day Ahmed came to the pastors' meeting, beaming from ear to ear. "Well, it's finally happened," he said. "Everyone in my mosque is now a baptized follower of Jesus Christ."

The same miracle was unfolding in the mosques of Ahmed's fellow imams. One day, all five men came to the pastors' meeting. They explained that their mosques were full of disciples of Jesus Christ. They were teaching from the Ingil and breaking bread together as they celebrated the Lord's Supper. One senior pastor, who taught at the Bible school, encouraged the other pastors to visit the "Jesus mosques." He said with a smile, "I come away from their services more inspired to live my life fully for Jesus than I do when I go to our churches."

---

[2]   The Qur'an identifies Christians as "the People of the Book."
[3]   Jesus, as named in the Qur'an.
[4]   The Gospels, as referred to in the Qur'an.

After this warm welcome, the imams of the Jesus mosques made a request. They said, "Our mosques are full, and the people are walking from a nearby town where there is no mosque. When we built our mosque, we got financial help from the Middle East. But we won't get money from the Middle East to build a Jesus mosque. Will you help us?"

The pastors prayed with them and agreed to help. When the Jesus mosque was completed with the traditional dome, a little red cross was placed on the top. Today that mosque is full of those who have come to know Jesus Christ as their Savior and Lord.

All because Kofi—an ordinary disciple of Jesus, a farmer and pastor equipped to train other disciples—had been willing to surrender his own fears to Jesus and die to himself.

Most of us in North America do not face the same kind of challenges as Pastor Kofi. We aren't receiving phone calls from people who want to kill us because we are Christians. We aren't risking death because we obey the call of God in our lives. But, regardless of the potential ramifications, every one of us is called to die to ourselves—to lay down our earth-bound ambitions and to be raised into fullness of life in Christ.

Is It Really Worth It?

From the moment we make the decision to invite Jesus to be Lord of our lives, we declare that the treasure we have found in Jesus is of greater value than all other treasures we may have accumulated. As we discover fullness of life in the kingdom of our God, Jesus says that this joy is "like a treasure hidden in a field, which a man found and covered up. Then in his joy he goes and sells all that he has and buys that field" (Matthew 13:44 ESV).

Does what you have discovered in Jesus and in his kingdom give you that kind of joy? That feeling of exuberance, a desire for more of what you've found and a willingness to give up everything so it can be yours?

Lucas and Riya were a well-to-do couple in India. Lucas was a banking executive, and Riya was a successful businesswoman. After getting to know Jesus, their desires and priorities began to change. Their concern for serving those in need began to surpass their desires for luxurious cars, a fine home, and exotic vacations. On weekends, they often went and served in a leper colony. As their opportunities grew in ministering to those in need and sharing the good news of Jesus with the outcasts and disenfranchised, Lucas and Riya did what they couldn't have imagined a few years earlier: they quit their jobs and moved to a modest home near the leper colony.

As I sat listening to these ordinary disciples tell their stories of God at work, their joy was contagious. God was doing miracles as they helped care for those with leprosy, led Bible studies, and prayed with men and women who had lost fingers, noses, ears, toes, and more. As they prayed, they saw facial features restored and fingers and toes grow back—including fingernails and toenails! With tears of joy flowing down her cheeks, Riya told me, "We left much behind, but we have gained so much more than we could have ever imagined!"

I am convinced that in our churches we often bypass or downplay Jesus' teaching on "dying to self" because it sounds uncomfortable. So, instead we slip into assuming living for self is more fulfilling and satisfying than living fully for Christ. It reminds me of the words of C. S. Lewis as he contemplated the desires that often war within us:

> It would seem that Our Lord finds our desires not too strong, but too weak. We are half-hearted creatures, fooling about with drink and sex and ambition when infinite joy is offered us, like an ignorant child who wants to go on making mud pies in a slum because he cannot imagine what is meant by the offer of a holiday at the sea. We are far too easily pleased.[5]

But according to Jesus, dying to self—following him instead of our own desires—is the prerequisite for abundant life in Christ.[6]

That's so clear in the powerful imagery of baptism.

As we make our public declaration that Jesus is Lord of our lives, our old self is buried in the water, and we are raised to new life in Christ.[7]

---

5   C. S. Lewis, *The Weight of Glory, and Other Addresses* (New York: HarperCollins, 2001), 42.
6   John 10:2–10.
7   Galatians 2:20.

After he went through a mid-life crisis, my father became totally disillusioned with the church. He subsequently made a series of unwise choices. Thankfully, he was befriended by a coworker who was in love with Jesus and had a desire to see my dad restored. I never knew this coworker, but I am eternally grateful to him. One day, my dad told me he was going to be re-baptized.

"Really?" I responded. "Why?"

His response was simple—and profound, "I lost my way. I was doing what I thought I wanted. Now that I'm back on track with Jesus, I want to spend the rest of my life doing what God has for me to do. And I want to make that statement clearly to my family and everybody else."

And everyone who knew Dad noticed the change! I was married and no longer living at home, but I didn't need to hang around long to notice his softer, kinder tone of voice with my mother and my younger siblings. There was a playfulness and joy in interacting with our little kids, his grandchildren. Grandpa was back and reengaged as a gentler, more patient, and more loving man than before.

Oh, some of the same old tendencies were present; he could still be stubborn about some things in ways I didn't understand. But his hot temper had cooled again—even more than before his mid-life crisis. As we interacted, I had this overwhelming sense that Dad was now at peace with himself, with his God, his wife, and his family.

Dad had always tended to be critical of those who saw things differently than he did. But after his baptism, he died to self and let go of the need to be right. And he took on the attitude of a servant in ways I had never seen before.

My dad passed away about eighteen years ago, but recently a woman from his church recalled a childhood memory of him: Each week my dad would go around all the Sunday School classes, making sure all the pencils were sharpened. She mentioned Dad's name to illustrate how, as a child, she was impacted by the servant heart of the congregation.

It's such a small thing, but I confess I shed a few tears as I heard her recount this memory. It's just that—well, you had to know Dad to fully appreciate that story. Dying to what we want and being raised into abundant life with Jesus brings transformation in every aspect of life.

Although you may not feel led to be baptized again, remembering the moment when you were buried with Christ in death and raised to walk in newness of life can have a profound impact on your daily walk with the Lord.

Dying to self is the way of the cross and is the access point to all the other elements of discipleship we'll explore throughout this book. But dying to self is not a common theme in most of our churches. We tend to focus more on self-actualization, on realizing our dreams, and pursuing our ambitions. It's often about being all that we can be and chasing after our desires. There's something to this. After all, we were all created uniquely by God with different gifts and abilities. Since none of us are the same, we can be who God has created us to be by pursuing the things that best utilize our gifts and are most satisfying to us. But our highest calling is not self-satisfaction, self-actualization, or enjoyment of life. Our highest calling as disciples of Jesus is obedience that fosters and flows from intimacy with our Lord. This requires that we lay down our selfish desires and pursue God. Thankfully, as we do so, we discover an abundant life we may never have imagined possible.

Choosing Surrender

When we talk to North American churches about what God is doing globally, how he's moving in communities that have never heard of Jesus, and breaking down the strongholds that hinder the gospel, a pastor will often ask, "What are the strongholds here in the US?"

We've found that the challenge in North America has some similarities to one particular challenge in India. Hinduism says, "Bring your Jesus as one of the many gods, but don't tell us Jesus is the *only* God." In the US and Canada, we may not have the thousands of named gods and goddesses found in Hinduism, but we do have gods. It's just that our gods are more subtle. Our gods are gods of luxury, entertainment, sport, celebrity, health, safety, and comfort. We often give our hearts to these idols as much, if not more, than we do to Jesus. Though we may never utter these words, our hearts cry out a similar mantra to that of Hinduism: "Bring your Jesus—but only as one of the many other things that brings me fulfillment, happiness, and satisfaction."

We are easily preoccupied with our individual desires—the things we want to have, want to accomplish, or want to experience. Unlike most of the world, we have unlimited choice, and our individual freedom to choose whatever vocation or interest we want to pursue makes surrendering our personal ambitions more difficult. Dying to self is hard in an individualistic culture.

We are bombarded by advertisements, friends, and social media with things that promise fulfillment, joy, and satisfaction. The idea of saying no to those things for the sake of a higher calling can be downright difficult. People raised and nurtured in materialistic societies find it hard to die to the possibility of having or experiencing something they've dreamed of and worked for.

When North American believers ask me why we aren't experiencing the spiritual renewal and powerful moves of God taking place in so many other countries where Global Disciples works, my short response is: "When we rely on our things and our many options, complete surrender is hard."

In the last half of the first millennium AD, followers of Christ in the Eastern Roman Empire came under increasing pressure from the emergence of Islam. Meanwhile, the Celtic churches in England, Ireland, and Scotland were perpetrating a vibrant missionary spirit. The Holy Spirit put the Celtic nomadic streak to good use. After years of study and preparation to take the gospel to the lost, Celtic missionaries were commissioned by their village and placed in a coracle—a small circular leather boat on wicker frames, capable of riding the waves—and pushed out from the shore with the prayer that the Lord of the wind and the waves would take them to the very people he wanted to save.

Coracles were used by fishermen at that time and were propelled with a paddle, but the missionary monks were not given an oar. They were entirely dependent on God, the wind, and the tides. Wherever they ran aground, they were to be ambassadors of peace, preaching the gospel, and building kingdom communities.[8] This type of total and complete abandonment of

---

[8] This story was drawn from Richard Showalter, *Introduction to Christian Mission Since Pentecost* (Columbus, OH: Rosedale Media, 2018), 45.

any control of our life's direction may seem absurd. I mean, why would anyone do that? But in choosing to follow Jesus, we all are called to surrender our will to the plans and purposes of our God. We may not float away in a coracle, but there are parts of ourselves that we must let die. It might be a safety net or a particular plan or dream for how our life was going to turn out. Maybe it's a toxic habit or unforgiveness. Maybe it's something we've been using as an escape to avoid the calling we know that God has on our lives.

For me, it was ranching. As a young man, I loved horses and dreamed of someday owning a horse ranch in the wide-open spaces of Wyoming or Montana. It was the desire of my heart. But, as I surrendered my life to the Lord, my dreams and desires and ambitions changed. With all due respect to horse and cattle ranchers, I'm glad that God changed that desire of my heart. There is nothing I would rather do—or can imagine would be more fulfilling—than providing leadership for Global Disciples. I wake up every day eager to get to work, wherever in the world I may be.

I experienced first-hand the promise of Psalm 37:4, "Take delight in the Lord, and he will give you the desires of your heart." God gives us the desires of our heart when we delight in, or surrender to, the Lord. As we realign our lives with God, we develop the right desires, and God will give us the desires of our heart.

As we pursue what we want to do or what we dream of being, it's so easy to lose sight of the goal of being an obedient, responsive disciple of Jesus— his desire for us is to be fulfilled in him, and we only truly discover this by wholeheartedly pursuing God and giving him every part of our life. When we do that, we discover a life marked by hope, purpose, and joy.

Not my own dreams.

Not my own desires.

God's desires.

Here are some helpful questions to bring to God in prayer, together with others in your faith community, to help discern where God might want to lead you:

- God, what are your dreams for me?

- Lord Jesus, what are you calling me to pursue?
- God, what are you calling me to surrender?

We can't truly surrender ourselves to God's purposes and plans for our lives without first dying to our own personal ambitions and desires. That begins by surrendering our lives to Jesus, not only as our Savior, but as our Lord. It's a huge step to say, "Lord Jesus, I surrender my dreams, my hopes, my ambitions and my desires to you."

We get a sense of how important surrender is to our discipleship journey when we read Jesus' words in Luke:

> "Whoever wants to be my disciple must deny themselves and take up their cross daily and follow me. For whoever wants to save their life will lose it, but whoever loses their life for me will save it. What good is it for someone to gain the whole world, and yet lose or forfeit their very self? Whoever is ashamed of me and my words, the Son of Man will be ashamed of them when he comes in his glory and in the glory of the Father and of the holy angels."

> Luke 9:23–26

This teaching gets intensely personal a few verses later when individuals want to follow Jesus but are forced to confront parts of themselves they're not willing to let go or give up; things they simply cannot let die:

> As they were walking along the road, a man said to him, "I will follow you wherever you go."
>
> Jesus replied, "Foxes have dens and birds have nests, but the Son of Man has no place to lay his head."
>
> He said to another man, "Follow me."
>
> But he replied, "Lord, first let me go and bury my father."
>
> Jesus said to him, "Let the dead bury their own dead, but you go and proclaim the kingdom of God."
>
> Still another said, "I will follow you, Lord; but first let me go back and say goodbye to my family."

Jesus replied, "No one who puts a hand to the plow and looks back is fit for service in the kingdom of God."

Luke 9:57–62

These responses are common today. Each one sounds different, but they reveal what our hearts are holding on to. The first person wanted to follow Christ, but he didn't realize it would mean laying down a comfortable life. It would take him away from the security of home and the safety of the familiar. It might upend his priorities, his goals for success, his status or education or position among his own circles. Jesus was honest with him, and he turned away.

The second and third men didn't want to lay down their family ties and what came with them. They said, "I will follow you, Lord, but ..." In our own culture, as well as those around the world, the ties of family often influence our choices. We put our family's safety as priority one; we use caring for our kids, our parents, our future needs for retirement, or the responsibility of a family business first. If Jesus calls us to set aside these ties or responsibilities, it's easy to balk and fumble and find ways to refuse, just as those two men did.

Jesus owned nothing. He never owned a home or a place to call his own. He lived his day-to-day life trusting God to provide for all his needs.

Unless our eyes are open to see the joy in dying to self and relying on Jesus, it is hard to give up all our earthly desires and dreams. God knows us so much better than we know ourselves. And when we surrender everything to Jesus, and walk in intimacy with him, our desires are shaped by his desires, and our deepest joy is bringing glory to our Lord and Savior, our dearest friend.

Four Changes in Mindset

Change won't happen overnight, but there are four adjustments we can make to our mindset that will help us move to a point where we are willing to die to self.

Mindset Change #1—Nothing Is Ours

In a culture of materialism and possessions, it's hard for us to get our heads around the fact that nothing is really ours. Often, it's only when we face extreme circumstances that this reality hits home.

Years ago, my friend's twelve-year-old son was killed when he was hit by a car while riding his bike. It left all of us who knew him with a great sense of emptiness.

In a raw moment as I sat with my grieving friend, I said, "I can't imagine the kind of pain you're going through. I don't know how you can experience this and keep going."

He thought for a moment, then told me something I'll never forget.

"You know, when our son was born, we held him in our hands and said, 'Thank you, God.' And we dedicated him to the Lord." He paused. "If I focus on the fact that I've lost my son, I feel so sad, so helpless. But if I focus on the fact that God entrusted us with the son whom we enjoyed twelve whole years with, then I remember that my son belonged to God from the very beginning."

When my own son was born, our first child, I, too, remember holding him and saying, "Lord, he's yours. Thank you for this gift, for as long as we have the privilege of enjoying him."

God provided my friend an amazing grace of peace in that terrible time of loss. In everyday situations, it can often take a long time to choose to surrender fully to the Lord. When we do, though, we can trust that God will be just as present with us as God was with my friend.

It took me (Tefera), ten years to give up the security of my monthly salary as a schoolteacher. I was teaching high school while also giving leadership to a church-planting movement. I was trusting my monthly paycheck from the government more than I was trusting God to provide. Year after year, I promised the Lord that the following year, I would let go of the job and the income. But fear crippled me. Then the Lord challenged me through a dream, making it clear that if I was not willing to give up my teaching profession, I would miss the opportunity he had given me.

When I shared this with my wife, she said, "It is better to obey the Lord now than to ask for another year." And I submitted my resignation. If I had not been willing to surrender, I don't think I would be where I am today. I thank God for the wise counsel my wife gave me to willingly surrender.

Whether it's our children, our career, a business we built, an education we invested in, a home or any of the many other things we consider "ours," it's all in God's hands.

Mindset Change #2—Suffering and Loss Is Part of the Journey

I (Tefera) came to know Jesus while living in Ethiopia under a dictatorial communist government, so the message of comfort wasn't a familiar concept in my culture. I was taught that if I gave my life to Christ, I would have eternal life, but I would have to pay the price. We were well acquainted with the words of Paul, "For it has been granted to you on behalf of Christ not only to believe in him, but also to suffer for him" (Philippians 1:29). I have been jailed three times, and both my legs were in chains for the sake of the gospel of Jesus Christ.

After I became a Christian, I began helping many young people who were excommunicated from their parents because they had chosen to follow Jesus Christ. I remember visiting one big village, where I met seven women who lost their marriages because they had decided to follow Jesus and refused to deny him. I was amazed as I visited from house to house, listening to their stories one after the other.

One woman specifically told me how she had been terribly ill and in bed for four or five years. She was wasting away and in such a horrible state that her husband wouldn't even approach her room. She was alone. It was there that Jesus found her. Christians came and prayed for her, and Jesus saved her life. In her words, "My beauty came back. I'm no longer sick. Jesus healed me."

Her husband continued to demand that she recant her faith, deny Christ, and then he would move back in with her.

"How can I deny Jesus," she asked, "and choose my husband—the one who wouldn't approach me—when Jesus did approach me, even in my illness?"

Each of those seven women who lost their marriages had given up everything for the sake of the gospel, following Christ even when it meant that they would suffer the loss of their husband, their family, their place in their community, and everything they owned.

If we are going to die to self, we must be willing to suffer. Thankfully we are not alone when we suffer. Just as God was with the woman in the village, God is with us.

Although our suffering and loss may not look like those in Tefera's Ethiopian community, following Jesus should cost us something. As we take seriously the call to die to self and rely on Christ, it could cost us clients and customers—and thereby income and security for our family. It could open us up to criticism, attacks on our reputation or character, or fractured relationships with coworkers, friends, and even family who choose another way and reject the path we've taken. It is a costly and, at times, lonely road, but the joy we discover in the presence of Jesus is beyond what we lose.

Mindset Change #3—This World Is Not Our Home

In Colossians 3:1–4, Paul writes,

> Since, then, you have been raised with Christ, set your hearts on things above, where Christ is, seated at the right hand of God. Set your minds on things above, not on earthly things. For you died, and your life is now hidden with Christ in God. When Christ, who is your life, appears, then you also will appear with him in glory.

The earth is not our home—we must keep our mind on kingdom things. Jesus taught us to pray to our Heavenly Father, "Your kingdom come, your will be done, on earth as it is in heaven" (Matthew 6:10). That is true prosperity. God's kingdom is where our life, our treasure, our everything is found. This world is the place where we must go about our Father's business, but at the end of the day, it is not our home. Keeping this in mind leads us into a place where we can give up everything.

In 2 Corinthians 5:1–8, Paul describes our life in this world as living in a tent. For most of us in North America, if we use a tent, it's for camping, and it serves us for a few days. It is a temporary dwelling, just as our life here on earth is temporary. God opens our eyes to see our life in this body as temporary, a short-term living space, compared to our life in heaven. Heaven is not some illusion out there; it is a real place that Jesus, our Savior and Lord, has prepared for us to be with him for eternity. When he comes back to take us home, he will take our weak, mortal bodies and change them into glorious bodies like his own.[9] The writer of Hebrews reminds us of this when he refers to our forefathers—Abraham, Isaac, and Jacob—who lived in this world as foreigners.[10] When we understand that this world is really not our home, we are free to rejoice in the Lord even in the midst of difficult or unpleasant experiences.

We will unpack this idea in more depth in the next chapter when we explore the kingdom of God.

Mindset Change #4—Rejoice in the Lord ... Always

Paul didn't live an easy life; he wrote some of his letters from prison cells! He was well acquainted with hardship and suffering. Yet in Philippians 4:4, he writes, "Rejoice in the Lord always." We are not told to rejoice in our circumstances, but in the Lord, who is sovereign over our life and situations. When we fix our eyes on Jesus, we rise above our situation to rejoice in the Lord as Paul did.

James, who also laid down his life for the gospel, writes,

> Consider it pure joy, my brothers and sisters, whenever you face trials of many kinds, because you know that the testing of your faith produces perseverance. Let perseverance finish its work so that you may be mature and complete, not lacking anything.

> James 1:2–4

This is the beauty of dying to ourselves, that even in difficult circumstances, we can be filled with joy! In fact, there is greater joy for the disciple who lays

---

[9]   Philippians 3:21.
[10]   Hebrews 11:9.

down their life than for someone who spends their life pursuing their own comfort and well-being.

Untold blessings await those who will lay aside their own aspirations and choose to follow Christ.

Dying to Self ... Over and Over Again

Dying to self is not a one-time decision. It's not something we work up the courage to do once, make the decision and then—thank goodness!—we're finished with that. No, dying to self is a choice we must make every single day. That is why Jesus said, "Whoever wants to be my disciple must deny themselves and take up their cross *daily* and follow me" (Luke 9:23, italics ours). It is a daily surrender of our will to do the will of our Lord and Savior. As we die and decrease daily, Jesus increases his influence in us.[11]

A friend of mine pointed out, "Jesus never asks me for everything at once, but every day, just a little more."

The challenge is to allow God to develop the fortitude within us to give a little more of ourselves to him every day; choosing to give him our time, our money, our dreams for ourselves or our children, our work, our service, our possessions into the Lord's hands.

Kofi picked up a phone and realized he had to choose in that moment to die to self. For all he knew, it would cost him his life. Instead, by dying to self, he became part of the amazing work of God in the lives of Ahmed, his fellow leaders, and entire communities.

Lucas and Riya found that giving up their success and position was no match for seeing the powerful work of Jesus Christ move among the outcasts with leprosy.

The ancient Celts laid down control of their lives and left it to the winds and waves of God, to the benefit of many lost and wandering souls.

My father lived with a renewed heart and greater joy in his surrender, and everyone who knew him felt the influence of that change.

---

[11] John 3:30.

Each and every one of these individuals were ordinary disciples who chose to die to self and rely on Jesus.

In chapter ten, we will walk through a thorough self-examination to further equip you to discern where God is inviting you to die to yourself each day. For now, consider these questions in your own time of reflection and, ideally, with other ordinary disciples on this journey with you.

Reflect and Discuss

- What inspired you in this chapter?
- What challenged you?
- What is God inviting you to do in the coming days?
- What obstacles are keeping you from accepting and acting upon this invitation?
- How will you live differently today because of what you have just read?
- What practical actions will you commit to doing soon?
- What questions do you still have?

Additional Study

- **The Cost of Discipleship:** Luke 9:57–62; 14:25–33; John 12:24–25, Acts 4:2–3.
- **Dying to Self:** Philippians 3:10–14; Romans 6:5–14; Galatians 2:20.
- **Whole-Life Stewardship:** 1 Peter 4:10–11; 2 Corinthians 9:6–15; John 10:10.
- **The Lordship of Christ and Obedience:** Philippians 2:5–11; Romans 10:9; John 14:15–21.

2

Adopting a Kingdom Mindset

The vast Amazon jungle seemed to go on forever as I gazed through the window of our tiny four-seater plane. I couldn't stop wondering what this stretch of jungle would have been like back in the 1950s when Nate Saint, Jim Elliott, and their coworkers flew their little Piper Cub to establish contact with an unreached tribe living in that part of the world.

These missionaries dreamed of learning to communicate, making friends, and eventually sharing the good news of Jesus with the community. Using an ingenious rigging that Nate designed, they would lower a bucket at the end of a long rope, and by circling the plane, they could keep the bucket still long enough to exchange items with people from the tribe on the ground.

Eventually the missionaries made enough "bucket contacts" that they were ready to try personal contact with the tribe. They picked out a sandbar where Nate could land the small plane, a spot on the river close to the village of the Waodani people.[1] It would be risky, but it was for opportunities such as this that the missionaries had moved with their wives and small children to Ecuador—leaving behind friends and extended families in their homeland.

I was only twelve years old when I first heard this story, soon after I made the decision to accept Jesus as my Savior. My mom knew I needed some good books to read, and one was called *Jungle Pilot: The Story of Nate Saint, Martyred Missionary to Ecuador*.[2] Reading that little book profoundly impacted my life. I had never considered being a missionary before, but something about the adventure of connecting with people who'd never had an opportunity to hear the good news of Jesus gripped my heart.

I bought a little wooden plaque with Jim Elliot's famous words, written when he was a college student preparing to be a frontier missionary, and I hung it on my bedroom wall: "He is no fool who gives what he cannot keep, to gain what he cannot lose."[3]

Now, years later, here I was, flying into the place where the story happened. We swooped down over the jungle, and a winding river came into view.

"We're almost there," our pilot informed us.

This wasn't just any pilot. This was Steve Saint, son of Nate Saint, and he was taking us back to where his father and four fellow missionaries were killed. On that fateful day, when they made their first personal contact with the Waodani people, they were ambushed and speared to death.

Steve began telling the story of what happened in January 1956, as he banked the plane sharply over a sandbar on the river and pointed out the window.

"There's the place he died," he said. We all fell silent.

We gained a little altitude, then began to circle for our landing. Narrowly missing the treetops, the plane shot into a little clearing, and the wheels touched down as we bounced along the dirt runway. A small crowd of Waodani ran down the path from their village toward the sound of the plane.

---

[1]   Waodani are an indigenous people who live among the jungles of Ecuador and neighboring countries.
[2]   Russell T. Hitt, *Jungle Pilot: The Story of Nate Saint, Martyred Missionary to Ecuador* (Grand Rapids, MI: Discovery House, 2016).
[3]   Elisabeth Elliot, ed., *The Journals of Jim Elliot* (Grand Rapids, MI: Fleming-Revell, 2002), quote from October 28, 1949, at Wheaton College.

These were the people Steve's father had so desperately wanted to know and to reach with Jesus.

When the engine cut off, we crawled out of the plane. An old man hurried up to Steve and greeted him enthusiastically. Steve turned to me and eagerly said, "I'd like to introduce you to Mincaye, the man my children call *Grandpa*."

I knew that name from my conversations with Steve, but I also recognized it from Steve's book, *End of the Spear*.[4]

Mincaye was the man who had speared Steve's father to death.

As we walked the trail back to the village, those who had come to greet us led the way. I followed along behind Steve and Mincaye as they laughed, catching up, hands on each other's arms. Like a couple of schoolboys reuniting after a long summer vacation, they talked over each other, so excited to share the latest news in their lives.

I wiped a few tears away.

Only in the kingdom of God, I thought. *Only in the kingdom of God can the man who killed your father be embraced as Grandpa by your children.*

I remembered the quote on my bedroom wall as I was growing up. Jim Elliot understood what it meant to die to self—to give up something he could not keep, to gain something he could not lose.

Saying no to self and yes to God and his kingdom—God's rule and reign—won't lead most of us to be a missionary martyr. But it is a prerequisite for our lives if we are to be ordinary disciples with extraordinary influence for Jesus. Jim Elliot, Nate Saint, and their coworkers profoundly impacted generations of people, the scope of which we cannot fully know on this side of heaven.

If we are to say yes to God's rule and reign—his kingdom—we need to understand what his kingdom is like and how we can participate in it.

The Kingdom of God

The kingdom of God is breaking out in some of the least expected places around the world. Undefined by national identities or geopolitical

---

4   Steve Saint, *End of the Spear* (Carol Stream, IL: Tyndale House Publishers, 2005).

boundaries, Jesus reminds us that his kingdom is a mystery whose secrets are understood only by those who are part of it.[5]

If the kingdom of God is truly lived out in its fullest biblical expression, we will see an explosion of kingdom communities emerging in surprising and unusual places. But before we explore the nature of the kingdom more fully, let's clarify what we mean by the kingdom.

Jesus uses the phrase the *kingdom of God* in all of the Gospels except for Matthew's Gospel, which uses the *kingdom of heaven*. Matthew chose to use this phrase out of sensitivity to his Jewish audience who often tried to avoid the word *God* in their writing. They believed the character of our holy, eternal, infinite Creator cannot be described with a single word. The *Gospels* of Luke and Mark, however, are written to a broader audience and generally use the term *kingdom of God*. Most scholars believe the two phrases are theologically identical. They both define the reality of God's reign—where what God wants done is done.

The Pharisees questioned Jesus about the kingdom of God and when it would be established, and he replied, "The coming of the kingdom of God is not something that can be observed, nor will people say, 'Here it is,' or 'There it is,' because the kingdom of God is in your midst" (Luke 17:20–21).

The kingdom of God cannot be found on any map or easily observed or understood because it is a spiritual reality, not a physical kingdom. In Romans 14:17, the Apostle Paul declares, "For the kingdom of God is not a matter of eating and drinking, but of righteousness, peace and joy in the Holy Spirit."

Early in his ministry here on earth, Jesus taught his disciples to pray what we traditionally refer to as the Lord's Prayer. As recorded in Matthew 6:9–13, he instructs his disciples to pray to their Father in heaven, "*Your kingdom come*, your will be done on earth as it is in heaven" (italics ours).

In many ways the Lord's prayer describes the norm, the nature, and the character of God's kingdom:

---

[5]   Matthew 13:11.

- In the kingdom, God's will is honored and obeyed; *"Our Father in heaven, hallowed be your name."*
- In the kingdom, we are thankful for God's provision; *"Give us today our daily bread."*
- In the kingdom, we forgive as Jesus has forgiven us; *"And forgive us our debts, as we also have forgiven our debtors."*
- In the kingdom, the Holy Spirit guards our hearts, minds, and choices from the ways of the evil one; *"Lead us not into temptation, but deliver us from the evil one."*

So how can we see this kingdom?

The evidence of the kingdom is reflected in the character, integrity, and demeanor of those who are kingdom citizens. The compassion of Jesus is expressed; there is good news for the poor, freedom for prisoners, recovery of sight for the blind, the oppressed are set free, and God's favor is released in the lives of more and more people.[6] Physical realities are impacted by the presence of God's kingdom through the lives of kingdom citizens.

We are becoming more kingdom-minded when we say no to our personal desires and yes to the desires of God. We submit to the King as the supreme authority in our life. We seek his direction and plan in every aspect of life—in the big and small things. We listen to him when we're thinking about where we will live or what job we will do, who we will marry, or how we will use our money. When we choose to surrender our life, our future, and our aspirations to the rule and reign of God, we begin living as kingdom citizens.

Jesus explained to his disciples it would be difficult for those who are not willing to give up their possessions to enter the kingdom of God.[7] But he goes on to say, "Everyone who has left houses or brothers or sisters or father or mother or wife or children or fields for my sake will receive a hundred times as much and will inherit eternal life" (Matthew 19:29).

---

[6] See Luke 4:18–19.
[7] Matthew 19:16–26.

Kingdom Citizenship

When I (Tefera) became a United States citizen in 2012, I gathered with a group of people at the same point in the process, and we went through the steps required for naturalization. At one point, we had to stand and recite this oath:

> I hereby declare, on oath, that I absolutely and entirely renounce and ab-
> jure all allegiance and fidelity to any foreign prince, potentate, state, or
> sovereignty, of whom or which I have heretofore been a subject or citizen;
> that I will support and defend the Constitution and laws of the United
> States of America against all enemies, foreign and domestic; that I will
> bear true faith and allegiance to the same; that I will bear arms on behalf of
> the United States when required by the law; that I will perform non-com-
> batant service in the Armed Forces of the United States when required by
> the law; that I will perform work of national importance under civilian
> direction when required by the law; and that I take this obligation freely,
> without any mental reservation or purpose of evasion; so help me God.

In doing so, we were assuring the United States government that we had no allegiance to any other nation; any prior loyalties we had to another country were being rescinded; and we would put the best of the United States at the forefront.

Reciting this was a solemn, sacred act, because not only were we renouncing things—we were also taking up new responsibilities. We weren't only laying down old loyalties to other countries—we were also pledging that we would take on a new loyalty to the United States, one that involved action.

The United States doesn't want to give citizenship to someone whose allegiance is going to remain with another country. The United States doesn't want split allegiance. If you are going to receive the benefits of being a US citizen, then you must also commit to the responsibilities that come with it.

What strikes me about this oath ceremony is that it really does mirror the kind of allegiance we have to give to God. In Matthew 22:37–39, Jesus says:

"'Love the Lord your God with all your heart and with all your soul and with all your mind.' This is the first and greatest commandment. And the second is like it: 'Love your neighbor as yourself.'"

If we are disciples of Jesus Christ, our primary citizenship is in the kingdom of God, not in our homeland. Our citizenship in any particular nation is temporary—it is only for this life. But when we invite Jesus to be our Savior and King, we enter an eternal kingdom that will never end.[8] As we explored in the previous chapter, the earth is not our home—and the kingdom reminds us of that. This is modeled so beautifully by most of the disciple-makers we help to equip around the world. They are willing—even eager—to leave the comfort and familiarity of their homes and possessions to go share the good news of Jesus among those who have never had an opportunity to hear and respond to the gospel.

The Church and the Kingdom

Tefera and I love the church, the body of Christ. We know it can be a dynamic, living expression of the gospel of the kingdom. We believe the church is key to God's strategy in multiplying disciples and creating new fellowships of believers around the world. But sometimes the church gets distracted, loses its primary focus, and misses out on amazing opportunities to represent and point to the reality of the kingdom of God. The church is an imperfect expression of the kingdom because we are imperfect people.

At times, it's disappointing to see how the church—at any level—can misrepresent the kingdom. Most of us have had experiences which make it clear that this organism we call church is not always a good or joyful expression of the kingdom. Sometimes that's painfully clear. But it is still the body of Christ that Jesus died for, that God our Father loves, nurtures, and chooses to work through to build his kingdom.

As Global Disciples, we use a simple working definition of the church

---

[8] Luke 1:33.

as we assist local clusters of churches in many countries to plant new fellow-ships of believers among least-reached people groups. We say:

> The church is a community of disciples of Jesus Christ, empowered by the Holy Spirit, and focused on advancing God's kingdom. They love one another, are devoted to God's Word and to prayer, and joyfully share life together, celebrated in worship, communion, and baptism.

Churches come in many sizes, shapes, and expressions. Whether a mega church, a house fellowship of a dozen disciples, or a few believers gathered under a tree, the proof of the pudding is in the sincerity of the disciples gathered, their love for the Lord and for one another, along with the basic components mentioned in the definition of church above.

In our experience as Global Disciples, we are seeing an emergence of re-freshing new expressions of the kingdom of God in many parts of the world. These expressions are beyond the influence of any one leader or organization and are made up of ordinary disciples, living out the kingdom. Their influ-ence reaches beyond any particular entity, denomination, or movement.

As we walk alongside these fellowships, we have observed a move of the Spirit, which we believe will revitalize traditional congregations and unleash new, viable, authentic church expressions of the body of Christ that will re-engage those who are disillusioned with the institutional church. These fellowships come in many shapes and sizes, living like the church in Acts 2, and drawing in those who are hungry for hope and relationships with people who truly care for one another, even though "church" has never been a part of their lives.

In places with many generations of Christ followers, the focus often shifts from "the kingdom of God" to "the organization of the church," which in turn leads to an inward, narrower focus and a tendency to institutionalize the gospel. When our primary focus becomes how well our congregation, denomination, or church association is doing, we are moving away from being kingdom-minded to being "tribally-minded." We define our "church tribe" by our church name, our style of worship, our building or house of worship, our theological stream, our lead pastor, our predominant age group or ethnic identity—and the list could go on. We rarely think of it as a negative thing. "It's just how it's done."

But our focus can easily become our church identity rather than our kingdom identity in Christ. What forms might that take?

- We may invite people to attend church instead of inviting them to a relationship with Jesus. This isn't a bad thing; we want people to "come, see, and experience" and enjoy the caring community. But the kingdom is foundationally about Jesus and our relationship with him—that's where it starts.
- We may measure commitment by the church activities we're involved in, instead of investing in being a disciple of Jesus who makes disciples. Yes, regular involvement with a local fellowship of believers is healthy and biblical. Hebrews 10:25 reminds us to "not [give] up meeting together as some are in the habit of doing," but it's for the sake of being equipped to utilize our gifts as ambassadors of Jesus.
- We may only pray for and focus on the ministry and congregation we're involved in instead of praying for and caring about those in the kingdom who are outside our immediate circle. We're not alone in the kingdom nor are we the only ones doing kingdom work.

The Apostle Paul pleads for a kingdom-minded perspective: "One of you says, 'I follow Paul'; another, 'I follow Apollos'; another 'I follow Cephas'; still another, 'I follow Christ.' Is Christ divided?" (1 Corinthians 1:12–13a). We're not building a case against denominational affiliations, church associations, or networks. But we *are* building a case for our primary citizenship being in the kingdom of God and for our primary identity being in Jesus Christ. We serve a God who places us in families. Being in a family—or a family of congregations or fellowships—is a good thing, but it shouldn't prevent us from relating freely and openly with other families of fellowships.

If your experience has eroded your trust or hope in the church, we encourage you to take a fresh look. Turn your focus to the kingdom of God and pursue, with others, the relationship that gives us entrance into the kingdom. You will discover so much more than religious rituals—you'll discover life, and hope, and dynamic new relationships with others springing up all around you.

Seeking God's Kingdom First

After his prayer in Matthew, Jesus instructs us to "seek first his kingdom and his righteousness" (Matthew 6:33). In the four Gospels, the kingdom is mentioned 119 times. The theme of the kingdom is at the heart of everything Jesus said and did.

So, let's consider some principles we must embrace if the gospel of the kingdom is to be transformational in our everyday lives.

The Kingdom of God Is About Relationships

If the kingdom of God is about the rule and reign of God on earth, then we can be confident the kingdom is all about relationships. Our God is a God of relationship. We will explore what kingdom relationships look like in chapter seven, but there are three spheres of relationships that are important to bear in mind as we consider the kingdom:

- Our relationship with God
- Our relationships with brothers and sisters already in the kingdom
- Our relationships with those who are not yet part of the kingdom

Our relationship with God. No matter what our culture or background may be, entering the kingdom of God is all about an extraordinary relationship we can have with our Heavenly Father and his Son, our Lord Jesus Christ.

Through this relationship we experience all the blessings God offers: forgiveness, joy, peace, purpose in our lives, restoration, the promise of life after death, and an understanding of who we are and why we are in this world. These all come through this relationship with God. When we invite Jesus and the Holy Spirit into our lives, we enter into a dynamic, life-transforming relationship with God. A relationship like no other!

The beauty of our new identity in the kingdom compels us to live it out, instead of hiding within the trappings of a religion. "We have to unwrap the Christ out of Christianity," as E. Stanley Jones said.[9] Do we have the courage to pull off the religious wrappings and baggage that sometimes prevent us from seeing this marvelous gift of relationship with Jesus? We must dust off the gift and reveal its true beauty. The truth is that God has rescued us from the kingdom of darkness and transferred us into his kingdom through Jesus, who purchased our freedom and forgave our sins.[10] Our new identity in the kingdom of God is a life of love, meaning, and purpose in which we share in his glory. It is Christ living in and through us. Once we glimpse the riches of God's glory in this life and the next, we will never be the same.

Our relationships with brothers and sisters already in the kingdom. This extraordinary relationship with Jesus opens the door to relationships with others who have discovered this same remarkable, life-transforming relationship with our Creator God—this priceless treasure that surpasses all else.

One of our Global Disciples board members is a successful business leader. At an event, I met a relative of his, who pulled me aside to ask, "What have you done to my brother-in-law?"

Confused, I asked what he meant. He said, "It used to be when we got together for family gatherings, the conversation was all about business opportunities, new projects, and developments. Now when we get together, it's all about people coming to Jesus and reaching people who never heard the gospel before. He has some amazing stories but … it's just different."

I smiled and said, "Be careful. It seems that what he's caught can be quite contagious!"

Our relationships with our brothers and sisters in the kingdom are valuable. As we serve and encourage one another, we sharpen one another to become more like Jesus. Our influence on one another is contagious.

---

[9]   E. Stanley Jones, *The Christ of the Indian Road* (Nashville: Abingdon Press, 1925).
[10]   See Colossians 1:13–14.

Our relationships with those who are not yet part of the kingdom. When we discover the treasure, that pearl of great price, it changes our conversations, it adjusts our priorities, and it turns some things in our lives upside down.

Bonnie and Matt are ordinary disciples of Jesus, living a normal, suburban life in the US. Matt's an engineer, and Bonnie works in our Global Disciples office; and they have two grade-school children. They have a deep love for Muslim people, and a desire to see them come to faith in Jesus Christ.

Several years ago, Bonnie and Matt had an opportunity to build relationships with those not yet in the kingdom by sharing their home with an immigrant Muslim family from the Middle East. The two families shared the kitchen, enjoyed many meals together, shared their lives and stories, building a relationship of influence. Hospitality, concern, compassion, and care spoke volumes—and having the opportunity to see up-close what it looks like to follow Christ had a significant impact on this couple.

Commenting on their journey with this Muslim family, Bonnie said, "By the wonderful grace of God, the couple who lived with us accepted Christ two weeks after moving to the neighborhood. This came after years of searching, questioning, and the testimonies of Arabic-speaking Christian friends in the area. We were not the ones to lead them to Christ, but we had the blessing of being part of their journey and watching years of toil bring forth fruit."

And what this couple had observed—in friendships, in marriages, in relationships with Jesus Christ—helped them want to be part of the kingdom.

Each one of us is an expression of the gospel. As the Apostle Paul reminds us, "You yourselves are our letter, written on our hearts, known and read by everyone. You show that you are a letter from Christ [...] written not with ink but with the Spirit of the living God, not on tablets of stone but on tablets of human hearts" (2 Corinthians 3:2–3).

The Kingdom of God Is Loving

A distinguishing mark of true kingdom-minded disciples is the love that they have for one another. In John 13:34–35, Jesus tells his disciples that their love for one another is going to show the world they belong to him.

Jesus also taught that loving only our fellow disciples is not true unconditional love. In his parable of the Good Samaritan, Jesus shared his expectations for kingdom-minded disciples to show genuine kindness and love toward their neighbors, those still outside the kingdom, still in need of the redemptive work of Jesus.[11]

John and Matt had been good friends a long time—the kind of friends who would do anything for each other. When John came to faith in Jesus in his early 20s, Matt was thrown.

Speaking of that time in their life, John said, "Matt wasn't a bad guy; he just had some resentment toward God. And we got into hundreds of conversations about the existence of God, the validity of Jesus' message, and everything else he wanted to argue about! At times, my frustration was overwhelming!"

When John decided to move away to attend seminary, his friends threw a farewell party. And Matt handed him a card in which he had written: "God is not real."

"Leaving the party, with that card in my hand," John said, "I just sat in my car and sobbed. My friend was so far from God and did not want to change. I committed to praying for Matt daily, asking the Lord to remove his heart of stone and replace it with a heart of flesh."[12]

For the next few years, John carried on his conversations with Matt, sending along books and videos he thought might help. At times, he dreaded those conversations; he knew it was going to be a battle. But he continued to be a good friend and prayed for Matt's salvation—and recruited his church fellowship to pray too!

In one conversation, Matt explained that when he was younger, he was kicked out of church for asking too many questions. In his mind, they kicked him out because they didn't have the answers, but he was also hurt—the church represented Christ, and to Matt, Christ had kicked him out. John tried to console him, "I told him he had to get to know Jesus for himself."

Finally, the two friends were living in the same state again and found

---

[11] Luke 10:25–37.
[12] See Ezekiel 36:26.

a time to get together. John said, "I arrived at Matt's apartment, and took a deep breath, praying that God would give me patience for the inevitable onslaught. But when Matt answered the door, something seemed ... *different*. As we were talking and laughing, I heard him say, 'God is good.'

"'What did you say?'

"'I said, God is good, John.'"

For John, the tears began as Matt explained that he'd started looking into Scripture for himself and felt God changing his heart. "It's real. Jesus is real!" Matt said.

"I put my hand on his shoulder, and for the first time, I wasn't praying *for* Matt," John said, "I was praying *with* him. We still joke about that going-away card—Matt admits it came out of his anger and hurt. He needed to figure out how to connect with God. Today that message would be: 'God is so good and so real.'"

Kingdom love is lived out in patience and prayer; in connecting people who don't know Jesus to the life and truth he offers. John had the opportunity to live out kingdom love, and eventually Matt experienced it too—moving from outside to inside the kingdom.

The Kingdom of God Transcends Culture and Geography

Jesus demonstrated love and respect for the culture and situation into which all people were born, and he calls us to do the same. It is God, after all, who determines where and when we are each born:

"The God who made the world and everything in it is the Lord of heaven and earth [...] he himself gives everyone life and breath and everything else. From one man he made all nations, that they should inhabit the whole earth; and he marked out their appointed times in history and the boundaries of their lands. God did this so that they would seek him and perhaps reach out for him and find him, though he is not far from any one of us."

Acts 17:24–27

As the gospel is shared freely and winsomely, accompanied by the love and compassion of Jesus, many cultures, religions and regions embrace Jesus Christ as their Savior and Lord. It's all part of God's amazing strategy of establishing his kingdom in every tribe, ethnic group, and language around the world. As I travel in difficult parts of the world, I've often wondered what life would be like if I had been born into a Muslim or Hindu family. Instead, I was raised in a family that loves Jesus. What if I had been born in the slums of Mumbai or Cairo? Would God love me the same? Does he love those people any less?

Of course not.

But do *we* love them less? We have all been created in the image of God, made for relationship with our Creator God, and, as uncomfortable as it may make us, Jesus—an Asian by human birth—shared, "I am the way and the truth and the life. No one comes to the Father except through me" (John 14:6).

The God who created the world and everything in it, the God who determined the place of our human birth and the religious or nonreligious affiliation of our parents, longs for relationship through Jesus with each one of us. This underscores how important it is for those in God's kingdom to show love and respect to all people.

We began this chapter with a story from the jungles of Ecuador, an incredible embodiment of the power of forgiveness and restoration, and the life-changing reality of God's kingdom. If you grew up hearing missionary stories, you've probably heard similar stories along the way.

We celebrate that through three hundred years of the modern mission movement, millions upon millions of people throughout Africa, Asia, Latin America, and beyond, have become followers of Jesus Christ. Their fear of "the gods" and the need to appease the dark spirits through sacrifices and religious rituals have been broken as the kingdom of God became reality among them, transforming their lives, their families, and their communities by the power of the gospel.

Are you aware of the new phenomenon in recent decades? We are now seeing large Jesus-movements—hundreds of new fellowships and thousands of new Christ-followers among the major religions of Hinduism, Buddhism, and Islam. The story of Ahmed and the Jesus mosques we shared earlier is just one example among many.

God is doing something new in our time! And here's why this is so relevant for us to consider: The dominant theme in these movements lines up with the central theme of Jesus' teaching and ministry—the good news of the kingdom of God. It all comes back to that extraordinary relationship with Jesus, which opens the door to relationships with others who have discovered this same remarkable, life-transforming relationship with our Creator. Like us, they are discovering this priceless treasure that surpasses all else.

Most movements of Christ emerging from Islam, Hinduism, and Buddhism are growing and flowing through natural family and relational networks. These networks are key to reaching whole ethnic groups with the gospel. As we consider respecting other cultures, we're immediately confronted with an important question: When a Hindu, a Muslim, a Buddhist, or a person of another faith and identity comes to faith in Jesus Christ, what needs to change?

Does their culture need to change? No, except in areas that may compromise their loyalty to Jesus Christ and obedience to his Word.

Do they need to change how they dress? No, unless there are issues of modesty in their culture that the Bible addresses.

Often, maintaining cultural patterns that do not compromise loyalty to Christ will allow a new believer to share their faith more freely and effectively within their families and communities. We believe questions about cultural adaptation and change are generally best answered by brothers and sisters in Christ who grew up and lived within those cultures. We have observed many disciples from other religious backgrounds tackle these questions with integrity, seeking Holy Spirit guidance, wisdom from the Bible, and counsel from fellow believers in their context. The Holy Spirit who led the apostles with discernment at the Jerusalem Council in Acts 15 is the same Spirit leading our brothers and sisters to clarity and truth in the kingdom of God today.

Let's think about how cultural adaptation issues might play out in the more dominant cultural groups in North America. How do we show love and respect to those who come to faith in Christ and still wear the scars or marks of drug abuse, gang membership, prison, prostitution, poverty, and more? What needs to change for them? And for us in the body?

When a person enters into a living relationship with Jesus Christ as their Savior and Lord, and the Holy Spirit floods their life, that's the most significant change. That is what is different.

This is the beauty of God's kingdom—it flourishes and grows healthy and strong within so many different cultures and environments.

The Kingdom of God Is Joy-Filled

One of the most common and easily recognized marks of the kingdom of God is joy! "God's glory is most fully revealed through the Christ-centered joy of his people."[13] This joy is brought on through this remarkable, indescribable, and life-transforming relationship with Jesus Christ who first loved and modeled fullness of life for us. And he made the way through his crucifixion and resurrection for us to enjoy life in his presence forever!

As we walk in relationship with our Creator, Savior, and Lord, we find delight in all he created for us to enjoy: the trees and flowers, the birds and animals, rivers and the seas, the sunrises and the sunsets, the sun, moon, and stars. These and so much more are reminders of our God's infinite power, inexhaustible creativity, and unconditional love for us.

Those who have come to know our loving Heavenly Father and Creator have this unquenchable desire to express our love, adoration, and praise to him. No matter where in the world the citizens of the kingdom of God gather, praise wells up within us—even in hard times.

I'm often amazed by the example set by the Apostle Paul. He and his coworker Silas had been beaten with rods and severely flogged, then put in a high security cell in prison—with their feet in stocks—all because they were preaching the gospel and had cast a demon out of a fortune-teller.[14] And what were they doing? "About midnight Paul and Silas were praying

---

[13] John Piper, *God's Passion for His Glory* (Wheaton, IL: Crossway Books, 1998).
[14] See Acts 16:16–24.

and singing hymns to God" (Acts 16:25). Joy, even in difficult situations, is a mark of citizens of the kingdom.

The Church and the Kingdom Are Advancing

Our primary identity is in Christ; our primary citizenship is in the kingdom of God. The more we tune our focus to the kingdom of God, the more clearly and frequently we will experience amazing glimpses of his kingdom.

It is a kingdom that bridges cultural and geographic boundaries, that builds relationships across language and history. A kingdom that welcomes new citizens through faith in the King. A kingdom whose God is the Lord, and whose people value one another and walk in love, compassion, and forgiveness.

Only in the kingdom could I have witnessed the scene that day on the jungle path, as Steve Saint cheerfully walked with Mincaye—the man who killed his father was now forgiven, loved, enjoyed, and known by Steve's children as Grandpa.

Only in the kingdom of God!

Reflect and Discuss

- What inspired you in this chapter?
- What challenged you?
- What is God inviting you to do in the coming days?
- What obstacles are keeping you from accepting and acting upon this invitation?
- How will you live differently today because of what you have just read?
- What practical actions will you commit to doing soon?
- What questions do you still have?

Additional Study

- **The Kingdom of God and Our Citizenship:** 1 Peter 2:9–12; Philippians 3:20.
- **Our Place and Identity:** Romans 8:37–39; John 1:12; 2 Corinthians 5:17–20.
- **Fellowship and Accountability:** Hebrews 10:24–25; Acts 2:42–47.
- **Functions Within the Body:** Romans 12:3–8; Ephesians 4:1–16.

3

Aligning with God's Word

Darsh was a poor shepherd in the rolling hills of central India. As he was tending his sheep one day, he spotted something black in the grass, a short distance away. He discovered it was a worn leather book cover with no pages inside. He picked it up, brushed it off, and placed it in his bag, wondering how it got there and what it had contained.

When he got home that evening, he showed the black leather cover to his wife. They decided it must've been an important book to have such a nice cover, so he placed it on a small table by the door in their modest little home of sticks and mud.

A few days later Darsh's wife commented on how peaceful their home had been since he brought the book cover into their house. They agreed they needed to find out what book this cover represented.

When Darsh was at the market, he started asking people at a few book-stalls if they knew what kind of a book the cover belonged to. No one had a clue; they had never seen a book cover like that before. Then Darsh spotted a stranger with a book in his hand, and the cover was similar to the one that had brought such peace to their home. Timid but excited, Darsh approached the stranger.

"Sir, excuse me, but can you tell me what kind of a book this leather cover belongs to?"

The stranger smiled. "Of course, I can," he responded. "That's the cover of a Bible. Have you ever seen a Bible before?"

Darsh said no but explained how he found a book cover as he was tending the sheep on the hills outside of town. He described the strange and unusual peacefulness his family had experienced ever since he brought it into his house.

Pleased, the stranger asked if he would like a copy of the book that belonged in the cover. Darsh was thrilled!

"Yes, yes, I certainly would!" he replied.

The kind man reached into his shoulder bag and pulled out a brand-new Bible for Darsh.

From there, the story goes quickly—the stranger began visiting Darsh in his house and teaching him about the Bible. Darsh came to faith in Christ and started the first prayer house for followers of Jesus in his Hindu town!

By the time we visited Darsh, he was teaching at a discipleship-mission training that Global Disciples had helped establish, and the disciples he trained had started more than twenty prayer houses where Jesus Christ is worshipped in the surrounding towns and villages.

All this kingdom influence came about because an ordinary man named Darsh found a leather cover, then the book it belonged to, and a new friend who helped him understand it. Eventually Darsh decided to align his life with the Jesus he discovered within that marvelous book.

You probably have a Bible within reach, even now. It's on a shelf, in a pocket, even on your phone. You're used to having it around, to picking it up and reading it whenever you want. It's not an object of curiosity like it first was for Darsh. Perhaps you have become so familiar with it, you take for granted its influence and power.

The Bible is the written, recorded Word of God to us. Through the redemptive work of Jesus Christ and in the power of the Holy Spirit, we draw on the Bible, often in community, to be our consistent guide in living the kingdom life and dying to self each day. A disciple of Jesus will seek to live their life in a way that is consistent with the Word of God.

God's Word Changes Lives

Inspired by the teachings of Jesus recorded in the Bible, many of us have made decisions that are considered counter-cultural or, in the eyes of others, unwise. Imagine you are a follower of Christ living in the same town as terrorists opposed to Christianity or anything they perceive as Western influence. How would you live your life, speak about Jesus, and worship with your fellow believers? What would "church" mean to you? Would you feel led to share the gospel or keep quiet and reduce your risks? Would you go out, or stay in your house as much as possible, praying for the day the terrorists leave your town?

Some of our friends in one northern African country found themselves in exactly this situation—they lived close to Al-Qaeda training camps. But they didn't hide in their homes or go underground. They didn't let fear turn to hate; they didn't respond as many of us might have.

In fact, the constant threat of attacks from the terrorists only increased the resolve of these nearby churches. Instead of answering the ever-present brutality with violence of their own, this group of ordinary Christ-followers decided to equip their young leaders to respond with the love and peace of Christ.

Kaleb was directing a discipleship-mission training for his cluster of churches. And after a lot of thought and prayer, he and other leaders chose to locate their discipleship-mission training in an ordinary, out-of-the-way house in town, just down the road from a terrorist training camp. The young men in the discipleship training were boyhood friends of several young men in the terrorist compound. They knew their names. They had grown up playing together.

Now their childhood friends had become Al-Qaeda members, seeking to exploit disorder, oppose Western influence, and harm Christians. But those in the discipleship training were not intimidated. In fact, the young disciple-makers convinced Kaleb to give them his blessing to visit the terrorist camp during some of their free evenings.

At first, the Al-Qaeda leaders saw these guys as potential recruits and gave them permission to hang around. However, these young men had not come into camp empty-handed; they had their Bibles tucked in the back of their belts and concealed by their shirts. As they talked with their childhood friends—now part of one of the most hated and violent terrorist groups in the world—the disciples bravely introduced them to the teachings of Jesus, using their smuggled Bibles.

It turned out that these fighters-in-training felt overwhelmed and distraught by the violence and brutality they were being indoctrinated into. They hated what they were forced to see and do. Some found life nearly unbearable, weighed down with depression, loneliness, and guilt.

Yet in these smuggled Bibles, they found the teachings of Jesus refreshing and uplifting. Kindness? Gentleness? Goodness? The fruit of the Spirit was in complete opposition to the terrorist training they were receiving. They found the message of the gospel compelling, and something stirred in several recruits.

After a few weeks of visits, several guys in the Al-Qaeda camp invited Jesus to be their Savior and Lord—and in that decision, they realized they could no longer continue along the path they were on. One evening, under the cover of darkness, their boyhood friends who were Christ-followers helped to orchestrate their escape from the terrorist training camp, knowing that if any of them were caught, they were dead.

They made it out, and once away from the camp, the young disciples arranged a place where their friends could hide as they were further introduced to the truth of God's Word and the teachings of Jesus. Their lives were radically transformed as they studied God's Word together. In secret, they also completed their discipleship-mission training, and then these former terrorist recruits were sent as witnesses to the work of Christ in their lives to towns and villages where the good news of Jesus had not yet taken root.

"It was amazing to watch," recounted Kaleb, the training director. "They went with the same boldness, determination, and tenacity they had learned in the Al-Qaeda training—but now armed only with the love and grace-filled message of Jesus Christ."

We were there when two of these former Al-Qaeda fighters came to a small business development training offered through Global Disciples. One young man was intent on starting a Christian music store. His plan was simple—set big speakers outside the door of the shop and play the music loudly. Someone in the small business training responded, "That sounds like a good way to get killed, doing that in the town where you're serving."

"No problem," he responded, "There's no greater reward in heaven than the reward of being a martyr for the cause."

After a moment of stillness, the small business instructor reminded him that followers of Jesus Christ do not accept the Muslim teaching that a man martyred for defending the faith will receive the reward of seven virgins when he reaches heaven. He went on to explain that our goal as Christ-followers is to stay alive as long as we can, so we can welcome as many other people as possible into the kingdom of our Lord Jesus Christ.

The mindset and worldview of these former Al-Qaeda fighters contin-ues to be transformed by the truth of Scripture and the power of the Holy Spirit. Before they met Jesus, their principal aim in life was to incite violence against those viewed as the enemies of Islam. Now they are radically trans-formed into advocates for peace and reconciliation with God and all people.

How did all these things come about?

Because several young men decided, no matter what, they would align themselves with God's Word.

Although realigning our lives with the Word may not require us to risk our lives like these young men did, it does often lead us to do things that are considered radical in our culture. It might mean relocating to a less desirable neighborhood, deciding not to take someone to court over a dispute, mov-ing into a less prestigious job, giving a car to someone in need, or sacrificing some form of comfort or convenience for the sake of another. Whatever it looks like for each one of us, responding in obedience to what God says to us through his Word and by the Holy Spirit will not always be understood or seem reasonable to those around us.

However, engaging wholeheartedly with the Word of God will give us more clarity on what it means to die to ourselves. And the Lord will use our responsiveness to the Word to continue to form us into people who are rec-ognizable as joy-filled, obedient, and influential citizens of God's kingdom.

There's Nothing Like It

When we read the Bible, we are reading powerful words, inspired by the Holy Spirit. These words can profoundly impact our lives and the lives of others, as many of us have experienced personally and witnessed in others. We have seen this as true in our lives, especially when we study the Bible and reflect on it with other disciples, much like Kaleb and the former Al-Qaeda trainees in the stories above. Authentic, transparent relationships among wholehearted believers, coupled with an openness to Scripture and the voice of the Spirit are like iron sharpening iron.[1]

Take a closer look at the valuable work of the Word that Paul laid out in his instructions to his disciple Timothy:

> But as for you, continue in what you have learned and have become convinced of, because you know those from whom you learned it, and how from infancy you have known the Holy Scriptures, which are able to make you wise for salvation through faith in Christ Jesus. All Scripture is God-breathed and is useful for teaching, rebuking, correcting and training in righteousness, so that the servant of God may be thoroughly equipped for every good work.
>
> 2 Timothy 3:14–17

There's so much packed into these four short verses.

Paul exhorts Timothy to continue in what he already knows. Keep going, Timothy! Stay confident in what you've learned! You know what you're doing—don't start doubting yourself and the things you've been taught. You know who you learned from, and how true these Scriptures have always been. As a mentor used to tell me, "Keep believing your beliefs and doubting your doubts. We get in trouble when we start doubting our beliefs and believing our doubts."

There's more here in these verses than a simple word of encouragement, and it starts right in the middle of the passage with the words, "which are

---

[1] Proverbs 27:17.

able to make you wise for salvation." What a fascinating concept—the Bible is able to make you wise through faith in Jesus! It's not just about gathering information; wisdom is the foundation of discerning truth and responding in obedience wherever Jesus might lead.

We're given this wonderful image of Paul explaining to Timothy that his alignment with Scripture, combined with his faith in Christ, will make him wise. Not only will Timothy know what he needs to know, the "God-breathed" Bible will thoroughly prepare and equip him for every good work that he undertakes.

When Global Disciples meets with church leaders around the world, they often ask us for a discipleship training curriculum. Our response is simple: is there a better curriculum than the Bible? The Bible *is* the textbook, the foundation for the discipleship-mission training that Global Disciples makes available. What other curriculum would you need for multiplying Christlike disciples? It is our ultimate authority and source of life. The Holy Spirit uses the written Word of God to transform us to reflect the image of Jesus in our daily life and ministry.

We align with Scripture because Scripture aligns us with God.

All Scripture is God-breathed, which means it flows out of the very heart of who God is. We need to honor Scripture as an expression of God's heart for us and for the world our God has created.

Jesus says, "You are my friends if you do what I command" (John 15:14). We are called to follow the example of Christ, to die to self and live in the kingdom of God now. To follow his example requires that we understand his heart—and to understand his heart, we must go to Scripture.

The writer in Hebrews goes even deeper in explaining exactly what makes the Scriptures so powerful.

> For the word of God is alive and active. Sharper than any double-edged sword, it penetrates even to dividing soul and spirit, joints and marrow; it judges the thoughts and attitudes of the heart. Nothing in all creation is hidden from God's sight. Everything is uncovered and laid bare before the eyes of him to whom we must give account.

Hebrews 4:12–13

The point here is clear: the Word of God has come to us in a way that cannot be disregarded or ignored.

The Word of God is applicable for all people of all times. Other books and writings may pass quietly into obscurity, but the Word of God is something every person must face, and its offer, ultimately brought to us through Jesus, is one that we must each accept or reject.

The Word of God is active and effective. When people take God's Word seriously, things begin to change. When Johannes Guttenberg began to print the Bible on the printing press in the sixteenth century, lives and society were transformed, and the Reformation era followed. Today, when an individual takes the Word of God seriously, lives, families, and communities are transformed.

The Word of God is powerful to create and recreate. Genesis 1 tells us that God created heaven and earth by speaking it into existence. "God said, 'Let there be light,' and there was light" (Genesis 1:3). The Gospel of John explains that the power of God's spoken word is found in Jesus: "In the beginning was the Word, and the Word was with God, and the Word was God. He was with God in the beginning. Through him all things were made; without him nothing was made that has been made" (John 1:1–3). Jesus revealed the power and authority of his spoken word during his earthly ministry. By it, he healed the sick and raised Lazarus from the dead. He rebuked the raging storms and silenced them by the power of his word.

The Word of God is penetrating. It impacts the physical, spiritual, emotional, and psychological aspects of who we are. It addresses the whole of our lives, thoughts, actions, and relationships. And in the end the Holy Spirit, through the Word of God, scrutinizes our desires, intentions, and motivations. Nothing is hidden from God; through encountering his Word, our lives are laid bare, and we must all give account.

The Word of God is reliable and trustworthy. The questions sometimes raised about possible contradictions, even within the four Gospels, are easily answered by the simple acknowledgment that various witnesses of any event or incident will see things from a different angle and each will highlight different aspects that stood out to them. Even when the words that are written are Holy-Spirit inspired,[2] the personality traits and gifts of the writer are beautifully evident in their writings.

Written over a period of fifteen hundred years and with sixty-six books making up the Bible, it's remarkable that there are at least fifty-five prophecies about Jesus the Messiah recorded throughout the Old Testament, hundreds of years before they were fulfilled in his birth, life, death, and resurrection.[3] "When we compare the reliability of the Bible with other historic documents of its time, utilizing the same criteria, we find the Bible is not only reliable—it is more reliable than other comparable works."[4]

To those who know and understand the character of our loving Creator, we know his words are to be heard, to be trusted, and to be received. God's words require a response, a change of heart or action!

So much of Scripture is a call to honor and worship God. The entire Old Testament could be summarized as God calling people to worship him; God's people getting distracted by giving their primary attention to other things; and their long, slow journey back to God.

Since the story of Scripture is the story of a people distracted from God, we must ask ourselves:

- What distracts us from worship?
- What distracts us from honoring God?
- What distracts us from surrendering our lives to God?

We can turn to Scripture and invite the Holy Spirit and those in our faith community to help us discern the answers to these questions, so we can realign our lives.

We have become the most informed people in the history of the world. From the moment we wake up to the moment we close our eyes at night, we are bombarded with information—facts, rumors, theories, suppositions, predictions, and opinions that someone believes we should

[2]   2 Timothy 3:16.
[3]   "55 Old Testament Prophecies about Jesus," *Jesus Film Project*, https://www.jesusfilm.org/blog-and-stories/old-testament-prophecies.html.
[4]   "Is the Bible Reliable," *Compelling Truth*, https://www.compellingtruth.org/Bible-reliable.html.

know ... immediately! Most of us carry around a device in our pocket that constantly floods us with this information. Even our Christian community can overload us with the thoughts, opinions, and interpretations of any leader who has a platform.

How do we discern what's true, what's reliable, what will address our needs and questions? Where do we go to find the truth we can lean on each day? We go to the Word of God. We measure and filter what we see and hear through what God says, leaning into the Holy Spirit's guidance. And we don't have to do it alone—we can engage the Word together with fellow disciples of Jesus. Let's follow the example of the Bereans in Acts 17, who searched the Scriptures to check what they heard against what God said. Let's choose to make the Word our foundation and our first line of defense.

Think for a moment about those young Christ-followers who willingly entered an Al-Qaeda camp. The camp was filled with people who would kill them in an instant if they knew why they were there or what book they carried. When these ordinary disciples decided to take on that mission, when they chose to return hatred with love, they set aside all distractions.

They had decided to completely die to themselves and align their lives with the kingdom of God by engaging wholeheartedly with God's Word.

Four Ways to Align Ourselves With God's Word

We know from personal experience what life is like when we're drawn away from, or misaligned with God and his Word. It's easy to get distracted, to feel discouraged, or weighed down by trying to do everything ourselves. Our spiritual energy drags; we're tempted to focus only on our needs and solutions; and we lose sight of the life God offers through his Word, through Jesus, and his Spirit. We've seen examples of those who have aligned themselves with Scripture, and in our heart of hearts, we want to live like they do. We want to experience God the way they have.

When we choose to align our life with the truth of God's Word, it will have a powerful effect on our own life, and through us to the lives of our family and those we serve.

When I (Tefera) served as an elder in one of the local churches we planted in Ethiopia, one of our deacons was studying at the Bible Institute. His theology professor gave an assignment to go and interview leaders of cults and write a paper on their false teaching. This deacon interviewed a cult leader, who did not believe in the Trinity. After the interview, the leader also gave the deacon some of their teaching materials. Soon the deacon came to me and asked me to help him.

"What happened?" I asked.

He told me what had happened and how he was now confused about what he believed. For each of his questions, I simply asked him to open the Word of God, directed him to certain verses, and then asked him to explain what he was reading. Through study and in conversation with each other, he began to find his way back. I saw his face was shining, and his spiritual life was restored after a couple of hours in God's Word.

At the end of our conversation, he said, "I would never have expected to find such an immediate solution to my questions and doubts." It was all there—in the Word of God. Since then, he has devoted himself to study the Word carefully, and he has helped many disciples to also grow in the Word.

It's important to continually align our lives with God's Word—here are four practical ways we can do that.

Study

You can't align yourself with something you know nothing about.

Did you know that less than 30 percent of Christians worldwide will ever read through the entire Bible? Or that over 82 percent of Christians in America only ever read their Bible on Sundays at church?[5] Even so, many Christians in America are familiar with the Bible. And in our familiarity, we can easily take it for granted, or forget to give it our wholehearted focus. I

---

[5] "Christians Don't Read Their Bible," *Ponce Foundation*, http://poncefoundation.com/christians-dont-read-their-bible/.

wonder if you have found yourself skimming over the Scripture passages we have included so far because you've seen or heard them before?

If you want to be changed by encountering God's Word, the first thing you must do is engage with it. Read it. Study it.

At the time I (Tefera) made the decision to follow Christ, it was illegal to have a Bible under the communist regime, and there were no Bibles to purchase in any shops. When I received a Gideon New Testament, I was very happy and started reading it in secret, page after page, but I couldn't understand why an innocent man like Jesus suffered and was crucified. When I started to read it over again and really study it, the Holy Spirit opened my eyes to see all that Jesus had done was for my salvation, and the salvation of the entire world. The Holy Spirit is always within us to teach us the truth when we study the Bible. That is when I recognized the words of Jesus, "The words I have spoken to you—they are full of the Spirit and life" (John 6:63).

Since carrying the Bible was illegal, the only option for us was to study the Bible in secret and memorize it verse by verse. We wrote out the verses that spoke to us from our daily reading and carried that small paper or card with us in our pockets until we memorized it and made it part of our lives. Our daily activity and prayers were shaped by this study and memorization.

I still remember when the Holy Spirit clearly spoke to me from Psalm 91:14–16. During my morning Bible reading, I heard a whisper that this Bible text was for me, so I wrote it on a piece of paper and kept it in my pocket. I memorized it throughout the day and into the evening.

When I came home from a Bible study, as soon as I reached the gate in our fence and entered, I heard a voice say, "I will not miss you tomorrow even if I miss you today." I didn't know what was going on, so I opened the gate and saw the leader of the district communist youth holding a pistol. Shocked, I called on the name of Jesus, ran into the house, locked the door, and knelt by my bed to pray! Immediately, the Holy Spirit reminded me of what he had spoken to me all day long through Psalm 91:14–16.

> "Because he loves me," says the Lord, "I will rescue him; I will protect him,
> for he acknowledges my name. He will call on me, and I will answer him;

I will be with him in trouble, I will deliver him and honor him. With long life I will satisfy him and show him my salvation."

This Bible verse became my life's theme.

I didn't go out alone at night for some time after that incident, although I did return to teaching school the next day. I was protected from many threats to my life by the power and authority of this word.

God longs to speak into the reality of our lives, whether that's the job he wants us to do, the choices we make with our money, how we raise our children, schedule our time, or serve in our church and community. He often uses his Scripture to do that.

Community

The University Christian Student Fellowship community nurtured my spiritual life and shaped who I (Tefera) am today. Every Tuesday and Thursday evening, there was a youth group in a Protestant church within walking distance of the university. If someone missed an evening, after the service, we would all go and find that person and pray over them. That meant you had a choice: go to the youth event twice a week or be visited by your Christian friends later in the evening and prayed over.

We also had a weekly Bible study under a tree or in an empty field. As I mentioned, we had to memorize the text we were going to study since we were not allowed to carry a Bible. In that faith community, we openly shared our understanding of the Bible text we studied, and we also prayed those texts over each other.

As I look back on that time, accountability and transparency were the key elements that helped me grow as a disciple of Jesus. As I shared life with my brothers and sisters in the university fellowship, I learned that I am not alone in my spiritual journey, and I have support from all my friends. Having others speak into our lives from within our community goes a long way to helping us live lives that align with Scripture. In that community, when my friends saw me doing something that ran contrary to the Word of God, they openly challenged me and corrected me in love. When I graduated from the university, I lost that intimate community until I started leading others to Christ and built that same DNA of community in them.

Right now, I lead a Bible study group of transplanted Ethiopians that started when I moved to the US in 2007. We have a weekly meeting to share life, study the Word of God, and celebrate the goodness of God together. At the end of our study, we share tea and snacks and build trusting relationships among ourselves. Currently, everyone in this small group is strong in their faith and involved in their local church's ministries.

When we recognize the need for community and create an environment in which everyone grows in their faith in Christ, it enables them to become disciples who will make disciples. When we intentionally create a small group in which each person feels respected and their ideas are valued, it will provide an opportunity to utilize everyone's spiritual gifting, and each person will be equipped and encouraged to play their part to advance the kingdom.

Meditation

Meditating on Scripture is one of the most helpful ways to align ourselves with God's Word. A simple definition of meditation is a practice that allows the Word of God to sink into our inner being by reading, reflecting, and thinking on a Bible passage. As we read and reflect on God's Word in meditation, it starts to saturate our life, and it becomes like a mirror showing us who we are and what is missing from us as a disciple of Jesus Christ. Through meditation we hide the Word of God in our heart, and it serves as a guardrail for our lives as disciples.[6] That's why Paul reminded the Philippians to think of what is true, what is noble, what is right, what is pure, what is lovely, what is admirable—anything that is excellent or praiseworthy.[7]

If we develop the simple habit of setting aside at least fifteen to twenty

---

[6]   Psalm 119:11.

[7]   See Philippians 4:8.

minutes daily to prayerfully read, reflect, and think on the Word of God, it will greatly impact our life. When we allow the Word of God to sink into our inner being and settle, it becomes part of who we are, and it completely changes our perspective. That is why the Bible clearly tells us to be filled by the Word, "to admonish one another with all wisdom through psalms, hymns, and songs from the Spirit, singing to God with gratitude in [our] hearts" (Colossians 3:16).

When Joshua was appointed to replace the great leader Moses, God told him to meditate on the Law that he gave to Moses day and night, so that he would succeed in all he did.[8] In the same way, our success in making disciples is based on taking quality time to meditate on the Word of God.

When Jesus met with his two disciples on the road to Emmaus, he simply helped them to meditate on what was written about him in the whole Scriptures, and it made their hearts burn within them.[9] I pray for the same Lord to open the Scriptures to us as we meditate on it daily. For additional help on meditating or listening to the Word, see Appendix B, page 215.

Obedience

The purpose in aligning our life with God's Word is to be obedient in whatever ways he invites us to die to ourselves, so we can live fully in the kingdom of God.

If obedience is missing, then simply reading the Bible will not help us at all. If we do not obey the Word we study and meditate on, we are like the foolish builder in Matthew 7:26–27:

> "But everyone who hears these words of mine and does not put them into practice is like a foolish man who built his house on sand. The rain came

---

8   Joshua 1:8.
9   Luke 24:32.

down, the streams rose, and the winds blew and beat against that house, and it fell with a great crash."

Those who listen to the words of Jesus and obey are compared to the man who built his house on a rock. Nothing could bring it down.[10] That is why Jesus said, "If you hold to my teaching, you are really my disciples. Then you will know the truth, and the truth will set you free" (John 8:31).

If we read the Word of God as God's love letter to his children, then we can respond in obedient love. When we obey the truth revealed to us, he continues to teach us new things one after another. Jesus said it clearly to his disciples: "If you love me, keep my commands [...]. Whoever has my commands and keeps them is the one who loves me [...]. I too will love them and show myself to them" (John 14:15–21).

Reading and memorizing page after page of God's Word will not benefit us unless we respond in obedience. Reading and preaching the Word of God is one thing, being obedient to the Word is another.[11]

What would happen to our body if 100 percent of the food we ate daily went right through us? It wouldn't nourish us. In the same way, if we are not obedient to the Word of God, it doesn't help us or anyone else. Reading the Word of God for information gathering doesn't make us spiritual, impact our lives, or allow us to influence others for the kingdom.

In the US, we often focus on accumulating information. However, many disciples we work with in other areas of the world are reading and discussing the Bible, asking the question, "How will we live differently tomorrow because of what we are learning today?" They're talking about it and working at integrating the Word into their lives and routines—and holding each other accountable. We often refer to it as *obedience-based discipleship*. Remember Jesus' words in John 15:14, "You are my friends if you do what I command." It's a common theme.

Let us take to our heart what is recorded in James 1:22–25:

---

[10] Matthew 7:24–25.
[11] Ezra 7:10.

Do not merely listen to the word, and so deceive yourselves. Do what it says. Anyone who listens to the word but does not do what it says is like someone who looks at his face in a mirror and, after looking at himself, goes away and immediately forgets what he looks like. But whoever looks intently into the perfect law that gives freedom and continues in it—not forgetting what they have heard but doing it—they will be blessed in what they do.

We can commit to all these things, but if we do not make a commitment to obedience, we will never be aligned with God. We can know all the right things, be part of a community, and even meditate on Scripture, but it is only when we begin obeying Jesus and we respond to the Holy Spirit's every nudge that we will begin experiencing an alignment with the Word of God.

Aligning our lives with Scripture transforms us. It keeps us in line and in step with the Spirit of the Lord. And it's essential if we are to enjoy and deepen our relationship with God.

Reflect and Discuss

- What inspired you in this chapter?
- What challenged you?
- What is God inviting you to do in the coming days?
- What obstacles are keeping you from accepting and acting upon this invitation?
- How will you live differently today because of what you have just read?
- What practical actions will you commit to doing soon?
- What questions do you still have?

Additional Study

- **Authority and Power of Scripture:** 2 Timothy 3:16–17; Hebrews 4:12–13.
- **Biblical Interpretation:** 2 Timothy 2:15; Acts 8:30–33; 2 Peter 1:19–21.
- **Practice of Bible Study:** Joshua 1:6–9; Psalm 1; Psalm 119:104–106.
- **Centrality of Jesus Christ:** Luke 24:25–27; John 1:1–3; Col. 1:15–29.

PART TWO
HIGHER

Rise above the normal, the common and usual:
become intimate with Jesus as Lord and Savior,
experiencing extraordinary resurrection power,
like the disciples of Jesus in the early church.

---

*"I want to know Christ—yes, to know the power of
his resurrection and participation in his sufferings,
becoming like him in his death, and so, somehow,
attaining to the resurrection from the dead."*

Philippians 3:10–11

4

Pursuing Intimacy with God

I couldn't wait to see Ekeno.

Our plane descended toward a narrow strip bordering the desert in central Africa, and as the plane landed, I could see a cluster of trees, and beyond that a small town. We taxied along the bumpy tarmac, lurched to a halt, and the propellers stopped spinning. The pilot opened the door, and I saw a small bus shelter, one end closed in for the ticket counter. Our luggage was placed on a concrete slab just off the runway.

I spotted ten or twelve local men standing together, some dressed in Western garb, but most wearing the more traditional robe wrapped around the body and draped over one shoulder. Then I recognized my friend Ekeno. It wasn't hard—he was slender, taller than the others, and carrying a long walking stick. As soon as he saw me squeeze through the plane's small door and step to the ground, he broke from the group, his walk turning into a jog. I greeted the lanky church planter with a warm embrace, and we quickly exchanged news about our families.

As soon as there was a break in the conversation, Ekeno blurted out, "It's finally happened!"

"What happened?" I asked, grinning at Ekeno's eagerness.

He glanced around quickly to make sure no one except his fellow leaders and disciples were within earshot and then whispered loudly, "We now have more than a hundred churches planted in the villages of our tribe!"

"Praise God!" I said. A huge smile broke out across his face, which in turn lit up the faces of his fellow church planters as they gathered around us. Every one of them had paid a price to be a part of this movement to share Christ among their people. God had honored their sacrifice, and their joy was palpable. I smiled at Ekeno and couldn't help but think about his long, amazing journey.

His father had fifty-six children with multiple wives; Ekeno was one of the younger sons. Born hydrocephalic (with too much fluid on his brain), his grandmother had cared for him day and night. Without intervention, he would not have survived. One day, a pilot landed a missionary doctor's plane close to Ekeno's village, and his grandmother begged the doctor to take the baby. After a long conversation and much resistance, the grandmother stopped pleading, laid Ekeno down in the desert sand, and walked away. The missionary doctor relented and took him back to California, becoming his adopted mother. After surgery at a children's hospital, Ekeno grew into a healthy child.

At the age of six, Ekeno heard the voice of the Holy Spirit speak clearly to him, "Go speak and heal the nations." He didn't understand what that entailed, but he knew that one day he would return to his people and share the good news of Jesus with them. After graduating from high school, this word took root in his heart. Instead of following his friends off to university, he returned to his African home, bought a herd of goats, and began moving around with his nomadic tribe, telling them about Jesus.

My mind raced back over the years to when I first met seventeen-year-old Ekeno. This young man clearly had a powerful anointing on his life, as well as a humble, compassionate, servant-heart, that God honors. Ekeno had recently completed nine months of discipleship-mission training and outreach in an African training program that Global Disciples had helped launch. I remembered this winsome young man eager to go back to his people with the good news of Jesus.

Ekeno told me early on that his dream was to one day plant a hundred churches among his people—a nomadic tribe largely unreached with the gospel.

"Then," he said with a chuckle, "after we plant a hundred churches, I'm going to retire."

Ten years later, that goal had been reached, but as we met that day on a dusty airstrip, there was no talk of retirement. He was just getting started!

After a while, the celebratory tone of the conversation changed as we walked toward the small guest house where I would spend the night. Ekeno told me about two young church planters he had come across as he walked the desert. He found them dead only a few weeks earlier at separate places, each lying in the sand close to locations where there had been a small oasis before the rains had stopped.

A few days later, I stood with Ekeno in the two places where these young men had died. There was no memorial. No markers. Only memories and prayers ... and tears.

Ekeno himself had nearly lost his life over and over again. I remember him telling me about the day he walked into a village, where a man fired his gun point-blank at Ekeno's chest. In pain, Ekeno's impulse was to grab the spot where he had been shot and cry out to Jesus. When he removed his hand, the bullet fell to the ground. He showed me the scar, right at his heart.

I turned and asked him, "How do you keep doing this and not lose hope?"

He straightened up, brushed away a tear and said, "You see that village over there?" He raised his long, slender arm and pointed across the desert.

Straining my eyes, I saw through the heat waves a little dark speck in the distance.

Ekeno's voice cracked. "We keep going because the people in that village and many villages beyond there, have no idea who Jesus is."

What gives a man like Ekeno the courage required to keep going, to keep sharing, to keep making disciples, when his life, and the lives of those he loves, is on the line?

There is only one answer.

His deep intimacy with God. It's an intimacy that has infused his life with the same unrestrained love that we see in Jesus—a love that continues, even in the face of death.

From the early days of his ministry, Ekeno would go out to what he called his *prayer tree*. He would wait deep in conversation with God under his prayer tree, initially alone, then with a few fellow disciples, until the Holy Spirit told them to go. Then they would go. That's how they planted all those churches.

In the Gospels, Jesus often went out to a quiet place to spend intimate, powerful time with the Father. Frequently this act preceded amazing miracles and wonderful works of God. Ekeno's experience echoes that. What has come out of Ekeno's time under the prayer tree has been extraordinary. Since our conversation at the dusty airstrip, well over four hundred churches have been planted. As recently as the year 2000, his people group was considered 'unreached' with the gospel. Now there's a thriving movement of Christ! Ekeno and those he's discipled are now taking the good news of Jesus to neighboring tribes—even some that have frequently been at war with his own. It's hard, it's risky, and it has cost him so much, but Ekeno carries on because intimacy with God sustains him as a disciple.

There's a cost to intimacy with God: the cost of time invested, and the cost of dying to some of our own desires, as we surrender our will to his. But there is also abundant hope, joy, and the honor of being a witness to the life-changing work of Christ and an ambassador of the living God who is at work in and through us. When we are motivated by what motivates God, we find ourselves urged by the Holy Spirit to do uncomfortable, unplanned, and even dangerous things. Although intimacy with God leads us into new and sometimes unpredictable situations, it is this intimate, deeply personal relationship that sustains us and leads to a fruitful life.

Bearing Fruit

As disciples of Jesus, we are called to bear fruit. Sometimes we confuse fruit with success. But we are not called to be successful! As Henri Nouwen

pointed out, we must be aware that there is "a great difference between suc-
cessfulness and fruitfulness."[1] Success is about the trophies, the games you
win, the books you write, the awards you receive, the money you make. As
Christ-followers, that is not our calling.

In John 15, the branches on a vine or a fruit tree bear fruit because they
are connected to the vine. The image of the vine and the branches is one of
the most powerful analogies of intimacy with God. Without that healthy
connection, there's no fruit.

> "I am the true vine, and my Father is the gardener. He cuts off every branch
> in me that bears no fruit, while every branch that does bear fruit, he prunes
> so that it will be even more fruitful. You are already clean because of the
> word I have spoken to you. Remain in me, as I also remain in you. No
> branch can bear fruit by itself; it must remain in the vine. Neither can you
> bear fruit unless you remain in me.
>
> "I am the vine; you are the branches. If you remain in me and I in you,
> you will bear much fruit; apart from me you can do nothing."

John 15:1–5

If you're familiar with these words, I encourage you to read them as if they're
new to you and spend some time being guided by the Holy Spirit in listening to God's Word. Read them over and over until Jesus' words have soaked
in. Grab a notebook and jot down phrases or words that stand out to you, or
any responses you have as you read the text. If you truly received and lived
out these words as truth, how might they affect your life?[2]

It's clear from these verses that apart from Jesus, we can do nothing.

Apart from Jesus, we can't lead someone to Christ.

Apart from Jesus, we can't equip people to make disciples.

Apart from Jesus, we can't plant one single church.

Most of us want to be fruitful, but we often try and do it in our own

---

[1]   Henri J. M. Nouwen, *Bread for the Journey: A Daybook of Wisdom and Faith* (New York: HarperOne, 1997), 4.

[2]   For guidance in growing in this pattern of listening to the Word, see Appendix B at the end of this book.

strength. The verses don't say, "If you strive, you will bear much fruit." Our task is to remain in the vine, the True Vine, Jesus. That's what's expected of us: to seek out intimacy with God—through the Word and the voice of the Holy Spirit—and to obey. Only then will the fruit come.

The fruit refers not only to seeing people come to faith in Jesus. The fruit of the Spirit is also evident in God's transforming work in our lives. It can be seen in our character, our responses and reactions to others, and to difficult situations. Remember, the fruit of the Spirit is love, joy, peace, patience, kindness, goodness, faithfulness, gentleness, and self-control.[3] These two types of fruit—leading others to Christ and personal transformation—usually flow together.

Abiding or staying continually connected to Jesus as the vine is often difficult with our distracted lifestyles. Our phone dings with a message, a Facebook post catches our attention. Maybe you are trying to develop the spiritual disciplines of prayer and time in the Word, but distractions persist. Sometimes your job, school, family commitments, even service or ministry leave very little margin.

After I made a commitment to Christ as a teenager, I struggled tremendously to live in the way I knew the Lord was calling me to live. I promised I wouldn't do "this" again, and I wouldn't do "that" again. I promised to make all the changes I knew I wanted and needed to make. But I just couldn't follow through. I couldn't do it on my own. I felt like I was stuck in my old life. In utter frustration one day, I cried out to God and flipped open my Bible and began reading. Of course, my Bible flipped open to John 15. Through these verses, the Holy Spirit made it clear that I could keep trying and failing or I could develop and nurture a healthy relationship with "the Vine," allowing the same Holy Spirit that raised Christ from the dead to flow into me, enabling me to withstand temptations and bear fruit. When I discerned the Holy Spirit's prompting through that reading of John 15, I began investing time and energy in developing that relationship, that connection between me and Jesus. I began praying specifically for my high school friends who did not know Jesus. I wanted to bear fruit that would last. A few weeks later

---

[3]   Galatians 5:22–23.

in the gym lobby after soccer practice, one friend approached me and asked, "What happened to you? You're just different than you used to be."

I explained that Jesus was the difference and how getting to know him had changed so many things in my life. I didn't say that much, but my friend asked, "Could you help me get to know Jesus?" So, in the gym lobby we prayed, and she invited Jesus to be her Lord and Savior.

In the months that followed I saw her life change, much as mine had only a short time earlier. She was no longer swayed by peer pressure as she had previously been. She was bold in talking about Jesus. She joined our Fellowship of Christian Athletes (FCA) huddle and impacted the lives and behavior of many of her friends. She was an ordinary young disciple, who, instead of being negatively influenced by her peers, became an influencer for Jesus.

There's nothing quite so satisfying as walking in intimacy with God ... unless it's helping others discover that same life-transforming intimacy!

Submitting to Pruning

Pruning is not a pretty process. My father-in-law, now with the Lord, had many fruit trees, and sometimes I would assist him while he pruned them. The trees actually looked a lot nicer before the pruning took place, because the smaller, leafy branches filled out the tree. But they were unnecessary, even detrimental, to the tree's health and its ability to produce fruit. All those small leafy branches drew sap and nutrition away from the branches that could bear fruit.

Likewise, sometimes there are good, attractive things in our lives that aren't bearing fruit. Should we eliminate some of those things we enjoy? Maybe. But we don't need to worry about pruning ourselves; we just need to remain in the Vine. Our Heavenly Father, the Gardener, will address those things if we are attentive to God's Word, pursue intimacy with him, and re-main open to the Holy Spirit.

It's not often many of us talk about pruning, and it's certainly not an idea we usually embrace. But if we are to grow as disciples of Christ, pruning is absolutely necessary both for the strengthening of our faith and if we're to bear any fruit. Pruning can be very personal, and it can be uncomfortable. Sometimes God chooses to prune the very things on which we base our identity—whether that be the way we look, the things we own, or the talents we possess.

A few years ago, my role entailed training youth leaders, planning youth events, and speaking at retreats. One time when our congregation was planning a youth retreat, I was asked to help with the planning. I fully expected I would be asked to be the speaker too. But when that discussion came up, my name was never mentioned! God taught me some profound lessons through that little pruning experience. It turned out that the young man who was invited to speak for the retreat was a guy I had been mentoring. That weekend God taught me that there's a special joy in seeing those in whom we invest our lives grow and flourish. I've come to love the role of raising up others; encouraging them; offering feedback; and seeing them released to equip, encourage, and mentor others—and to celebrate when they excel in God's kingdom. As ordinary disciples, we will experience extraordinary influence when we walk in intimacy with God and invest freely in the lives of others.

But it won't happen without pruning.

As with fruit trees, pruning is not something that occurs year-round. The Master Gardener takes us through seasons of pruning—sometimes longer seasons than others. But if we cooperate with the Gardener, we can enjoy the seasons of greater fruitfulness that follow.

It's Time to Close the Door

Often the benefits of God's pruning in our lives are recognized in times of solitude. When we pour out our hearts and our frustrations, and then take the time to listen, the Lord has beautiful ways of bringing us around to his perspective.

When Jesus instructs his disciples to pray, he tells them to go into their room and close the door.[4] He explains that when our Father sees what is done in secret, he will reward us. When a married couple go into a room and

---

[4]   Matthew 6:6.

close the door, it's usually for the sake of privacy or intimacy. Behind closed doors, they talk about things they would not discuss openly, sometimes with laughter and sometimes with tears. They may use expressions that they would not use in other settings. And they pursue intimacy with one another in ways that they never would with anyone else, or if the door were not closed. I believe God wants you to communicate with him—just the two of you—in ways that you would not if the door were left open. Sometimes it may be with laughter or with tears. Sometimes it might mean talking with God in ways you may not talk with anyone else. That's intimacy. And I believe that's the kind of relationship God wants with each of us.

And what is the reward?

It's all that comes with intimacy: knowing deeply and being deeply known.

I believe that in the same way intimacy between a husband and wife leads to reproduction, so will intimacy with God lead to fruitfulness. Children are a blessing and reward from the most intimate moments a husband and wife experience together. Likewise, spiritual daughters and sons arise from our intimacy with God. God wants more and more spiritual sons and daughters. He wants all people to be saved and to come to a knowledge of the truth.[5]

Whether you're single or married, a businessperson, a member or leader in your local church, this is a call to intimacy with God. And it is a call to deep and caring relationships with one another in the body of Christ. Family is such a powerful image for the church. Around the world in Global Disciples, we address one another as sister and brother. Scripture builds on this family image beautifully with our Heavenly Father and Jesus as our elder brother. Jesus declares, "For whoever does the will of my Father in heaven is my brother and sister and mother" (Matthew 12:50).

Reproduction within the body of Christ happens as we allow our intimacy with God to transform us into caring brothers and sisters who reflect the character and compassion of Jesus. As we do so, our lives become more and more fruitful.

Jeff lives in middle America, and he came to Jesus amid many personal

---

[5]   1 Timothy 2:4.

challenges, including drug addiction. He eventually became a pastor, and later, crossed paths with Dan, a friend from the old days of drugs and parties. In the wake of his rough divorce, Dan asked Jeff if they could start a Bible study for "losers like me." So Jeff started a group with a bunch of guys struggling with addictions. One particular night, Dan opened up with a tirade on his wife's infidelity, spewing out his pain and anger. It was messy and uncomfortable, but it was the start of something new. From that place of pain, Dan continued to attend the group and grow in faith and intimacy with Jesus. He took part in the discipleship training Jeff's church held and went to Indonesia on a mission outreach. Dan has since helped to start three more addiction recovery groups. Several times, when someone has shown up to a recovery meeting and mentioned they are homeless, Dan will take them home with him. He has risked so much by moving strangers into his house and given much of his own money to help them out along the way.

What a powerful witness to the love of Jesus when these new members were born into the family of God. As Psalm 68:6 declares, "God sets the lonely in families, he leads out the prisoners with singing." Out of intimacy with our Heavenly Father, the compassion of Jesus is embodied in those who know him—and to those who haven't yet found that place of peace, joy, and freedom in Christ.

When Tefera and I were traveling in the Middle East, we met Desta, a young woman ministering to domestic workers who, in trying to survive on very meager salaries, have turned to prostitution. Desta's approach is simple. Around 1 a.m., she heads out to a few bars nearby, where she knows young women are looking for a pickup. As the crowd thins, the Holy Spirit directs her to specific women, and Desta invites them to come home with her. She gives them a good meal, a new outfit, and a comfortable place to spend the rest of the night. In the morning she introduces them to the One she represents: Jesus. If they choose Jesus, she'll begin discipling them and connect them with one of the local house fellowships.

"God sets the lonely in families, he leads out the prisoners with singing."

Some beautiful things happen in our lives when we desire and seek intimacy with our Creator—peace, hope, joy, patience, kindness, and love—all so evident in the stories of Dan's life and ministry, and in Desta's courageous work. But deepening our personal intimacy with God requires making some deliberate choices.

Five Ways to Deepen Your Intimacy With God

I (Tefera) am a workaholic. A few years ago, I took a two-week vacation: one week to paint rooms in our house and a second week for family time. The painting took more time than I planned, and my family was unhappy because I didn't give them the time they needed. I was offended, too, because I had worked hard to make them happy, and I thought they would understand that I did it for them!

The next day, in our bathroom, I heard an inner voice telling me to slow down. Immediately I found my eyes fixed on our shower curtain. For the first time, I noticed it was decorated with beautiful pictures of birds, flowers, and butterflies. That shower curtain had hung there for over two years! Yet in my hurrying, I never noticed the beauty right there in front of me.

God spoke to me in that moment.

Do you understand how you missed seeing my beauty as you focus on work? You are trying to please your family by working hard, but what they actually want is to spend time with you. In the same way, you try to please me with your hard work, but I am longing to spend quality time with you. If you prioritize time with me first, then you will accomplish more in less time.

I am still on the journey of spending quality time with the Lord rather than working so hard. It is a difficult change to make, but an important one.

Any of us who experience intimacy in relationships with spouses, children, parents, or friends, know that healthy intimacy does not happen without effort. It requires time, initiative, and patience. Similarly, building intimacy with God requires some specific things:

Open communication. When we openly share our dreams, longings, victories, and struggles, it fosters intimacy. God knows everything about us and our situations, but as we draw near to him by being vulnerable and transparent about our struggles and weaknesses, our dreams and desires, God draws near to us.

Regular times of reading and meditating on God's Word. This kind of quality time reveals God's purpose and plan for our lives. The styles of literature in the Bible can speak to us in various ways, revealing God's character, his love for each one of us, and his responses to those who love and obey him, as well as his responses to those who don't.

Listening well. While most of us understand listening is essential in human communication, sometimes we overlook the importance of listening in developing our intimacy with God. Often our prayer time is one unending stream of requests and concerns. But God wants to speak to us, too. Jesus says in John 10:27, "My sheep listen to my voice; I know them, and they follow me." We suggest always having a journal and pen nearby to record what God is speaking to you when you set aside this important time to listen.

Does God really speak to us in our generation? Absolutely. He speaks to us in many different ways.[6] Throughout this chapter and the stories in this book, you will notice all of the different ways God speaks to us. Sometimes it may be through a still small voice, or he may fill us with peace about what to do in a certain situation that causes us anxiety. He speaks through his Word—with a recurring phrase or reference. Or even in an audible voice. He also speaks to us through his people or in circumstances by opening or closing doors of opportunity. Perhaps for many of us, the better question is, "Am I listening?" rather than "Does God speak?"

Expressing appreciation and love. This is foundational in developing intimacy in any relationship. As we develop personal intimacy with God, we will express our love and appreciation freely through prayer and worship. As we express adoration, praise, and worship to God, the warmth of intimacy often wells up within us and overflows into other areas of our lives.

Times of privacy and being alone together. Dedicated time away from other distractions and concerns can foster intimacy in relationships. When it's just you and God together, it removes the concern of what others may

---

[6] Job 33:14–18.

think if they hear the conversation or observe what's happening. God is not interested in whether your communication with him demonstrates how "spiritual" you are to others around you. Jesus modeled the way for us by setting aside time alone with his Father, sometimes early in the morning, and other times throughout the night.[7]

Amazing things happen when we spend time focused on these five ways of developing intimacy with God. We don't need to concern ourselves with the fruit or what might need pruning. God will take care of those things as we grow deeper in our relationship with him.

The fruit will come.

The fruit that Ekeno has seen among his least-reached tribe is difficult to explain apart from the work of God. His early strategy—by his own initiative and the leading of the Spirit—was simple. He carried flour from the main town to the surrounding villages. At each village, he would exchange the flour for goats, and tell people about Jesus. He took along several young guys to carry the flour and then herd the goats. Once he completed his circuit, they would herd the goats back to town and sell them, using the proceeds to buy more flour, and return to the villages once again. This formed Ekeno's income stream, because in the early days he supported himself in his witness for Jesus. Like so many of the disciple-makers Global Disciples trains, he learned to use what God had placed in his hands to build relationships and provide for his needs.

After a few witch doctors tried to kill him, Ekeno learned when he entered a village it was wise to first ask to speak with the witch doctor who controlled the area through fear and black magic. He now tells the witch doctor that he is not there to harm him but to give him a better understanding of the God who created the sun, the moon, the stars, and everything in the universe.

Then he often asks, "Is there anyone in your family you have not been able to heal?" Inevitably there is someone the witch doctor has been unable to help—someone who couldn't walk or an individual with a debilitating disease. Ekeno or his coworker prays for that person in the name of Jesus,

---

[7]   Mark 1:35; Luke 6:12.

and almost without exception they are healed. This opens the door, and in many villages, the witch doctors have been the first to believe in Jesus!

Ekeno may sound like he's some sort of super-disciple, but any disciple of Jesus can develop and experience an intimate, fruitful, transformative relationship as we learn to listen, to communicate, to express our hearts and spend time with God. Out of his intimate relationship with Jesus, Ekeno carries an unshakable confidence and faith in what God can and will do. He also leans into the amazing resource God has given to every disciple—the presence and power of the Holy Spirit.

Reflect and Discuss

- What inspired you in this chapter?
- What challenged you?
- What is God inviting you to do in the coming days?
- What obstacles are keeping you from accepting and acting upon this invitation?
- How will you live differently today because of what you have just read?
- What practical actions will you commit to doing soon?
- What questions do you still have?

Additional Study

- **Solitude and Time Alone with God:** Mark 1:35; 6:31,45–46; Luke 4:42.
- **Prayer:** Matthew 6:5–18; Philippians 4:6–7; Isaiah 58:6–8.
- **Worship and Confession:** John 4:24; Romans 10:9–10; 1 John 1:5–10.
- **Scripture Meditation and Listening:** Joshua 1:8; John 10:14–15, 27.

5

Living in the Power of the Holy Spirit

"If you don't get out of here, we'll kill you," the man snarled as four others pinned Salim against the wall. He could smell their sweat, their anger. They punched him repeatedly in the face and stomach, and although they gave no reason for the beating, he knew why. He had been found out. And now he wondered if he was about to die.

As the five men finally backed away, Salim fell to the ground, his nose bleeding, his body in pain. When his attackers disappeared around the corner, he pulled himself to his feet and ran away down the street.

Looking over his shoulder the entire way, Salim hurried back to his room. He couldn't pack quickly enough. After cramming his sparse belongings into a bag and cleaning himself up, he headed out of town the fastest way he knew how. Surely those men were following him, but every time he glanced back, he saw only shadows in the darkness. As he fled the city, he knew he would not go back. Never. He'd be a dead man if he returned to the city to preach the gospel.

He caught a bus that took him to a friend in a neighboring town. Feeling lucky to be alive, Salim winced as he felt the tender bruises on his face and body. Looking out over the rocky wilderness, he thought of the eerie scenes he had witnessed in that spiritually-charged region. He pictured some of the men who wandered the streets armed to the teeth, automatic rifles slung over their shoulders, pistols in their waistbands.

What if one of his attackers had carried a gun? Would he be on this bus, running away, or would he instead be lying in an alley in a pool of his own blood? Shuddering at the thought, Salim vowed again that he would never return.

Salim arrived at his friend's house, still trembling in fear. His friend, another Christ-follower, welcomed him warmly, served him a meal, and invited him to stay with his family for as long as he wanted. Salim nearly wept with gratefulness, and he told his friend everything that had happened since they had last seen one another.

The previous year, Salim was commissioned by his church to begin discipleship training with some new Muslim converts in a Muslim-dominated area. He had arrived full of excitement and passion. This was what he had always wanted to do—train new believers in how to share their faith! Salim felt a deep sense of purpose. He knew this was precisely what God had called him to do, and that the Holy Spirit had led him to this very city.

He was sure of it.

On the surface, moving there in the first place was not a smart decision—it was an increasingly dangerous area for Christians, especially those who shared the gospel. Aware of the dangers, Salim met with new converts secretly and tried to stay under the radar. As the Holy Spirit prompted him, he met with people one-on-one to talk about Jesus. His courage came directly from the Holy Spirit—a courage he had rarely felt before. He thought he had been doing a good job of staying out of harm's way, making smart decisions about when to walk the streets and when to meet. No one had confronted him. But someone had noticed, someone determined to stop the work he was doing. Now, safe in his friend's house, Salim couldn't sleep. He was restless and unsettled. But why? *I'm safe here,* he kept telling himself. *I don't have to worry, and I don't have to go back.* Yet he couldn't fall asleep. All night, the Holy Spirit seemed to ask him the same question.

"Who gave you permission to leave?"

Salim didn't have an answer.

The next morning over breakfast, Salim told his friend about this repeated question from the Holy Spirit. He explained that he had gone to such a risky place out of his determination to follow the Holy Spirit's leading in his life … but when he ran, when he grabbed that bus out of town, he had not been following the Spirit. He had listened only to his fear.

"I'm going back," Salim told his friend, determined. He knew he had to follow the Spirit's leading. He would never find peace otherwise.

"You're crazy!" his friend told him. "You were just attacked. If you go back, and they find you, they'll kill you!"

"I can't leave a place the Holy Spirit has led me to. I can't do that, not until I'm told to leave." The moment Salim said it out loud, an incredible sense of peace flowed through him. It wasn't a peace promising he would be safe or even that many would come to faith. No, he felt peace from God because he knew what the Holy Spirit was telling him to do—go back—and he was willing to do it.

Though Salim's friend was firmly against the idea, after talking and praying together, he sent Salim away with his blessing.

When Salim tells his story now, it is with a twinkle in his eye and joy in his face. "The five men who threatened to kill me are now part of our fellowship. They've all become followers of Jesus."

Something radical happened in their lives, and it changed their hearts and everything they understood. These men went from wanting to kill Salim because he was a Christ follower to following Christ themselves. And not only that, Salim reports they are now active witnesses to others of the saving grace of Jesus Christ.

Because Salim was willing to die to himself and follow the guiding of the Holy Spirit, these men had the opportunity to turn from their old ways and live vibrant lives in the kingdom of God. In such hostile environments, there is sometimes a greater sensitivity to the Holy Spirit's leading, a sensitivity that develops out of necessity. In those settings, we need to know what our next move should be because it is a matter of life and death.

For those of us in North America, our task is to learn to be attentive, sensitive, and responsive to the voice of the Holy Spirit. Sometimes our thick cloud of comfort is the very thing that stops us from being alert to what God wants to say to us. Or we rationalize away a voice or message or a recurring thought that comes seemingly out of the blue. Our culture focuses on what's provable, visible, repeatable, and reasonable. When something falls outside of those criteria, we become uncomfortable, and we doubt or dismiss it. We find it difficult to act in faith—accepting that we may not fully know or understand all that the Spirit of God is doing. Sometimes we may shy away from the Holy Spirit if we believe we're being asked to do something impractical, and so we rationalize it away. Or we know what obeying will cost us, and we're not ready to pay the price. We know it's the right thing to do, but we also fear that our friends, our family, or our coworkers won't understand or will misjudge us.

Getting to Know the Holy Spirit

Walking by faith and not by sight is a real test for many of us. Yet, as we saw in previous chapters, we are called to continually die to ourselves—and to our culture of comfort—as we live into the kingdom of God. The Holy Spirit will help us discern what to do from moment to moment and will empower our obedience as we practice abiding in Christ. As he determines appropriate, God gives us each gifts with the power source of the Holy Spirit within us—not only for our benefit, but for shaping, serving, and adding to his kingdom.

The Holy Spirit is not some vague power. He is the third person of the Godhead who was and is with God the Father and God the Son from the very beginning. Too often the Holy Spirit has been viewed as simply a spiritual concept rather than fully God.

The Holy Spirit is sent by God the Father at the request of Jesus the Son to be with us until the end of the world.[1] Scripture describes the Holy

---

[1] John 14:26; 16:7.

Spirit as the one who speaks, teaches, testifies, convicts of sin, guides, and intercedes.[2]

When Jesus ascended into heaven, he sent the Holy Spirit to live within us. That is why Jesus told his disciples to wait until they received the power that the Holy Spirit gives them to be his witness.[3] The Spirit comes to be our advocate, to help us, instruct us, empower us, and be with us forever.[4] The same Spirit that raised Jesus from the dead now lives within every person who invites Jesus Christ to be their Savior and Lord.[5]

The character of our Father God, of Jesus, and of the Holy Spirit is the same. There is nothing about the character of the Holy Spirit that differs from the character of Jesus. There are no words we might use to describe the nature of God that are not consistent with the nature of the Holy Spirit. The Holy Spirit will not instruct us to do things that are inconsistent with what God wants us to do or has instructed in the Bible.

It would have been easy for Salim to succumb to the voice of the enemy, to fear. If he had remained in fear, he wouldn't have experienced the peace of God. He wouldn't have returned to the city he fled. And he wouldn't have seen his five attackers come to Christ. Salim not only knew how to follow the Holy Spirit's leading; he also knew the amazing things that could happen when he was empowered by the Holy Spirit.

Confronting the Enemy

Years ago, I (Tefera) lived in the northern part of Ethiopia. At that time, only a few followers of Christ lived there, and no one in town was willing to rent a house to me and my family because we were followers of Christ. If someone did rent their property to us, they and their family would be excommunicated from the community.

We eventually managed to rent a house from a family that had moved to the capital city. A year later, they decided to sell the house, but I had no

---

2   John 14:17; 15:26; 16:8–15.
3   Acts 1:8.
4   John 14:16–18; Acts 1:8.
5   Romans 8:11.

money to buy it. I asked them to give me at least one month to find a new place. Graciously, they were willing to give me that amount of time. But the buyer, who practiced witchcraft, did not agree. The owner told me that the buyer would not give me the month I had requested, because he needed to move into the house immediately.

I went home and told my wife the sad news.

That evening, I knelt down to thank the Lord for the day before I went to bed. While I was praying, the Holy Spirit came upon me in a way I had never experienced before, and I started speaking in a tongue I had never spoken. Immediately, I received the interpretation of what I had been saying:

The house you live in belongs to God, for his service. But you have handed it over to the enemy without a fight.

I started crying and weeping, and the Holy Spirit empowered me to fight against the evil spiritual power that was using the buyer to snatch away the house God had entrusted into my hands. As I prayed, I felt in my spirit that I was in a physical battle. As Scripture tells us, our struggle is not against enemies of blood and flesh, but against the rulers, against the authorities, against the cosmic powers of this present darkness, against the spiritual forces of evil in the heavenly places.[6]

Around 3 a.m., when the Holy Spirit finished groaning in me, I sensed the battle was over and went to bed. At 5 a.m., I had a dream: I saw the cancellation of the sale as I had sensed in my spirit during my prayer time. I woke from my dream and knew beyond a shadow of a doubt that Jesus was going to allow us to stay in this house.

After my morning devotion, my wife gave me breakfast and urged me to try to find a house to rent. She was very concerned—if we didn't find a place to live, our family of four would become homeless.

I told her there was no need to look for another house, because in a dream God had shown me that the sale would be canceled, and we wouldn't have to move.

She thought I was out of my mind.

"What do you mean?" she asked.

---

[6] Ephesians 6:12.

I told her, "The battle is over—this house belongs to us."

She laughed. "Stop teasing and go look for a house."

I went to school to teach, and when I came home for lunch, my wife asked again if I had found a house. I said again, "This is our house."

She still didn't believe me.

"The battle belongs to the Lord," I said quietly.

That afternoon at 2 p.m., the owner of the house came and told me the news: the sale had fallen through at the last minute. My wife was overwhelmed with the unexpected, good news, and she started weeping with joy.

We lived in that house for two years and eventually bought it and used it to serve the Lord until we finished our ministry in that region in 2001.

This is just one of many examples we could share about battling with the enemy. Time and again we have observed that the battle does truly belong to the Lord. As believers, we stand in the authority of Jesus. All authority in heaven and on earth has been given to him,[7] and that same authority is available to us through the power of the Holy Spirit. This empowers you and me to be light and to proclaim the light of Christ over darkness. This is not child's play. In Christ we have the authority to enter spiritual battles to dispel the forces of evil.

I (Tefera) have a plaque in my office that reads, "Don't doubt in the dark what God has shown you in the light." When God speaks to us through the Holy Spirit—directing us on what to do, where to go, or what to say—the enemy's first strategy is to try and convince us it was a dumb idea. If we can be convinced of that, we won't do it. We'll back down. We'll rationalize ourselves out of it. All these battles are going on in our minds—that is why we need to daily renew our mind by the power of the Holy Spirit and the Word of God.

The foundational truth about the work and character of the enemy was declared by Jesus in John 8:44: "[The devil] was a murderer from the beginning, not holding to the truth, for there is no truth in him. When he lies, he speaks his native language, for he is a liar and the father of lies."

Declaring truth from Scripture is a wise and effective way to confront

---

[7]   Matthew 28:18.

the lies of the enemy. In John 10:10, Jesus reminds us of the nature of the spiritual conflict in which we are all engaged and the victory that is ours in Christ: "The thief comes only to steal and kill and destroy; I have come that they may have life, and have it to the full."

Often, this spiritual battle occurs when the enemy of our souls tempts us as he tempted Jesus in the desert, when Jesus was "full of the Spirit" (Luke 4:1) after his baptism.[8] Like Jesus, we are tempted to allow Satan to satisfy our appetites, to fulfill our urge to be in full control, and to fuel our egos. These three same basic temptations that Jesus experienced in the wilderness are described in 1 John 2:16 as: "the lust of the flesh, the lust of the eyes, and the pride of life."

The "lust of the flesh" goes far beyond our sexual desire, although that's certainly included. If we're honest, most of us want things our way. We want pleasurable and satisfying experiences. The temptation to take short-cuts to satisfy our appetites for intimacy, for wealth, for pleasure, and for control will lead to emptiness, brokenness, and sorrow. As Jesus reminded Satan by quoting Deuteronomy, "Man shall not live by bread alone."[9] The next portion of that verse, from Deuteronomy 8:3, says, "but on every word that comes from the mouth of the Lord." We are satisfied and find lasting fulfillment and joy as we do things God's way.

The "lust of the eyes" correlates with the second temptation Jesus experienced as he was preparing to launch into his public ministry. We all have a tendency to want things for ourselves. How many times have you seen a new car, a convenient gadget, a beautiful house, a fun-loving friendship, or the latest smartphone and said (or at least thought), "Wow, I wish I had one of those"? The tempter took Jesus to a place where he could see the kingdoms of the world, claimed they were his, and offered their splendor and authority to Jesus—if Jesus would only worship Satan. Jesus, quoting from Deuteronomy 6:13 and full of the Holy Spirit, stands firm, declaring that only the Lord our God deserves our full devotion or worship. Anything short of that is idolatry.

---

8   Luke 4:1–13.
9   Luke 4:3-4; Deuteronomy 8:3.

The "pride of life" identifies a common temptation for many of us. We all want significance, and we are tempted to do things to appear important. We see authority or influence in others that we want for ourselves. If Jesus had jumped off the highest point of the temple in Jerusalem without being injured, it would have been a shortcut to fame and notoriety. In the third temptation of Jesus, the tempter himself quotes Scripture in an attempt to deceive Jesus. But Jesus again refutes Satan, quoting from Deuteronomy 6:16, "Do not put the Lord your God to the test."

As disciples of Jesus, we see this sequence of temptations as reminders to stand strong in these same areas in which we are tempted today—to want things our way, to want so much for ourselves, and to want significance. Jesus withstood all the temptations he faced by being full of the Holy Spirit and relying on the truth and power of Scripture. It's this same God-inspired duo that gives us joy, victory, and freedom in our lives today. 1 Corinthians 10:13 reminds us: "No temptation has overtaken you except what is common to mankind. And God is faithful; he will not let you be tempted beyond what you can bear. But when you are tempted, he will also provide a way out so that you can endure it." We can tell the tempter to back off—in the name of Jesus. God isn't going to allow our temptation to go beyond what we can handle by the power of his Holy Spirit within us.

Living Into the Power of the Holy Spirit

Beyond helping us battle the enemy, the Holy Spirit leads us into the life of a disciple. He brings the power we need to live each day; he gifts us with the tools we need for kingdom work. And when we learn to listen and follow the Holy Spirit, our lives and the lives of those around us undergo powerful changes. In the previous chapter, we talked about the transformation of Dan and his community of those struggling with addiction. It was the Holy Spirit who brought that transformation, and it was also the Holy Spirit who led Desta in her ministry with women in the Middle East.

And it was the Holy Spirit's transformative power at work in the life of the Apostle Peter. The changes in Peter's life and the incredible fruit he experienced in his ministry show what can happen when we dedicate ourselves to following the Holy Spirit instead of making decisions based on our own understanding. Two specific scenes in Peter's life illustrate this shift from fearful follower to dedicated disciple.

We find the first in Luke. Jesus has been arrested, and Peter is afraid. Peter's resolve is tested late that very same night, and it quickly becomes apparent he's relying on his own strength:

> A servant girl saw him seated there in the firelight. She looked closely at him and said, "This man was with him."
>
> But he denied it. "Woman, I don't know him," he said.
>
> A little later someone else saw him and said, "You also are one of them."
>
> "Man, I am not!" Peter replied.
>
> About an hour later another asserted, "Certainly this fellow was with him, for he is a Galilean."
>
> Peter replied, "Man, I don't know what you're talking about!" Just as he was speaking, the rooster crowed. The Lord turned and looked straight at Peter. Then Peter remembered the word the Lord had spoken to him: "Before the rooster crows today, you will disown me three times." And he went outside and wept bitterly.
>
> Luke 22:56–62

Three times Peter denies knowing Jesus. Yet only hours before this, Peter had declared, "Even if all fall away on account of you, I never will" (Matthew 26:33). This fickle indecision is the natural result of trying to do what we're called to do with only our willpower. When hard things come up, we'll bail, just like Peter did, and like Salim initially did. We'll run for our own safety, comfort, or peace.

Peter was bold and quick to speak. But in his own strength he failed. He became fearful, as most of us would in his situation. He did not have the courage or strength to follow through his commitment.

Without the power of the Holy Spirit, none of us are any different. I can't count the number of times as a young believer I prayed, "Oh God, please forgive me, and I promise I'll never do that again." Maybe you've been there. Maybe you still are. That was Peter, before the Holy Spirit.

Each one of us needs to not only hear the Holy Spirit, but to live and move and act as disciples who are filled with the power of the Holy Spirit.

This is the same power the early believers experienced in Acts 2:

> When the day of Pentecost came, they were all together in one place. Suddenly a sound like the blowing of a violent wind came from heaven and filled the whole house where they were sitting. They saw what seemed to be tongues of fire that separated and came to rest on each of them. All of them were filled with the Holy Spirit and began to speak in other tongues as the Spirit enabled them.

Acts 2:1–4

What an incredible scene: the entrance of the Holy Spirit! These signs and miracles are amazing in and of themselves, but let's keep reading to find out what impact the power of the Holy Spirit had on those present, and especially on Peter:

> Then Peter stood up with the Eleven, raised his voice and addressed the crowd: "Fellow Jews and all of you who live in Jerusalem, let me explain this to you; listen carefully to what I say. These people are not drunk, as you suppose. It's only nine in the morning! No, this is what was spoken by the prophet Joel:
> "'In the last days, God says,
> I will pour out my Spirit on all people.
> Your sons and daughters will prophesy,
>   your young men will see visions,
>   your old men will dream dreams.
> Even on my servants, both men and women,
>   I will pour out my Spirit in those days,
>   and they will prophesy.'"

Acts 2:14–18

Where did Peter's courage come from? This was a man who had recently denied Christ. How does he now proclaim his new faith in the city where his leader and Lord was so recently executed? It is only by the power of the Holy Spirit that Peter could speak with such authority and courage. In fact, he was so filled with the Spirit, so in tune with the power that was available to him, that the fruit of this sermon became immediately apparent. The people listening were "cut to the heart" (v.37) and wanted to know what to do. Peter called them to repent and to be baptized in the name of Jesus. And "those who accepted his message were baptized, and about three thousand were added to their number that day" (Acts 2:41). Three thousand people baptized in one day! By the power of the Holy Spirit flowing through a bold disciple like Peter, a vast number were added to the kingdom. And it didn't stop there. The new disciples devoted themselves to the apostles' teaching and to fellowship, to the breaking of bread and to prayer. They continued to meet in homes and temple courts, and the Lord added to their number daily.[10] These new disciples went out making new disciples—and this dynamic expression of God's kingdom through the early church continued to expand in size and influence.

What can we learn of how this multiplying, first expression of the church in Acts spoke of and engaged with the Holy Spirit?

First, they were entreated by Peter to see the Holy Spirit as a gift that comes with repentance and baptism.[11] Let's make sure we, as ordinary disciples, don't miss acknowledging the constant presence and activity of this gift of the Spirit in our lives and relationships. Being continually aware of and responsive to the Holy Spirit leads us toward a healthy daily dependence upon and empowering by the Spirit—which often results in extraordinary influence.

Second, the Holy Spirit's activity in the lives of the early believers led to a radical rearranging of their priorities, a reduced importance of

---

[10]   Acts 2:42–47.
[11]   Acts 2:38.

possessions in their lives, compassion for others in need, and ultimately to full surrender. They had "everything in common" (Acts 2:44). This is the kind of life-transforming impact the Holy Spirit can have. But it only happens when we move beyond letting our peers define what a "normal" Christian looks like—and instead begin to look to Scripture and Holy Spirit inspiration for our understanding of what it is to be an obedient, wholehearted disciple of Jesus.

The failure to daily acknowledge and surrender to the presence and work of the Holy Spirit in our lives can lead to a dulling of our spiritual sensitivities. Jesus declares, "My sheep listen to my voice [...], and they follow me" (John 10:27). It is through the Holy Spirit that we hear the voice of Jesus. How well do you recognize his voice?

Knowing the voice of Jesus, through the Holy Spirit, comes with practice over time. One of the beauties of living our lives in the context of a faith community is that it provides a safe place where we can test what we sense the Holy Spirit is saying with others who are developing the same spiritual sensitivities. We call it discernment. It often starts with, "I sense the Holy Spirit is saying ..."

Our sensitivity to hear what Jesus speaks to us through the Holy Spirit can be hindered by unconfessed sin in our lives or a lack of forgiveness often evident in a broken relationship.

Obviously, our theological frameworks also shape our understanding of the work and ministry of the Holy Spirit. If you or others in your faith community believe that some gifts of the Spirit expressed in the Book of Acts are not applicable for us today, there will be less of a tendency to ask for those gifts. The next chapter takes a more extensive look into what we can learn from the Book of Acts and what we can learn as ordinary disciples of Jesus, eager to influence others for his glory.

Throughout our work across the globe, we have observed that when we allow the Holy Spirit to move in and through our lives, we experience spiritual and numerical growth. If we have largely ignored the Holy Spirit in our lives or in our churches, perhaps it's time to repent and allow the Holy Spirit to move in our midst as he did in the early days.

When the Holy Spirit Works

We have seen how the Holy Spirit brings power to our lives and does battle with our enemy. But there is more. Let's return to Salim's story to see more of the ways the Holy Spirit operates.

- Prior to this story, *the Holy Spirit convicted Salim of sin and his need to accept Jesus* as Savior and Lord.
- *The Holy Spirit led Salim's church to send someone* as a disciple-maker to this predominantly Muslim town.
- *Salim was convinced by the Holy Spirit that he was the one to go,* so he accepted his church's invitation.
- *The Holy Spirit drew the young men Salim was discipling into Christ* and gave them the desire to grow in Christ.
- *The Holy Spirit repeatedly spoke to Salim through the night, which led to Salim returning* and risking his life.
- *The Holy Spirit empowered Salim to overcome the fear the enemy was using* to pull him away from the place and the work to which God had called him.
- Over time *the Holy Spirit convicted the five men of their need to receive Jesus* as their Savior and Lord.
- We don't know how, but *the Holy Spirit gave someone courage to witness to these five men.*

Isn't it amazing to step back and evaluate all the ways the Holy Spirit was at work in this situation? None of this would have happened by Salim's strength and determination alone.

God calls you and me to be witnesses for Christ and ambassadors for his kingdom. And it is almost always the Holy Spirit who personalizes that call. We will never be effective in disciple-making so long as we ignore the Holy Spirit's power and influence in our lives and in the world.

Several years ago, I was traveling through India and stopped to visit one of the discipleship-mission training programs we had helped a cluster of churches to launch. They asked me to teach for a morning, and since I had the time in my schedule, I agreed.

At that time, they were focusing on the gifts and ministry of the Holy Spirit. So, as I taught from 1 Corinthians 12, I told stories of how God is at work healing people and moving miraculously in some of the hardest and most resistant places around the world, to draw people into relationship with Jesus.

After the teaching session, Kabir, the director, thanked me and said, "I should have told you that some of the stories you are telling included things that our churches don't teach." Kabir didn't seem upset, just concerned that I had told stories that didn't line up with their understanding of what the Holy Spirit does in our world.

I apologized for not asking before I taught, then added, "In these trainings, I always encourage the leaders to be true to God's Word, to honor the doctrine of their churches, and to have open conversations with the appropriate leaders if they have questions or concerns." I continued, "But it's important to allow the ways we see God at work to continue to shape our theology."

A few months later, Kabir was at a Global Disciples Annual Equipping Event for local training directors. When he spotted me, he came running over. "Well," he said with a big smile, "God is continuing to shape my theology."

Kabir explained how they encourage the disciple-makers they train to pray for people, no matter what the situation. One church-planting team was sharing the gospel in a village where there were no followers of Christ. A young girl approached them and asked them to come to her house and pray for her mother.

When they arrived, they found the mother lying in bed close to death. Her doctor had told her that her kidneys were failing, and she would die. He gave her an oxygen tank and some pain medicine and sent her home. The disciple-makers asked if they could pray for her in the name of Jesus. She nodded. So, they prayed that God would spare her life for the sake of her young daughter since it was just the two of them to care for each other. They saw no immediate change in her condition, but they exchanged cell phone numbers to keep in touch. The disciple-makers went on to the next village.

The next day the young girl contacted them, "My mommy's feeling better today. She actually ate a little food." A day later, they heard from her again. "I helped my mommy get out of bed today. And she said she's feeling better." The third day, the news got even more encouraging. "My mommy cooked some food for us today. She was out of bed almost all day. She doesn't use her oxygen tank anymore. Would you like to talk with my mommy?"

The woman got on the phone with the disciple-makers and said, "Your Jesus healed me. Thank you for coming and praying. I want to have a celebration with my neighbors. Will you come and celebrate with us and tell us all about your Jesus who healed me?"

The disciple-makers went back to celebrate with this woman, her daughter, their extended family members, and neighbors. In the middle of the feast, she invited one of the disciple-makers to tell everyone about the Jesus who had healed her. A church was born in that Hindu village that day; this woman and her daughter were the first to be baptized. Many more people followed, and today there's a thriving fellowship of believers in that little community.

"So," Kabir declared loud enough for everyone around to hear, "how we are seeing God at work is shaping my theology."

As ordinary disciples seeking to live and move in the power of the Spirit, we need to dig into the teaching from 1 Corinthians 12–14. It is foundational for understanding the work and ministry of the Holy Spirit. As my Indian friend Kabir learned—through both study and experience—it is transformational. Our North American emphasis on self-reliance, independence, and fixing things for ourselves often draws us away from this dependence and connection to the work of the Holy Spirit. Perhaps that's why so many we serve deal with burnout and discouragement—they use their gifts without a relationship with the Holy Spirit and without connecting with his power.

It's so important that we read 1 Corinthians 13, which focuses on love, along with 1 Corinthians 12, which focuses on spiritual gifts. Our approach to using these God-given gifts must always center around love. Without a grounding in love, our gifts can cause damage instead of building up.

Faith, hope, and love are more important than any of the other gifts God gives us. And if we use our gifts to build the kingdom with love, we will see many more people coming into the kingdom of our Lord Jesus Christ. This is how ordinary disciples, like Salim in northern Africa or Kabir in India, have such extraordinary influence.

And it can be similar for you too.

Have you given up too soon on the promise God has given you? Are you afraid to do the things the Holy Spirit is leading you to do? Did you set out on a new path laid out for you by God, only to be discouraged? Are you burnt out or weary from trying to do it all on your own?

Don't give up.

The Holy Spirit is your source of strength, of power, of comfort, and he is living within you! Living in that reality will influence or reshape every area of your life.

As we have already seen from the early church in Acts 2, and through stories like Salim's and Kabir's, the Holy Spirit reshapes not only our individual lives, but can transform whole communities of believers. Let's dig deeper and see what else we may learn from Acts that will lead us to a new level as disciples, as intimate friends of Jesus with extraordinary influence in our world.

Reflect and Discuss

- What inspired you in this chapter?
- What challenged you?
- What is God inviting you to do in the coming days?
- What obstacles are keeping you from accepting and acting upon this invitation?
- How will you live differently today because of what you have just read?
- What practical actions will you commit to doing soon?
- What questions do you still have?

Additional Study

- **The Divine Person of the Holy Spirit:** Acts 5:3–4; 1 Corinthians 3:16; 6:19; John 14:7; 15:26.
- **Gifts and Ministry of the Holy Spirit:** 1 Corinthians 12:4–11; Romans 12:4–7; Ephesians 4:11–13.
- **The Fruit of the Holy Spirit in Daily Living:** Galatians 5:22–26; Ephesians 5:8–11; 2 Corinthians 3:18.
- **The Role of the Holy Spirit in a Spiritual Battle:** Ephesians 6:10–18; 2 Corinthians 10:3–6.

6

Reclaiming the Ways of Acts

Akayu was frustrated. He wanted to believe the Holy Spirit was guiding him when he received the government assignment to become a schoolteacher in this broken, out-of-the-way place in southern Ethiopia. But it was hard. He was a visionary young man with big plans; he wanted to see the school revitalized and the community transformed through the little church he planted.

He never imagined it would be this difficult. Even local government officials had given up on the people. Alcoholism and violence dominated the region. The district had the highest unemployment rate, the lowest percentage of school-age children in school, and the highest homicide rate of any district in the country.

People lived in fear and tried to appease spirits who, if angered, would harm them. They paid homage to a local witch doctor who seemingly had power to leverage the spirits. For the right price, the witch doctor would protect them or curse others. Sometimes those who were cursed would become sick or even die. This only added to their fear and hopelessness. It was a broken, desperate place.

Akayu was one of only a few Christians in town. He had done well at the school and was promoted to oversee several schools in the region. But the church he led was not growing. He was weary of the heartache. Alone and discouraged, he wondered if people would ever be open to the gospel. Did anyone care about this wretched place? Was it worth all his hard work, prayers, and tears? He longed for the church to make a difference in his community.

One day he heard that his denominational office had begun working with Global Disciples in developing a training for disciple-makers and church planters in least-reached areas. Hopeful that this training would help their region, Akayu selected and sent two young men, Abel and Geme, to take part in the training.

A few months later, Abel and Geme returned, passionate and renewed in their commitment to prayer, and believing God would pour out his Holy Spirit to transform their broken community. They prayed diligently and pursued every opportunity they could to share the good news of Jesus. For two years, they prayed as they tried to identify men and women of peace.[1] They pleaded with the Lord for a fresh move of his Holy Spirit. Akayu and his tiny church joined them for prayer, sometimes praying all night long. But outside of their small church community, people continued to resist their witness and reject Jesus.

One day God spoke to these disciples as they prayed. The Holy Spirit instructed them to go and warn the local witch doctor that if he did not repent of his evil ways, he would die within a week.

It was not a message they were eager to deliver.

Yet God gave the young men courage, and so they made an appointment with the witch doctor. Within a few days, Geme, Abel, and Akayu stood before the witch doctor to deliver the message: "Our God has told us that if you do not repent of your evil ways, you will die within the week."

---

[1]   From Luke 10:6, a person of peace is open to receiving a disciple, welcomes them in and/or provides a link or connection to the wider community.

Irate, the witch doctor threw them out of the house and told them never to return.

A few days later, he died.

Akayu and the disciple-makers had only just heard this shocking news when there was a knock on the door. Shaken and trembling, the witch doctor's apprentice stood on the doorstep. He had witnessed the meeting and heard the message they delivered.

"Tell me," he pleaded, "who is the spirit that you worship? I've seen my master put curses on people who then became sick and sometimes died. But you didn't put a curse on my master. You just spoke to him softly. And now he's dead. Obviously, the spirit that you have is stronger than the spirits of my master. Who is that spirit?"

Akayu invited him in, gently reassuring the young apprentice that there was no need for fear. He explained how they served the living God—the one who created the earth and the sky, the sun and the moon and the stars, and all people. And he explained that the Holy Spirit of this one true God lived within them. Akayu went on to explain that if he were to denounce all the spirits of his master and surrender his life to the one true God, this same Holy Spirit would come and live within him—not to harm him or others, but to give joy and peace, purpose, and meaning in his life. The witch doctor's apprentice asked many questions. Finally, he boldly and clearly denounced the spirits of his master as the two young men prayed for his deliverance. It was a battle, but the victory was won in Christ Jesus.

In the weeks and months that followed, the witch doctor's apprentice was discipled and taught the ways of Jesus, and soon became a coworker in the kingdom of God. The oppressive spiritual bondage over the region was broken. People who had rejected the gospel became responsive and eager to learn more about this Jesus who was transforming so many lives in southern Ethiopia. The whole spiritual climate changed. Within a short time, five new churches were planted!

I visited their first discipleship-mission training after this breakthrough. All twenty-five training participants were persistent in prayer and fasting, and followed the prompting and guidance of the Holy Spirit that flowed from their times of prayer. Scattering across the region, they visited towns and villages unreached with the gospel. They spent time building relation-ships, giving witness to the transforming work of Jesus in their lives, and leading people out of brokenness into whole-hearted relationship with Jesus. In the first year, they planted new fellowships of believers in seventy of the seventy-five communities.

When the training participants shared their testimonies, I recall one young woman telling her story of how she was demon possessed and had cut herself and even threw herself into the fire. I saw the scars on her face and arms where she had cut herself, yet now her eyes and smile glowed with the joy of Jesus. "My family didn't know what to do with me," she said. "Then they heard about some followers of Jesus who prayed for people, and they were healed. So, they took me to these people. They prayed for me, and I was set free. Now I tell everyone I can about Jesus. He saved my life. And now I'm free."

The transformation in her own life prepared her to be God's agent of transformation to others. The young woman who used to cut herself and throw herself into the fire became the most effective evangelist and disciple-maker in Akayu's region.

ACTS: Reclaiming the Ways of the Early Church

Akayu found himself in an impossible and hopeless situation. For years it seemed nothing had changed. Perhaps you feel similarly discouraged. Maybe you believe God wants to do something new in your fellowship—or maybe in the North American church more broadly—but it seems so slow in coming. Sometimes change happens differently than we imagine. We can't predict the way God works, and he doesn't always answer our prayers in the way we hope, as C. S. Lewis once noted: "It would be rash to say that there is any prayer which God never grants. But the strongest candidate is the prayer we might express as the single word 'encore.'"[2] God is always do-ing something new. But there is also consistency in how he works. We see

---

2   C. S. Lewis, *Letters to Malcolm: Chiefly on Prayer* (San Francisco: HarperOne, 2017), 35.

patterns in the ministry of Jesus, in the early church as recorded in Acts, and in many of the disciple-making and church-planting movements we have the privilege of serving in various locations around the world.

The Book of Acts has much to teach us about how we are called to live as the body of Christ. So, let's consider how disciple-making movements across the globe are reclaiming the ways of Acts—and what the North American church can learn from them. Every movement we have observed has four key characteristics, which can be expressed with the acrostic ACTS.

A: Accelerated Growth

The Book of Acts tells the story of a rapidly multiplying church. You'll remember from the last chapter that as they prayed in the upper room, the twelve disciples of Jesus and their friends experienced the outpouring of the Holy Spirit at Pentecost in a spectacular, powerful, and public way.[3] Peter, empowered by the Spirit, preached a masterpiece of a sermon right there on the street, and three thousand new believers joined that very first expression of the New Testament church.[4] Amazing!

Acts chapter two explains that more new believers were added to their number each day.[5] By chapter five we're told "more and more men and women believed in the Lord and were added to their number" (Acts 5:14). And a short time later "the numbers of disciples multiplied greatly in Jerusalem and a great many priests became obedient to the faith" (Acts 6:7 ESV). This was just the beginning!

The stories we have been telling you throughout this book have often resulted in Acts-like rapid growth. The movement that grew out of Akayu's prayers, efforts, and subsequent equipping of disciple-makers, illustrates this well. Akayu continued training and sending out disciples who were prepared to make disciples. Small, locally sustainable fellowships of believers sprang up across the region. Within a decade of the initial breakthrough,

---

[3]   Acts 2:1–4.
[4]   Acts 2:14–41.
[5]   Acts 2:47.

he saw 476 new churches scattered in small towns and villages across the region, with more than twenty-one thousand new believers worshipping in these fellowships. And the multiplication continues.

Miracles of healing and deliverance are commonplace and contribute to the rapid growth. In addition, Akayu and other leaders have been determined that the economic limitations of the people would not inhibit the growth of new fellowships. More than 140 of these church-planting disciple-makers are largely supporting themselves through their small business activities. Like the Apostle Paul, they have been able to move into new areas unrestrained by a lack of finances.

Ekeno and his team, whose story we told you in chapter four, have also experienced and continue to experience this accelerated growth. By equipping disciples to go and make disciples, they grew from eight small fellowships to more than 450 dynamic fellowships in fourteen years—across their arid desert region. Most places of worship were initially under trees, and then they eventually constructed thatched-roof pavilions. In the towns, they built more permanent structures.

As in the Book of Acts, the advance of God's kingdom today has been accelerated through the bold proclamation of the good news of Jesus, transformation of lives, and demonstrations of God's power through healing and deliverance. Ekeno and those he equips as leaders have intentionally modeled the way, taking younger leaders with them—and preparing them to do the same. As the Apostle Paul demonstrated, accelerated growth requires leaders who are reproducing themselves.

So what would need to change if our churches or fellowships of believers were to accommodate that kind of growth? Most of our churches in North America are not designed for rapid multiplication. Our buildings and our organizational structures are generally designed for incremental growth—and sadly, sometimes even for an anticipated decline. We tend to assume that next year's numbers will be similar to the previous few years. But when we read the Book of Acts, it appears that accelerated growth was anticipated, integrated, and welcomed.

In Acts, and the letters to the churches that follow, it is clear the early church lived, prayed, and worked with a "movement mentality." This was simply a continuation of the kingdom movement mentality so evident in the life and ministry of Jesus. Like Jesus, we need a view of God's kingdom that is big enough and dynamic enough to transform our neighborhoods, cities, and nations. We need to nurture a movement mentality that leads to ways of being church that can accommodate accelerated growth.

When I talk with business leaders, I explain that rapidly growing churches, and ministries like ours which serve them, need to be *scalable* or able to scale up quickly. *Scaling up* was first a common concept in engineering. It refers to how well a system can perform with much greater demands placed upon it. The term crossed over from the field of engineering to business as people began to say companies were "scaling up" to handle rapid growth well. Soon the word *up* was dropped and now we simply talk about *scaling*. If a new app comes onto the market, business leaders may ask, "Do we think this product can scale?"

For a business to be scalable means it has the ability, over time, to sustainably grow the business to whatever size your specialty allows in your market segment. By that definition, the church in Acts was scalable. Is that true of your church or the associated group of fellowships with whom you are relating?

In our work with Global Disciples, we evaluate whether a church, ministry, or training is scalable or has a movement mentality by asking:

- Is the basic entity (church, small group, or ministry) reproducible in similar settings?
- Can it be locally sustainable without the provision of ongoing outside resources?
- Is it developing leaders that are stepping out to lead the new reproducing entities?
- Can it thrive in existing buildings or in structures that are inexpensive and reproducible?
- Do the members own the vision for multiplication and are they actively engaged in doing their part to see the vision realized? And are they imparting that vision to new members?
- Are disciples being equipped to make disciples who will go and make disciples?

The last question is at the heart of *accelerated growth*. The churches we serve around the world that are experiencing accelerated growth are made up of disciples who are making disciples—who are then equipped and motivated to make other disciple-making disciples.

This naturally leads into the next characteristic we need to reclaim to fulfill our God-given mission.

C: Compassionate Witness

Throughout the Book of Acts, *witness* is one of the more prominent words. It appears at least twenty times in twenty-six chapters. We are appointed to witness through our words and deeds.[6] It is not one or the other—both word *and* deeds are needed. In a court, witnessing usually involves telling others about what one has seen, heard, or experienced. As Christians, no one can truly witness without hearing, seeing, or experiencing God.[7] All of us, who have experienced the love, joy, and peace of God, are responsible to give witness to all those who have never experienced it.

As witnesses of Jesus, we need to maintain a close walk and fellowship with Jesus on a daily basis—to see, hear, and experience him. As disciples, we are living letters, the gospel in human form, sent out to our world. To be effective witnesses, we need to walk with Jesus daily and be empowered by the Holy Spirit. And our witness should be born out of compassion for the spiritual needs of those who don't yet know him.

Michelle grew up in an ordinary North American family—one in which no one knew or followed Christ. She and her younger sister often debated the existence of God. Her sister was sure he didn't exist, but Michelle thought he did. One evening after high school, Michelle was hanging out with several good friends who were talking about going to see a movie. She asked if she could join them, and they sheepishly replied, "Sure, if you want to." It was 1978, and the movie was *The Late Great Planet Earth*, based on the book by Hal Lindsey. For the first time, Michelle heard someone declare that there

---

[6] Acts 1:8.
[7] 1 John 1:1–2.

is a God, that she could have a relationship with him through Jesus, and that there was a heaven and a hell. She was shaken, and felt convicted that she needed to respond in some way. Over drinks at a bar afterwards, Michelle grew angry when her friends began joking and laughing about hell. "I don't see what's so funny about this!" she flared at them. A few days later, this same group of friends were talking about an evening church service, and Michelle again asked to go along. "Sure, if you want to," came the response. That evening, the pastor gave a clear invitation for anyone who wanted to accept Jesus as their Savior and Lord. Michelle responded, surrendering her life to Jesus.

After the service, Michelle told her friends, "I knew there was something different about you. I saw it all through our years in high school. But why didn't you ever tell me how important it is that I know Jesus as my Lord and Savior?"

They responded, "We didn't think you'd care."

Michelle couldn't believe what she was hearing, "You didn't think I would care that I can have a personal relationship with God through Jesus Christ? That I wouldn't care where I was going when I die?"

Michelle was quick to witness about her relationship with Jesus. She told her sister, "There is a God, and he wants to have a relationship with you too." Her sister soon came to faith in Jesus, and then her sister's husband, and others. Michelle was not about to keep the good news a secret!

It's simple: if we do not witness, people will not receive the fullness of life God has for them right now and will instead die in their sins without hearing the good news of Jesus. There is no other way of salvation except through Jesus Christ.[8] The gospel is the power of God to transform lives.[9]

In Acts, we consistently see a strong commitment to the spoken witness of Jesus flowing together *with* compassion in caring for physical needs. In the early church, the appointment of leaders to provide for those in need and to serve in the daily distribution of food confirms this priority. "Choose from among you seven men who are known to be full of the Spirit and wisdom.

---

[8]   Acts 4:12.
[9]   Romans 1:16.

We will turn this responsibility over to them and give our attention to prayer and the ministry of the word" (Acts 6:3–4).

When we as the body of Christ combine the clear presentation of the gospel with a compassionate response to human need, we too will begin to experience the kingdom of God advancing in new, lifegiving ways. Did you know, the average horse can pull about eight thousand pounds? However, two horses teamed can pull about twenty-two thousand pounds. And with some training, the same two horses can move thirty-two thousand pounds. That's the power of synergy!

In the early church, people sold houses and properties and shared freely so "there was no needy persons among them" (Acts 4:34). And in Galatians 2:10, the Apostle Paul reports on the Jerusalem Council and declares that in his preaching and witness to the Gentiles, "All they asked was that we should continue to remember the poor, the very thing I had been eager to do all along." Paul was led by the Holy Spirit to share the same type of love Jesus demonstrated to those in need. We are also advised as God's chosen people, holy and dearly loved to clothe ourselves with compassion, kindness, humility, gentleness, and patience.[10]

Compassion is one of the dominant emotions Jesus expresses. It's visible time and time again as Jesus relates to those around him. Depending on the Bible translation, the phrase that is sometimes translated as "moved with compassion" is used between six and nine times in the Gospels to describe what Jesus was feeling.[11] It could literally be translated as "his stomach was wrenched with compassion." Have you ever felt that? You see a need, and you are deeply moved. It's not just pity. You feel it in your gut. You're moved with compassion.

I believe the Holy Spirit wants to plant the compassion of Jesus into our lives, compassion for people in need both spiritually *and* physically. It's not just one or the other. Lesslie Newbigin, long-time mission worker in India, states it rather bluntly in his little book, *Mission in Christ's Way*, "So words

---

[10]   Colossians 3:12.
[11]   Matthew 9:36; 14:14; 15:32; 20:34; Mark 1:41 (NLT, NKJV, etc.); Mark 5:19 (NKJV); Mark 6:34; 8:2; Luke 7:13 (ESV, NKJV, etc.).

without deeds are empty, but deeds without words are dumb. It is stupid to set them up against each other."[12] In the mission of Jesus, we see both the presence of the kingdom *and* the proclamation of the kingdom.

Too often in the body of Christ, there has been an unhealthy and unnatural separation of *evangelism* and *deeds of compassion*. Jesus healed the sick *and* proclaimed the kingdom of God. Jesus taught the crowds, cast out demons, *and* was moved with compassion because the crowd was hungry but had no food. With the touch of Jesus, a young boy's lunch of five loaves and a few fish fed the hungry crowds with plenty left over. Jesus didn't separate the presence and proclamation but integrated the two through every part of his life and ministry.

This integration of compassion and witness should never create "rice Christians." In other words, we don't want to see people "convert" to Christianity and accept baptism just to gain food, medical services, or other benefits. With the exception of crisis situations, natural disasters, and calamities, we believe the most compassionate thing we can do is to encourage and help build local sustainability. That's why our Global Disciples approach offers to equip the church networks we serve to facilitate their own small business development training.[13] Sometimes it's easy to mistakenly assume that money or gifts are the best ways to respond to need. One book that helps reframe a perspective away from this mentality is Brian Fickert and Steve Corbett's *When Helping Hurts*.[14] We usually recommend this book to those who are inclined to express compassion simply through providing handouts.

The Holy Spirit releases creativity and initiative among disciples of Jesus to make disciples who gather in sustainable, reproducible fellowships of believers. But it's something that only happens with persistent prayer. That's

---

[12] Lesslie Newbigin. *Mission in Christ's Way* (Geneva, Switzerland: WCC Publications, 1987), 11.

[13] Global Disciples' simple small business training curriculum is entitled, "What's in Your Hand?" We provide a biblical basis and foundational teaching on business principles and practices including marketing, markup, basic record-keeping, etc. Then each participant is guided in developing a small business based on the skills, background, resources or experiences they have that could be developed into a business.

[14] Brian Fickert and Steve Corbett, *When Helping Hurts: How to Alleviate Poverty Without Hurting the Poor or Yourself* (Chicago, IL: Moody Publishers, 2009).

why this next characteristic is so essential for North American disciples of Jesus to reclaim within the body of Christ.

T: Transforming Prayer

Prayer is another dominant theme in the Book of Acts. God does the impossible when his people pray. And we must reclaim prayer at a new level if we as the body of Christ are to experience the accelerated growth and the compassionate witness we are called to. We believe that God challenges and transforms us through prayer. And through prayer, he brings transformation in the lives of others too. Transforming prayer calls us away from self-involved or "wish list" praying and into a passionate pursuit of the presence of Jesus. Our minds are transformed and our priorities are reordered as we pursue intimacy with our Heavenly Father, through a relationship with Jesus, and by the power of the Holy Spirit.

Through prayer, God removes the blinders that prevent people from seeing the light of the gospel which displays the glory of Christ.[15] It is the Holy Spirit who softens hearts, opens minds, and draws people into relationship with Jesus.

Prayer and fasting, when coupled together, are two of the most powerful spiritual disciplines we can draw upon to conquer the strongholds of the enemy and to advance the kingdom of God. In prayer and fasting we are aligning our hearts with the heart of God, so, as the psalmist declares, "My soul thirsts for God, for the living God" (Psalm 42:2).

When we reclaim these practices of fasting and prayer, with a heart of submission and surrender, the Holy Spirit transforms our personal lives. But according to Scripture, fasting and prayer can also affect change on a much grander scale.[16] We believe that when God's people fast and pray with a broken, repentant, and contrite spirit—rather than for personal gain—God hears from heaven and moves to bring healing in our lives, our churches, our communities, our nation, and our world.

---

[15] 2 Corinthians 4:4.
[16] Mark 9:29.

Fasting and prayer were key in transforming the district in Ethiopia where Akayu worked. As more and more people came to Christ, the bars closed, violence subsided, kids attended school, family relationships were restored, and people became more hard-working and industrious.

Local government officials noticed what was happening and came to the church leaders saying, "We don't know what you did with these people. We thought they were useless." Because of the remarkable change, the government officials began giving Akayu and the church leaders land to divide among people to farm: a couple hundred acres here, five hundred acres there.

One by one, communities were transformed.

In history's great revival movements, it's clear that when God's people united in fasting and prayer, across denominational and association lines, it brought about a change in the direction in families, communities, cities, and nations and in the fulfillment of the Great Commission.[17] It still can!

Fasting in the Bible usually refers to abstaining from food for a period of time as a way of declaring our dependence upon the Lord, sometimes as an act of repentance. But more often in the Gospels and in Acts, it is a discipline to pursue a deeper intimacy with God or to seek direction in a decision or an area of uncertainty. In the church in Antioch, it was in a time of worship and fasting that the Holy Spirit instructed them to "Set apart for me Barnabas and Saul for the work to which I have called them" (Acts 13:2–3). Fasting is a biblical way to humble ourselves in the sight of God.[18] King David said he humbled himself through fasting.[19]

In my life, fasting brings me face-to-face with the motivations of my heart and enables the Holy Spirit to reveal my true spiritual condition, often resulting in brokenness, repentance, and God's transforming work in my life. I so easily get distracted from what matters most. In fasting, the idolatries that slip into my life are exposed. Regular fasting is like an exclamation mark in my prayers. It's saying to God, *My prayers are not just words; this is the true desire of my heart. I want you more than food. I want your ways more than*

---

[17]   See, for example, John Piper, "Revival and Fasting," desiringGod.org, June 6, 1986, www.desiringgod.org/messages/revival-and-fasting.

[18]   Psalm 35:13; Ezra 8:21.

[19]   Psalm 69:10.

comfort. I am hungry for more of you! Times of fasting allow the Holy Spirit to activate God's Word in my life, so it penetrates deeply into my heart, and his truth becomes more meaningful to me.

Regular fasting—whether a day a week, once a month, or periodically as the Lord leads—can transform our prayer life even if we can only take time to pray in short times throughout our day. It's an investment, a sacrifice that communicates our seriousness about our relationship with God—leading to a deeper intimacy with Jesus and a greater sensitivity to the Holy Spirit.

The essence of fasting is acknowledging and growing in our dependence on God. So rather than turning to the things that bring us comfort, we turn to him. Jesus assumed that his followers would fast. Twice in two verses within the Sermon on the Mount Jesus says to his disciples, "*when* you fast" (Matthew 6:16-18, italics ours)–not *if* you fast.

It's important to understand that spiritual fasting is not about skipping a meal or losing weight. It is instead about taking the time you would put into eating (or whatever it is that you're fasting from) and meditating on God and his Word through prayer. Fasting from food is particularly useful because throughout the day, as you think about food or realize you're hungry, that's your cue to return your mind to the goodness of God.

The length of time for fasting can vary. The most common is a twenty-four-hour fast, skipping two meals from dinner one day to dinner the next day. Some people fast for three days. On special occasions, some will be led by the Holy Spirit to fast for twenty-one days or forty days. The length of time does not increase our spirituality; fasting is a matter of the heart. In my practice, I find it meaningful to read God's Word and pray instead of eating during mealtimes.

For those who are pregnant, or who have medical conditions or eating disorders, fasting from food is not usually advisable. Thankfully, a fast doesn't have to be from food. You could consider fasting from social media, TV, Netflix, or anything else that distracts you from focused time in prayer, Scripture, and seeking the Lord.

As you fast and pray, you can confess not only the obvious sins that come to mind but allow yourself to linger in God's presence, giving him time to show you the less obvious ones as well.

Fasting is a way to deliberately invite God to prune things that are hindering our growth and witness in our lives, things we might not even recognize. While fasting, you may want to ask God to reveal any signs of self-centeredness, spiritual indifference, an unwillingness to share your faith in Christ with others, or insufficient time in God's Word and in prayer. He may want to reveal a poor relationship with your spouse, your parents, your children, your friends, or other members of your community.

To experience the best God has for us from a fast requires a firm commitment. Arranging a special time with God is crucial in attaining intimate communion with the Father. It requires devoting ourselves to seeking God's face, even during those times in which we feel weak, vulnerable, or irritable. Fasting is a practice to take seriously and prayerfully; not as a ritual to gain favor but a heartfelt seeking of God and his will and glory in our life and the lives of others. Through prayer and fasting, we take our eyes off the things of this world and focus on God.

If you wake up in the night, choose to meditate on the Lord, instead of scrolling through social media, or anxiously tossing and turning. Sing praises to him whenever you please. Focus on your Heavenly Father and make every act one of praise and worship. God will enable you to experience his command to "pray continually" (1 Thessalonians 5:17) as you seek his presence.

As Global Disciples, we have seen prayer and fasting opens doors among unreached people, and it prepares us to be more responsive witnesses of Christ and ambassadors for his kingdom wherever we may be.

Viraj came to know Jesus and participated in a Global Disciples training in a high-risk setting in India. He understands firsthand the transforming work of prayer and God's power. "I went into a village to share Jesus," Viraj told us. "A group of religious [Hindu] radicals came and began to beat me. One man had a knife. They decided to kill me, but first they asked what my last wish was. I told them I wanted five minutes to pray. I began praying for their families and crying out to the Lord for them. The leader heard this and said, 'Ok, we will not kill you today. You will come to my home and pray for my wife. If she isn't healed, then we will kill you.' His wife suffered from severe back pain and couldn't even walk. With great fear, I went to his home and prayed for his wife … and she was immediately healed!"

Viraj continued, "This leader repented and came to know Jesus. His home is on the main highway, and he opened it for others to know about Jesus. In a short time, sixty-eight people were baptized! This new brother then donated land, another sister gave money, and they built a place for the church to meet. The man who was going to kill me is now the pastor, and God is using this fellowship to establish other churches!"

As Viraj discovered, the spiritual sensitivity that grows out of the disciplines of prayer and fasting is important in directing our response to the needs around us. It is a gift from God, meant to draw us into deeper intimacy with Jesus through the Holy Spirit and help us become influential disciples in the kingdom. Prayer and fasting also swing wide the door for us to see signs of God's power, the fourth characteristic of the church in the Book of Acts.

S: Signs of God's Power

A few years ago, at one of Global Disciples' regional annual equipping events, Brother Akayu from Ethiopia, stood up to share his testimony. "It's been an amazing year of God's faithfulness," he said. "In reading through the Gospels recently, I realized that we have seen every miracle recorded in Matthew, Mark, Luke, and John, take place in the last year."

I had never heard anyone say that before, so I quizzed him a bit after the meeting—and he had a story for each miracle I asked about. That's incredible! But I guess I shouldn't be surprised. Jesus did say, "Very truly I tell you, whoever believes in me will do the works I have been doing, and they will do even greater things than these, because I am going to the Father" (John 14:12).

What we are observing is that where the church is experiencing accelerated growth, God is moving with signs of his power. I'm part of a congregation in Ephrata, Pennsylvania, and we begin each week with a short video testimony of someone who has experienced God working miraculously in their lives. Often these are testimonies of healing physically, emotionally, or relationally. When we began that practice, I wondered if we'd run out of these incredible stories of the signs of God's power. We haven't—and now I suspect we never will.

One of the "secrets" to what God is doing among my local fellowship is that for fifteen years we have hosted Gateway House of Prayer—a 24/7/365 non-stop house of prayer. It engages people from many different congregations across our region, and it's been encouraging to see the acceleration of God at work as many have come to faith.

I will never forget the first time I saw God demonstrating his power through a dramatic healing. I was fifteen years old, and my uncle offered to take me to a Full-Gospel Business Men's Fellowship event at a local hotel ballroom.[20] I had no idea what to expect. Though I grew up in a church in which we remembered sick people in our prayers, I'd never seen anybody miraculously healed. We walked into the hotel lobby, and my uncle pointed out to me the man who would be speaking that evening. As we walked in his direction, I heard him call out to a girl walking nearby.

"Excuse me, young lady, have you ever had someone pray for your leg to be healed?"

I saw the young woman he was talking to; she wore a steel brace on one leg with an elevated shoe with a sole about six inches thick. She timidly replied that no, she had not had anyone pray for her leg.

The speaker invited her to sit on a nearby chair and remove her brace, which she did. Then he pulled over a chair so she could prop up both of her legs. By that time a small crowd was gathering, and I was only a few feet away from her chair. Her polio-stricken leg was at least six inches shorter and much thinner than the other leg. The man talked quietly with her for a few moments, then laid his hands on her and began to pray. I'd been taught to close my eyes for prayer to avoid distractions, but I wasn't the only one with my eyes wide open for that prayer! And as I watched, her thin, short leg grew to the same size and length of the other leg. In a moment, the young woman was on her feet jumping and shouting and laughing and crying and celebrating—and the group observing erupted in joy and celebration. The speaker just smiled, said "Praise the Lord," and quietly headed to the ballroom.

That evening changed my life and my perspective. I became fully convinced that *those things* still happen, even in North America. I've seen many

---

[20] https://fgbmfamerica.org.

miracles since then and even had the opportunity to participate in a few. One thing is certain: Jesus is the Master-healer, whether medical doctors are involved or not. We don't see as many miraculous healings here as we do in areas that are unreached with the good news of Jesus. Maybe it's because we don't ask in faith as often. Maybe it's because we have more access to better medical care. Maybe it's because God especially loves to make his glory and power known in a way that people can understand and respond to—especially the one third of our world's population who have never before heard the good news of Jesus.[21]

Jesus communicates at the beginning of his ministry that God's heart is for the outsiders. According to Luke 4, Jesus returned to Galilee in the power of the Spirit after forty days of fasting and prayer in the desert. He went to Nazareth where he had grown up and, on the Sabbath, went to the synagogue as usual. Jesus was handed the scroll of the prophet Isaiah and found Isaiah 61:1–2 and read:

> "The Spirit of the Lord is on me, because he has anointed me to proclaim good news to the poor. He has sent me to proclaim freedom for the prisoners and recovery of sight for the blind, to set the oppressed free, to proclaim the year of the Lord's favor."

> Luke 4:18–19

Then Jesus said, "Today this scripture is fulfilled in your hearing" (Luke 4:21).

He knew his hometown folks wanted to see miracles like those he had just performed in Capernaum. But instead, he reminded them of two stories, both of which focused on God's heart for the "outsider." In the days of the revered prophet Elijah, it had not rained for three and a half years. There was a severe famine and many hungry widows in Israel. But God sent Elijah to provide food miraculously to a Gentile widow in Zarephath. And in the days of the prophet Elisha, there were many in Israel with leprosy, yet

---

[21] https://athirdofus.com

not one of them was healed. Instead, God used Elisha to heal Naaman, the Syrian military leader who had been attacking their towns and villages.

When Jesus finished telling these stories, the people in the synagogue were so angry, they took him to the top of the hill to throw him off the cliff, but Jesus slipped away.[22]

Could it be that we are seeing miraculous healings and signs of God's power demonstrated among people least-reached with the gospel because God's heart is for outsiders? Maybe. But that's certainly not a reason for those of us in North America to stop praying for God's miraculous demonstration of his power wherever we are—for his glory and for the advancement of his kingdom.

In an increasingly post-Christian environment, where there is less awareness of Jesus and the good news he offers, I believe we will see more and more signs of God's power revealed in our North American context. Jesus loves to make himself known in ways that challenge the prevailing worldview and open people's eyes to the treasure and the mystery of the kingdom of God.

With that in mind let's pursue and reclaim the forgotten ways of ACTS so that we can be a part of what God is already doing in the world right here in our own context:

Accelerated Growth
Compassionate Witness
Transforming Prayer
Signs of God's Power

We see these key characteristics demonstrated in the disciple-making and church-planting movements we serve around the world. These realities helped Akayu and his team impact a depressed, broken, and unreached region of southern Ethiopia, transforming it through Christ into the thriving hub of a multiplication movement and planting 476 new fellowships of believers in ten years.

---

22 See Luke 4:25–30.

What would it look like to see these key characteristics reclaimed from the Book of Acts in your community? In your city? In your neighborhood?

We believe it's God's desire to awaken these basic characteristics in the lives and faith communities of North Americans, so we will see Jesus transforming lives, families, and neighborhoods, and even reaching beyond, to impact other regions and nations.

Reflect and Discuss

- What inspired you in this chapter?
- What challenged you?
- What is God inviting you to do in the coming days?
- What obstacles are keeping you from accepting and acting upon this invitation?
- How will you live differently today because of what you have just read?
- What practical actions will you commit to doing soon?
- What questions do you still have?

Additional study

Sharing the Gospel and Witnessing: John 4:28–42; Mark 5:18–20.
Compassion For Those in Need: Matthew 9:35–38; Luke 10:25–37.
Evangelism and Making Disciples: Matthew 28:19–20; Mark 16:15.
Christ's Commission: Matthew 22:37–39; 28:18–20; John 20:21.

PART THREE
WIDER

Broaden your influence as a disciple:
overcome the hurdles of unhealthy
relationships and discover God's heart
for the world we are all called to love.

---

*"I pray for those who believe in me ... that all of
them may be one, Father, just as you are in me
and I am in you. May they also be in us so that
the world may believe that you have sent me. I
have given them the glory that you gave me."*

John 17:20–22

7

Getting Relationships Right

"I am so sorry. I don't know what to do," the community health worker apologized to Gabriel profusely. "Here, take this oxygen tank and get him to the hospital as soon as you can."

Gabriel looked at his wife, Ana, in desperation. They had already walked an hour, carrying their son, Caleb, as his asthma attack had left him struggling with every breath. Now the clinic had no medication to help.

Left with no choice, Gabriel reluctantly slipped the strap on the oxygen tank over his shoulder. Ana carefully placed the plastic mask over their little boy's nose and mouth. At least he would have some relief for the journey. They began the walk to the hospital, a long way from their home in the deserts of East Africa. There were no taxis, and even if there were, they had no money for the fare. So they set out on foot. The midday heat was almost unbearable, and even with the oxygen tank, Caleb's breathing remained labored and ragged. Gabriel knew they didn't have much time, so he decided to cut off on the dirt road through the territory of the Pokot tribe.

Their new route was not without risk. It ran through a desert area with a long history of raids and killings between the Pokot and Gabriel's tribe. In the past, when one tribe needed goats or camels to pay dowries for marriage, they would kill people from the neighboring tribe and steal their flocks. Resentment and animosity had intensified over the years, and the area was rife with conflict.

They had not been walking long when three men suddenly stepped out from behind the scrub brush along the path. One man pointed a gun at Gabriel, demanding money. Frantically, Gabriel pleaded for mercy and tried to explain they were in a hurry. They weren't there to cause trouble, but their little boy needed a doctor. For a moment, Gabriel didn't know if the men would shoot all three of them. He prayed to Jesus that the men would leave them alone. The bandits rifled through their things, took what little money they had, then grabbed the oxygen tank and took off running.

Distressed, but with no choice but to continue on their journey, they hiked a rough path. Caleb's breathing faded, and Gabriel and Ana pleaded with him to keep going. They were nearly there, and they began jogging, with their son on Gabriel's back.

Then Caleb's breathing stopped.

Gabriel and Ana collapsed in the shade of a small tree and wept, begging God to save their son.

But Caleb was gone.

Gabriel cradled their son's body in his arms, and slowly, they turned around and began the long trek home across the desert. When they finally returned home that night, they buried their little Caleb, as was their tribe's tradition.

Devastated by their loss, Gabriel's leaders and coworkers tried to comfort them, but the couple continued to struggle with deep grief.

Gabriel had come to know Jesus several years earlier and had been equipped as a disciple-maker and church planter through a training started by an indigenous movement of churches with help from Global Disciples.

Some months later his church leader talked to Gabriel about their mission efforts among the Pokot people—the men who had stolen Caleb's oxygen tank were from that tribe.

"I know this will be very hard," he said to Gabriel, hesitation in his voice, "but I'd like you to go with us to the Pokot. I'd like you to help us share the gospel of Jesus Christ among those people." His leader had known hardship and loss. He understood that for Gabriel to move through resentment and bitterness would require dying to himself and forgiving like Jesus.

But Gabriel wasn't ready.

"You must be crazy," Gabriel said. "I will never go back to that place."

However, he couldn't shake the request. He prayed, he wept, and he prayed some more. He found himself going back and forth between a hard-hearted denial and the whisper of a question:

Could this be what God wanted him to do?

Finally, Gabriel contacted his leader. He would do it. He would go and meet the growing number of Pokot believers. The dreaded day came, and they walked a long distance across the rugged desert to find a thatched-roof pavilion, full of Pokot people who had come to know Jesus as their Lord and Savior. Gabriel's leader greeted the group and began teaching them about Jesus and his love for each one of them.

Then his leader turned to Gabriel and invited him to share the testimony of how he came to know Jesus and whatever else God laid on his heart. Gabriel told the story of his conversion and what it meant to him to be a follower of Christ even in the hard times. Then he told the story of losing his son on the way to the hospital. Heartbreak and loss flowed from his voice as he explained the long desperate journey to get help for Caleb, and his devastation when the oxygen tank was stolen. The crowd in the pavilion was completely silent as Gabriel told his story. Some Pokot cried as they listened. When Gabriel finished his story, you could have heard a pin drop. In that space of quiet and reflection, three men in the back corner stood up together. One of them spoke.

"It was us," he said, his voice shaking. "We are the three men who stole the oxygen tank. It is because of us that your son is dead."

The man paused, and every eye in the house was on him.

"There's a gun here," he continued. "Take it and shoot us. Please. After what we did to you, your family, your little boy, we don't deserve to live."

There was a long silence. No one spoke. Gabriel began to walk through the crowd of Pokot, toward the men and the gun. In the silence everyone slowly turned and watched as he drew closer and closer.

As Gabriel stepped up to the man who had spoken, their eyes locked together. Everyone watching held their breath, wondering what would happen next.

They got their answer.

Slowly Gabriel reached out his hand … and placed it on the man's shoulder. Tears streamed down Gabriel's cheeks. He spoke slowly, each word an effort.

"In the name of Jesus, you are forgiven."

After a few moments, Gabriel moved over to the second man, and then to the third. And to each one he offered the same gesture. The same words.

"In the name of Jesus, you are forgiven."

Whenever I think about Gabriel's story, I think of Jesus, beaten, spat on, ridiculed, whipped, and stretched out mercilessly on the cross. I think of those crude nails pounded through his hands and feet, and how the cross was dropped with an excruciating thud into the hole prepared for it. Yet Jesus, the sinless, perfect Son of God, one-with-God since creation—in the midst of being tortured and killed for my sins—cried out, "Father, forgive them, for they do not know what they are doing" (Luke 23:34).

I don't know what I would have done if I had been in Gabriel's situation. What would I do if my own son had died at the hands of greedy and violent men and I then found myself in the presence of those men? Would I react in anger? Bitterness? Unforgiveness? Would I want to hurt them? I hope I would have the courage to do what Gabriel did.

The Undeniable Connection

For twelve years prior to my work with Global Disciples, I gave leadership to a discipleship-mission training program. Whenever we tackled this foundational teaching on forgiveness and right relationships, I saw profound transformation take place in the disciples we trained. So much so that we later incorporated it into our Global Disciples training. It is a key that unlocks our capacity for intimacy with Christ—and to be attentive and responsive to the promptings of the Holy Spirit. There is an undeniable connection between forgiveness and living fully into the kingdom of God.

We are social beings created for relationships: at home, with our families and neighbors, with our coworkers or classmates, and in the community of disciples. Those relationships can bring joy, meaning, and fulfillment to our lives when they're healthy, God-honoring relationships. And when broken by sin, personal offense, critical attitudes, or a lack of sensitivity, those same relationships are a source of pain and frustration.

Hebrews 12:15 warns, "See to it that no one falls short of the grace of God and that no bitter root grows up to cause trouble and defile many." To miss the grace and mercy of God through a lack of forgiveness prevents us from living fully into the kingdom of God. The bitterness that often accompanies unforgiveness not only negatively impacts our own life, but it also affects those around us.

When we are reconciled in our relationship with God, the Holy Spirit will be faithful in identifying areas of brokenness in our relationships with others. The deeper we go in our relationship with Jesus, the more freely the Spirit brings to mind our need for healing and reconciliation in our interpersonal relationships. This is an important part of the journey. To have a broad influence in the kingdom of God, you and I must go deep with Jesus. But the depth of our relationship with Jesus can clearly be inhibited by broken relationships with others. We find complete freedom in Christ only as we seek and receive forgiveness from God and from those negatively impacted by the choices we have made. We also need to be willing to forgive someone else for their hurtful behavior toward us.

Forgiveness and inner healing from past wounds are so foundational for discipleship. It takes courage and humility to acknowledge to others the choices we have made that created distance, tensions, or brokenness in our relationships. It also takes courage to extend forgiveness to those who have hurt us.

Jesus teaches us to pray, "forgive us our debts, as we have also forgiven our debtors" (Matthew 6:12). He goes on to say, "for if you forgive other people when they sin against you, your heavenly Father will also forgive you.

But if you do not forgive others their sins your Father will not forgive your sins" (Matthew 6:14–15).

Receiving Forgiveness

Getting our relationship with God right is a good first step toward right relationships with ourselves and with others. Some religious leaders asked Jesus which is the greatest commandment, to which he replied: "'Love the Lord your God with all your heart and with all your soul and with all your mind.' This is the first and greatest commandment." But without any additional explanation he said, "And the second is like it: 'Love your neighbor as yourself'" (Matthew 22:37–39).

A few years ago, I (Tefera) was teaching a session on right relationships. One of the participants came and shared how she struggled to forgive herself. I reminded her of the truth in Scripture: when we are in Christ, we are new creations, we are reconciled with God,[1] and there is no condemnation for us.[2] God has forgiven us, but we have a choice to believe his Word and extend his forgiveness to ourselves. That is why Jesus said, "Love your neighbor as yourself." Our love for others begins by knowing how loved we are by God. Only when we build our lives on that foundational truth can we truly love others and make peace with them.

Seeking Forgiveness

I will never forget the time when my son was on a seven-month discipleship training and mission experience, and he wrote a letter to me seeking forgiveness for his attitudes, choices, and behaviors that had created distance in our relationship. I wept. And I had my own attitudes to confess as I gladly extended forgiveness to my son.

If the Holy Spirit is bringing an unresolved relationship to your mind right now, stop and deal with it. Write an email, send a text message, make a phone call, or visit if possible. If these aren't possible, consider confessing to

---

[1]   2 Corinthians 5:17–18.
[2]   Romans 8:1.

a trusted friend. Jesus says it this way, "If you are offering your gift at the altar and there remember that your brother or sister has something against you, leave your gift there in front of the altar. First go and be reconciled to them; then come and offer your gift" (Matthew 5:23–24).

By confessing our sins and dealing with wounds from the past, we pave the way to move forward in our relationship with Christ and to partner with God to influence others for the kingdom. We want to be able to say, "There is nothing unresolved in my past that will prevent me from being who God is calling me to be today and in the future."

Extending Forgiveness

During a discipleship training program, a young woman named Pam came to me with Liz, her team leader. I had noticed her tears during the session, and now her voice quivered as she said, "I need to talk with you about something from my past. It's controlling me."

Later that day, with Liz by her side, Pam poured out her heart. Her pain was deep, and telling the story seemed unbearable. Sometimes she sobbed uncontrollably, but she fought her way through. It mattered too much to stop. As a teenager, her father had raped and sexually abused her. Repeatedly. She had told no one. For years, she felt so guilty, so dirty, so angry, so bitter. Some days she simply wanted to end it all.

"You were talking today about forgiveness," she said through her tears, "about not having anything from our past stand in the way of what God wants to do in our lives in the future. But…" Her whole body trembled as she spoke, "I can't forgive him! I can't. I hate him. He ruined my life! There's no way I can forgive him."

She wasn't ready to forgive. We sat in silence with tears. Liz held her gently in her arms. This was a holy moment. The journey toward healing of a beloved daughter of God was beginning. A few days later, at Pam's request, I met with Pam and Liz again. We prayed and listened to what the two of them had been processing together. There were a few smiles through the tears. God was beginning to do his work. No longer carrying the pain of this experience all alone was making a difference.

Liz was a godly woman who listened well, prayed with Pam regularly, and led her into the comfort and truth of Scripture. When they asked to meet me again some time later, they updated me on the journey.

"Pam has something to tell you," Liz said.

It wasn't easy but again, Pam fought her way through. She was determined.

"I'm–I'm ready to–to forgive my dad." Then a burst of tears. She tried to compose herself, "I don't want this or anything from my past to limit what God wants to do in and through my life." Empowered by the Holy Spirit, through tears and sobs, Pam prayed and forgave her father.

In the years since then, Pam has acknowledged that the decision to forgive is one she needs to make repeatedly, whenever the painful memories rise to the surface. But over time, this has become less frequent.

Sometimes the journey to healing and forgiveness is a long process. Sometimes we need to extend forgiveness when the guilty party doesn't seek forgiveness or even acknowledge the wrong. But it's always worth the investment because of the peace and joy it brings with it. Today Pam is free; a vibrant, joyful disciple, mother, and wife, serving the Lord with delight and clarity of purpose. The chains of shame, hatred, and anger have been broken. She has forgiven. Her life is a living testimony of the words of Jesus, "So if the Son sets you free, you will be free indeed" (John 8:36).

It's important to mention that in cases of abuse, it's often not safe or appropriate to reconnect relationally with the abuser. Forgiveness does not mean putting ourselves in situations where we may be subject to subsequent abuse. But it does mean releasing the pain and hurt to God and allowing him to take that from us. For Pam, that connection and resolution came later, accompanied by a trusted counselor.

God longs to reconcile us to himself and to others, no matter how big or small we may consider the wrongs we have done or how horrible or minor the sins committed against us. God wants to set us free from shame, bitterness, resentment, and a spirit of heaviness. You and I have been forgiven much! Apart from God's mercy and grace, expressed in the blood of Christ shed on the cross, we would face judgment and separation from God. So how can any of us withhold forgiveness from others? Even if it is a long journey to do so, it is worth taking the first step, and to invite the power of the Holy Spirit to press us on toward freedom.

Forgiveness—received and extended—is God's gift and reflects what he has made possible for us. God values right relationship so much that he gave us his only son so that we could be reconciled back to him. When we truly experience this love and forgiveness ourselves, we cannot help but pass it on to others. His love changes everything, including our decision to forgive others. Jesus illustrates this in the parable of the servant who owed the king a huge debt in gold.[3] When he was unable to pay it and prayed for mercy, the king forgave the debt completely. That same servant went out and found a fellow servant who owed him only a small debt in silver. Because he couldn't repay, he had that servant thrown into prison. You may remember the king's response when he heard about the exchange—it wasn't pretty. Jesus concludes by saying, "This is how my heavenly Father will treat each of you unless you forgive your brother or sister from your heart" (Matthew 18:35).

The magnitude of the debt we have been forgiven through Christ helps us understand why the most common and powerful expression of God's redemptive work is the Christ-centered love and joy of his people. We've been called from a kingdom of darkness to walk in the kingdom of light and extend his forgiveness wherever we go.

Forgiveness Unlocks Doors

When there is brokenness in our relationships with other people, it creates brokenness in our relationship with God. At the end of his teaching on how to pray, Jesus addressed how forgiveness unlocks heaven for us. "For if you forgive other people when they sin against you, your heavenly Father will also forgive you. But if you do not forgive others their sins, your Father will not forgive your sins" (Matthew 6:14–15).

In other words, even if it takes a long time, we must extend forgiveness toward those who hurt us, or our relationship with our Heavenly Father will

---

[3]   Matthew 18:23–35.

be blocked; the door of heaven is locked on us. Our worship or offering is not acceptable until we go and make our relationship right.[4] Forgiveness is the foundational need of every human being, but it often feels like a hard choice. If a broken relationship needs to be restored, we choose to make it right by extending forgiveness or asking forgiveness. By choosing to forgive individuals or groups who have inflicted pain or difficulty in our lives, we not only open the door of heaven, but the doors to healthier relationships. Forgiveness can set us free from the bondages of bitterness, resentment, self-hatred, or disdain of others. As one young man told me, "I had lived so much of my life reacting to my father's lack of acceptance, trying to prove myself. Until I forgave him, I didn't realize the peace I was missing in my life. I feel like a new person. I'm free."

The Ministry of Reconciliation

When we are in right relationship with Christ, it brings a joy and freedom that we want other people to experience too. This is why I love the words from Paul to the church in Corinth:

> Therefore, if anyone is in Christ, the new creation has come: The old has gone, the new is here! All this is from God, who reconciled us to himself through Christ and gave us the ministry of reconciliation: that God was reconciling the world to himself in Christ, not counting people's sins against them. And he has committed to us the message of reconciliation. We are therefore Christ's ambassadors, as though God were making his appeal through us.
>
> 2 Corinthians 5:17–20

For those of us who are in Christ, these verses illustrate the kind of relationships we should seek with those around us. You and I are new creatures. The old you has vanished. The new you is here and ready for change. We have

---

4   Matthew 5:23–24.

been reconciled to God through Christ, but our new being isn't just about that vertical relationship between us and God. We're not called to disappear into the wilderness for the rest of our lives, living only with God.

No! God has "committed to us the message of reconciliation," which is simply letting people know that, through Jesus Christ, they can have peace with God. They can be reconciled with him and enjoy that right relationship. We are now responsible for reconciling others to Christ and to ourselves! We are Christ's ambassadors to the world and his witnesses to the gospel.

What an incredible responsibility and opportunity!

We are called to be agents of reconciliation wherever God has placed us. Some of us may be called to go to far-off places and reconcile ourselves to others and God, but most of us are called to live out this reconciliation with people around us, in our ordinary lives and routines: our family, our friends, and our church community, but also that irritating neighbor, or difficult co-worker, the hurting, broken, burdened or ostracized around us. Those in need of a right relationship with God and with others. This is where we start to get our relationships right.

And getting our relationships right is not always easy.

Cultivating Community

We've been created for relationships—with God, with others, and with ourselves—each to impact and influence the other. Forgiveness is key to ensuring bitterness doesn't grow in those relationships, but we also need to proactively cultivate the relationships God has given us. Most of us have discovered that we are happier and more satisfied when we are in healthy, authentic, and caring relationships. Those of us who are disciples of Jesus, living in right relationship with God, at peace with ourselves, and in harmony with others, should be the most joyful, fulfilled, and deeply connected people in the world. Sadly, that is often not the case. Even in our churches, we find lonely people gathered in the crowd for worship but feeling alone and disconnected.

Meaningful relationships develop over time with mutual interest and effort. That's why in any expression of the body of Christ, it is crucial to be part of a small discipling group in which we are known and loved. Whether it's a house church or a cell/small group within the larger body, at least four characteristics of your small faith community are essential for spiritual growth:

- *Trust* is built through openness and vulnerability, when what we share with one another is handled with care, sensitivity, and appropriate confidentiality. Being truthful and authentic with one another about our history and the journey we're on, along with our current joys and challenges, helps develop trust and friendship. When we relate to those whose trust was broken in the past, patience and affirmation are important expressions of love and concern as trust is established.
- *Spiritual Hunger* is as significant as our level of spiritual maturity. If we share a common hunger for more of Jesus, the desire to experience living in the fullness of the Holy Spirit, and a longing to bring God glory in all we do, we will draw into deeper and deeper fellowship with one another. Allow that spiritual hunger to draw you into the Scriptures. As our spiritual hunger is satisfied, it will translate into a growing desire individually and corporately to see others come to know Jesus as their Lord and Savior.
- *Accountability* takes us beyond ideas to application and action. In North America, we tend to treat discipleship groups as optional discussion groups. But when we choose accountable relationships, we're asking those around us to help us live out the things we are learning about in Scripture. Where the church around the world is experiencing rapid growth and multiplying disciples, it always involves accountability, sometimes referred to as *obedience-based discipleship*. Jesus reminds us, "You are my friends if you do what I command" (John 15:14).
- *Prayer* for one another within the small group or fellowship makes a real difference. We encourage you to pray with and for one another when you're together, but also regularly between meetings. There's so much more that God wants to do when we agree and pray together. Jesus makes it clear in Matthew 18:19–20, "Again, truly I tell you that if two of you on earth agree about anything they ask for,

it will be done for them by my Father in heaven. For where two or three gather in my name, there am I with them."

Community can be cultivated in the everyday spaces of life—in our homes, in coffee shops, gyms, or in our workplaces. Handoko was a successful business leader in Indonesia who came to Christ as an adult. His relationship with Jesus transformed his life. His businesses flourished with his new commitment to integrity and by operating in ways that built trust and brought glory to God.

He noticed his local church in Jakarta wasn't addressing the challenges he faced in business—a concern he also heard from other business leaders who followed Christ. So Handoko launched the "Priesthood of all Believers" business fellowship.[5] Every month several hundred business leaders and their spouses gathered in a hotel ballroom in Jakarta for worship, prayer, and solid biblical teaching relevant to business leaders.

I was introduced to Handoko by our Indonesian facilitator, and we quickly became friends. Handoko and his wife, Inge, launched Global Disciples' first National Foundation there in Indonesia. The foundation brings together local business and professional leaders, registered as a legal entity with their governments, for the purpose of praying, giving, and promoting the work of Global Disciples in their nation. This has now been multiplied into eight more countries, as local business leaders embrace our vision for local sustainability.

When I joined Handoko for those events during my visits to Indonesia, I was always inspired, challenged, and encouraged. The authenticity of the worship, teaching, and relationships was so refreshing! Part of this was born through personal adversity, and a willingness to stand with each other in the hard parts of life. As a community, they had prayed, comforted, and stood by Handoko and Inge when their eldest daughter died from a fatal reaction to a date-rape drug her boyfriend slipped her. When the young man came to ask their forgiveness, Handoko was faced with a painful, impossible choice.

"It was such a struggle to forgive," he said. "But that's what we do as the priesthood of believers—we forgive, and we declare forgiveness in the name of Jesus for those who repent."

---

5   Handoko drew this name from 1 Peter 2:9.

No wonder I had seen such authenticity and genuineness in those "Priesthood of Believers" business leader gatherings. These brothers and sisters were cultivating community and choosing to be real with each other—no matter how painful the reality was. They were faithful in bearing one another's burdens and committed to seeing their employees, coworkers, families, and neighbors reconciled to Christ. [6]

Nurturing Deep Friendships

As well as relationships in community, we also need relationships at the individual level: the one-on-one connections; the trusting, life-affirming, heart-to-heart friendships.

Most friendships are born of a shared experience or common interest—fans of the same team, sharing a workspace, a similar educational or business experience, even going through a crisis together. As disciples, we share the common experience of salvation through Jesus Christ and new life in him. Not only that, we share the same Holy Spirit. And it's through him that we can connect with each other on a deeper level. I think back to Salim's story in chapter five. When he was in crisis, running and afraid for his life, his friend was willing to step into his need, even in the middle of the night! He provided shelter, support, but also truth and love—speaking to Salim's fears and helping him consider what the Holy Spirit directed. And then blessing Salim when he chose to return to his place of service.

Developing personal Spirit-infused friendships requires time, energy, empathy, and awareness—things that most of us struggle to invest. The same distractions and agendas that eat away at our intimacy with God will get in the way of deepening our friendships as well.

Friendships can be messy and complicated. We're broken, imperfect people and even as disciples of Jesus, filled with the Holy Spirit, we don't always get it right. But forgiveness is a mighty tool, and if we seek to be faithful in our relationship with God and with others, we can enjoy deep, soul-satisfying friendships. In trust and humility, it is possible to build a friendship that is a safe landing place for confession. Good friends rely on each other for discernment

---

[6] Galatians 6:2.

in decisions or accountability in obedience. They provide spiritual "back-up" in the battles, and celebrate breakthroughs and milestones together!

This takes effort—from you and from the other person. It doesn't *just happen*. And this depth of friendship goes both ways—you give, and you receive; you step in to help, and you step back and ask for help. You speak truth with love, and you learn to humbly listen to truth spoken in love. You seek the Lord together, you rejoice when your friend rejoices, and your friend weeps with you when your tears flow.

I realize this is only scratching the surface in what it takes to enjoy Spirit-connected, Spirit-infused relationships. Many of us long to experience friendships like this, and the first step toward cultivating such a friendship is often praying for it. Ask the Spirit of God to direct you to people who are open to this type of relationship and to show you how to invest and build this kind of friendship together.

Look to the model Jesus gave us. John—who enjoyed a deep friendship with Jesus—put it this way: "This is how we know what love is: Jesus Christ laid down his life for us. And we ought to lay down our lives for our brothers and sisters" (1 John 3:16). Laying down our life is a daily call to prefer others above ourselves, to make decisions based on God's purposes and for their good, not our own. It may mean getting up in the middle of the night to meet your friend at the emergency room. Or being humble enough to ask for help. It may look like giving up your empty nest to make room for the one who's just lost everything. Or rejoicing with a friend when a long-awaited prayer is answered—even if you're still waiting on answers to your own prayers.

It can flow in tears and tenderness, as Liz, Pam's team leader demonstrated—listening well, standing beside her, fully present to support Pam in her distress.

Laying down your life is sometimes speaking the truth in a challenging situation—as Gabriel's leader spoke to him, calling him out of bitterness into forgiveness. Or it can be setting aside your own pride and your need to be right, in order to hear correction from a friend.[7]

It means wrestling together in prayer, seeking accountability in your spiritual walk, celebrating God's goodness with each other. Laying down

---

[7]   Proverbs 27:6.

your life for your friends can become a living witness to the gospel of salvation, the perfect summation of discipleship. Because of what Christ has done for us, we can and should be willing to lay down our lives for others.

Right Relationships

What characteristics will we demonstrate as witnesses of Christ, representing him well in our families, our communities, and workplaces?

In our Global Disciple Training, as we equip disciples of Jesus to make disciples, we consider the fruit of the Holy Spirit[8] to be the gold standard of right relationships. I encourage you to think through the people in your life and ask the Holy Spirit to reveal if your relationships with them exhibit these traits, so we can seek to reconcile our relationships whenever necessary.

- *Love*—Gabriel's act of forgiving the men who killed his little boy reminds me of these words: "Above all, love each other deeply, because love covers over a multitude of sins" (1 Peter 4:8).
- *Joy*—The joy and freedom I saw in Pam's life after forgiving her dad illustrates this. "If you keep my commands," Jesus explained, "you will remain in my love, just as I have kept my Father's commands and remain in his love. I have told you this so that my joy may be in you, and that your joy may be complete" (John 15:10–11).
- *Peace*—Gabriel and Pam each discovered peace that came from Spirit-empowered forgiveness. It didn't take away the pain, but it settled anger and brought a peace beyond what they each thought possible. "Finally, brothers and sisters, rejoice! Strive for full restoration, encourage one another, be of one mind, live in peace. And the God of love and peace will be with you" (2 Corinthians 13:11).
- *Patience*—Most of us find it hard to be patient and wait. But writing from a Roman prison cell, the Apostle Paul instructs, "Be completely humble and gentle; be patient, bearing with one another in

---

[8]   Galatians 5:22–26.

love. Make every effort to keep the unity of the Spirit through the bond of peace" (Ephesians 4:2–3).

- *Kindness*—You may not identify with the stories of violence and abuse in this chapter, but we have each experienced—or shown—a lack of kindness in subtle, yet hurtful ways. As disciples of Jesus, we are called to much more. "Therefore, as God's chosen people, holy and dearly loved, clothe yourselves with compassion, kindness, humility, gentleness and patience" (Colossians 3:12).

- *Goodness*—You are designed to fulfill God's good purposes—no question. "For we are God's handiwork, created in Christ Jesus to do good works, which God prepared in advance for us to do" (Ephesians 2:10). Lord, show us what those good works are! "I myself am convinced, my brothers and sisters, that you yourselves are full of goodness, filled with knowledge and competent to instruct one another" (Romans 15:14).

- *Faithfulness*—Are you being a faithful steward of the relationships God has entrusted to you? We often talk about stewarding our resources and abilities, but our relationships are a gift from God too. Do you care about the people he's placed in your life, investing in them, paying attention to their needs, listening to their heart, putting their interests above your own, keeping your promises, and calling them to a deeper relationship with God? That's faithful stewardship. And it comes with a reward, as Jesus taught in his parable of the faithful steward: "Well done, good and faithful servant! You have been faithful with a few things; I will put you in charge of many things. Come and share your master's happiness!' (Matthew 25:21). Imagine experiencing the warm embrace of Jesus as he speaks those words to you one day!

- *Gentleness*—Remember Gabriel reaching out to the men who killed his son. Or Liz embracing Pam in her distress. Salim's friend opening his door and his home in a moment of need. A gentle word or touch can be an instrument of healing and hope for our hurting world. From his dark Roman prison cell, the Apostle Paul writes, "Rejoice in the Lord always. I will say it again: Rejoice! Let your gentleness be evident to all. The Lord is near. Do not be anxious about anything, but in every situation, by prayer and petition, with thanksgiving, present your requests to God" (Philippians 4:4–6).

- *Self-control*—Few things do more harm to a relationship than a lack of self-control in how we respond to temptations and frustrations. An inability to control our anger, our words, and our selfish attitudes can damage even the best of relationships. Let's remember that God's grace offers salvation to all people and "teaches us to say no to ungodliness and worldly passions, and to live self-controlled, upright, and godly lives in this present age, while we wait for the blessed hope—the appearing of the glory of our great God and Savior, Jesus Christ" (Titus 2:11–13).

Let's pause right here and acknowledge that when we try to do this on our own, all of us fall short of these standards. But remember, when we rely daily on the power of the Holy Spirit, he empowers us to do the hard work of building right relationships, of forgiving and seeking forgiveness, of extending grace, kindness, and the message of reconciliation as influential disciples.

The world is watching. How we live in right relationship with each other as followers of Jesus Christ can speak volumes to lost, broken, hurting people. When Gabriel was faced with the men responsible for his son's death, he looked beyond his pain, beyond tribal lines and revenge, and he saw three individuals—just like every single one of us—who needed the message of reconciliation. He saw those men through the eyes of Jesus, and that made all the difference.

Reflect and Discuss

- What inspired you in this chapter?
- What challenged you?
- What is God inviting you to do in the coming days?
- What obstacles are keeping you from accepting and acting upon this invitation?

- How will you live differently today because of what you have just read?
- What practical actions will you commit to doing soon?
- What questions do you still have?

Additional Study

Right Relationship with God: Genesis 3:1–8; John 3:16–18, Romans 5:6–10.

Forgiveness and Inner Healing: Matthew 5:23–24; 6:12–15; 18:21–35.

Christlike Relationships with Others: John 13:34–35; Colossians 3:12–17; Ephesians 4:29–5:7.

Being Ambassadors of Reconciliation: 2 Corinthians 5:18–21.

8

Demonstrating God's Heart

Tet was chosen by his cluster of churches in Myanmar to develop a Global Disciples discipleship and mission training program. It was a big step for both Tet and his churches, and they were excited to see what would happen when he came back, ready and able to train others to make disciples.

After going through the training, Tet returned to his community, eager to begin equipping the local believers with the tools he had received. As planned, a dozen believers showed up for the first day of training.

So did a Buddhist monk.

Tet recognized him as Yeshe, the leader of the local monastery. Wearing his traditional red robe, austere and dignified, Yeshe strutted to the front row and sat on the floor mats with the others. Drawn by curiosity, Yeshe wanted to see what this young man was teaching in his community. He intended to stop the entire thing if it threatened his power or influence. Though Tet was nervous, he couldn't see any reason to ask Yeshe to leave, so he plowed ahead with the teaching. This Buddhist monk had a skeptical mindset and was prepared to do whatever was necessary to protect his community from Christianity. But he sat and respectfully listened to lesson after lesson about Jesus. As he learned that Jesus can save people from sin, his spiritual walls began to crumble. After the training, Yeshe had so many questions that he continued to visit Tet. They had conversations long into the night at Tet's home, and this Buddhist monk fell more and more in love with Jesus.

"Now that I have heard about Jesus," Yeshe told Tet, "I have trouble sleeping when I go home. I keep asking myself over and over if it's possible that I have been wrong for all of these years!"

One day, Yeshe disappeared. The other monks from the monastery came to Tet's house to ask him what he had done with their leader. Tet told them boldly and lovingly about Jesus. "I think your leader received Jesus Christ as his Savior," Tet explained. "I imagine that's why he left." Tet paused and looked around at the Buddhist monks in their red robes. "Jesus died for your sins, too. You should receive him, just as your brother Yeshe did."

The monks were stunned and didn't know what to say. Some months later, when Tet was delivering another training event, several more monks showed up. This time it was clear they came to harm Tet and stop the training. They were worried they would lose more of their monastic brothers, just as they lost Yeshe. Yet, as they listened to Tet sharing about Jesus, they brought up more and more questions. Tet told them, as he had told Yeshe, that Jesus died for everyone—including them—and they could receive the promise of John 3:16.

Unlike Yeshe, these men wanted proof. "If your God is real, then tell him to provide food for us and send rain when you pray. Then we'll believe!"

If Tet declined, they would ridicule Jesus and Tet's faith. So he agreed to meet them the following morning in a forest clearing, a quiet place the monks often used to meditate. Tet couldn't help but think of the Bible story of Elijah and the prophets of Baal on Mount Carmel when they challenged Elijah and tested God.[1]

The next morning, Tet met with the monks in the sacred clearing, and

---

[1] 1 Kings 18:22-24.

he began to pray. *Food and rain, God. Food and rain.* Around noon, after Tet had been praying for a few hours, a stranger stumbled into the clearing. He carried a huge pack on his back, and he was lost, in need of directions. After talking with Tet and the Buddhist monks, he took food out of his backpack and shared his lunch with them. Then he walked back into the woods and was gone. Tet was relieved—God had answered one prayer, bringing food in the middle of the forest. But still no rain. Tet continued to pray, until late in the day.

"No more," one monk said. "Your God is not as you say he is." With that, the monks left him and went home.

Tet was disappointed, but decided to head home, believing God was still in control. On the way, rain began to fall, eventually becoming a heavy, flooding downpour that lasted well into the night. God had answered Tet's prayer! He sat in his house and wondered what the monks thought of the sudden change in the weather.

He found out the next morning.

He answered a knock at the door, and there stood the Buddhist monks.

"Yes, yes," they said. "We believe in your Jesus."

Together, Tet and the monks returned to the clearing in the woods, and, in prayer, these monks surrendered their lives to Jesus, discarding their robes and their identity as followers of Buddha. They became living testimonies of the powerful, transforming work of God in the hearts and minds of those who hear and respond to the gospel of Jesus Christ.

Like Yeshe, these new followers of Christ knew it wasn't safe for them to remain where they were known as monks, so they "disappeared" too. Later, Tet received word that these new disciples had found another place to live, and were growing in their faith in Christ and serving the Lord by ministering among people addicted to drugs.

Through his Holy Spirit, God is active in pursuing relationship with people of various religions and backgrounds. And he works through those who, like Tet, are willing to boldly and lovingly give witness to Jesus. This is the very nature of the God we serve—he is love, and he longs for relationship with all people. God our Savior "wants all people to be saved and to come to a knowledge of the truth" (1 Timothy 2:4).

God's Desire to Make His Glory Known

When thinking about God's heart for the nations, many Christians immediately think of the Great Commission:

> Then Jesus came to them and said, "All authority in heaven and on earth has been given to me. Therefore go and make disciples of all nations, baptizing them in the name of the Father and of the Son and of the Holy Spirit, and teaching them to obey everything I have commanded you. And surely I am with you always, to the very end of the age."

> Matthew 28:18–20

But God's concern for the salvation of people of all nations extends beyond this New Testament concept introduced by Jesus and passed down to his disciples. Yes, Jesus did send his disciples out. Yes, this is an important commission. However, God reveals his love for all peoples throughout the *whole* of Scripture—beginning in Genesis and culminating in the incredible Book of Revelation.

Think about Adam and Eve, the first people created. They were placed in a utopia, every need met, surrounded by beauty … and they chose to disobey God. He could have destroyed them on the spot or separated himself from them forever. But how did God respond to this act of disobedience by the very beings he had created? He went looking for them.

> Then the man and his wife heard the sound of the LORD God as he was walking in the garden in the cool of the day, and they hid from the LORD God among the trees of the garden. But the LORD God called to the man, "Where are you?"

> Genesis 3:8, 9

God knew what Adam and Eve had done. He was fully aware of the situation. But instead of simply walking away or raining down fire on their heads, he called out to them, "Where are you?" God sought them out because he loved them and had created them with the capacity to enjoy a relationship with him. We repeatedly see throughout Scripture that God does not give up easily on his relationship with us. He pursues us out of his unconditional love even when we fail or turn our back on our Creator. Words are inadequate to express all the attributes, abilities, and accomplishments of God—Father, Son, and Holy Spirit—as described in Scripture. He is all powerful yet gentle; sovereign yet approachable; just yet abounding in love. "God is love," and "We love because he first loved us" (1 John 4:8, 19). When the Spirit of the living God enters in our lives, he imparts into us that same persistent love. Describing his compulsion for others to come to know his Lord, the Apostle Paul writes, "For Christ's love compels us" (2 Corinthians 5:14).

If we read the Bible only looking for promises for our own lives or the benefits of serving God, we can easily overlook what it reveals about our God's unfathomable love for *all* people. Consider the story of Abraham. God tells him that he will be blessed and through him all peoples will be blessed.[2] What is that blessing? Many years later the ultimate expression of that blessing is explained: "You are the sons of the prophets and of the covenant God made with your fathers, saying to Abraham, 'And in your offspring shall all families of the earth be blessed.' God, having raised up his servant [Jesus], sent him to you first, to bless you by turning each of you from your wicked ways" (Acts 3:25–26 ESV).

The blessing of Abraham was Jesus, descendant of Abraham but also the Son of God, who came to reconcile all people from all nations to God. It's the blessing we receive when we come to God through faith in Jesus Christ. And with this blessing—a relationship with God through Jesus—we accept the responsibility of passing that blessing on to others. We are blessed to be a blessing! This is the story line throughout Scripture, revealing the heart of our Creator God—that the blessing of salvation will spread to all the families of the earth.

---

[2]   Genesis 12:2.

God's Heart for All People

Since the beginning, God wanted—and planned—to enfold people of every nation, tribe, and language into his kingdom. He wanted them to be reconciled and restored to a relationship with him. To accomplish this, he chose first to work through Abraham's descendants, the Jewish people in the Old Testament, and then through the church in the New Testament. Many Old Testament passages point to the day when God will gather *peoples from all nations* to be included in his purposes and become agents of his kingdom.[3] Before his return to heaven, Jesus said the gospel of the kingdom would be preached among *all peoples* and then the end will come.[4] After his resurrection, he commissioned his disciples to go and preach the gospel by the power of the Holy Spirit and to make disciples of *all nations*.[5] In short, they were sent on a mission into the world as Jesus himself was sent by the Father.[6]

God's intent was always that we would become agents of his mission to all peoples. Making his heart and his glory known required his disciples to cross ethnic and religious barriers. At first the gospel moved from the people of Israel to the Samaritans, and then on to the Gentiles—diverse ethnic groups and followers of a variety of religious beliefs. And we know that one day before the throne of God, there will be "a great multitude that no one [can] count, from every nation, tribe, people and language, standing before the throne and before the Lamb" (Revelation 7:9).

Do we really demonstrate God's heart to all people, including those who are different from us in many ways and practices? Will we respond with love and truth with those whose belief systems differ to ours—as Tet did with the Buddhist monks? Our prayer should be that the Lord of the harvest plants his heart for all people into our hearts and the heart of every disciple, so we do our part to make sure the world knows him.

As Global Disciples, we have seen God, by his Holy Spirit, take initiative

---

3   Isaiah 56:3,6–8; 66:18–21; Zechariah 8:20–23.
4   Matthew 24:14; Mark 13:10.
5   Matthew 28:19; Mark 16:15; Luke 24:46–47.
6   John 20:21.

to draw people from many other religions into relationship with him through Jesus. All God needs is ordinary disciples who long to make him known. God often works in the most unexpected ways in the most unexpected places.

Jonah and Ali were two young men taking part in some discipleship-mission training in northern Africa. They had a clear sense of where God wanted them to make disciples—along an isolated stretch of road where there were several Muslim towns and villages with no known followers of Christ and obviously, no churches. After their training, Jonah and Ali began working their way along the road, stopping at the first village as the Holy Spirit directed them. But they found no receptivity to them or their message, so they moved on. The second village was as difficult as the first, with no person of peace emerging and no receptivity among those with whom they tried to build relationships. After a lot of prayer, they sensed it was time to move on.

As Jonah and Ali made the long trek to the third village, they wondered if they heard the Holy Spirit's directive clearly. Was it just their personal concern for this area or their own desire to see people come to Jesus? Or was God planning to do something special in one of these gospel-deprived places? As they walked into the third village, they saw small groups of people gathered on the dirt roadway. It was unusual to see men, women, and children gathered and casually talking in the middle of the day. As they drew closer, someone welcomed them and asked, "How did you know Anir?"

"Oh, we're sorry," Jonah replied, "We weren't aware it was a funeral day. We're just here to visit." That sparked interest since visitors were uncommon in their village, and the questions followed. Ali explained they had come to build friendships and to help them understand more about *Isa al-Masih* (as Jesus is referred to in the Qur'an). As they spoke about Jesus, two somber men walked up and listened quietly for a few moments, intensity on their faces building. Then one man demanded, "Who are you? And what are you doing here?"

Jonah and Ali were shocked by his angry outburst, but before they could respond, the other man joined in.

"Our brother has died," he shouted, his face contorted with anger, "and you walk in uninvited and start talking to us about some foreign god. Get out of here! We're getting ready to bury my brother, and we don't want you here! Get out."

Empowered by the Holy Spirit, Jonah and Ali remained calm. "We are so sorry," they exclaimed. "Please forgive us. We intended no harm. We will leave, but could we please first pay our respects to your brother? We would be honored to be able to express our sympathy and condolences to your brother's family."

Their respect and kind words diffused the anger of the brothers. The brothers told everyone the burial would soon take place, then they led Jonah and Ali to the house where the dead man's wife and children were mourning. They entered together, and Jonah and Ali explained to the widow that they were just passing through and wanted to express their sympathy.

Then Jonah, again responding to the prompting of the Holy Spirit, made a strange request. "May we pray for your husband?"

One of the brothers responded in disgust, "He's dead. Please just leave us alone."

But the widow interrupted, "Please, let them pray."

Jonah and Ali stepped up to the dead man, laying their hands on his cold, bloated body. With no embalming and in the heat of the day, it was obviously time to bury him. Jonah began to pray a simple prayer that God would reveal his glory and make his power known in this difficult situation, in the name of Jesus. As he prayed, the swollenness of the dead man's body began to decrease. Murmuring began around them, the mourners stopped wailing, and every eye was on the dead man's body. When his eyelids began to flutter, his wife let out a scream, "He's alive! He's alive!" She reached out and touched his arm as he moved and attempted to sit up. She threw her arms around him. By now the room was in chaos! The man's body had re-turned to normal proportions, and he stood up, still in his burial garb and confused by all the commotion.

The once-angry brothers now asked everyone to leave except the family—and Jonah and Ali—who they hugged as the family marveled in disbelief.

Today a church is thriving not only in that village, but in many nearby villages as well. The news that Jesus is more than a prophet spread quickly, backed by the evidence of Anir, a prominent village leader who was dead and now lives. Along with his brothers and their families, he is eager to give witness to the power of Jesus Christ to give new life, physically and spiritually. There are still doubters and those who violently oppose these Christ-followers. And while it may stretch your faith and imagination, we have confirmed the story, so we tell it with confidence.

God's heart for people of all nationalities and religious persuasions is evident throughout the Bible. And he continues to demonstrate his power and glory today through the name of Jesus Christ. In our postmodern pluralistic cultures, we're told all ways are equal or that truth is our own to make it what we will. It is good to be reminded that it's only through Jesus that we can come to relationship with God. As we relate to people around us with differing perspectives that can be hard to digest. As Jonah and Ali encountered, we may have conversations with those from religions where Jesus is considered a good prophet but not really the "only way." Our challenge is to speak truth and point people to the uniqueness of Jesus Christ (see Appendix C). That was the key to Tet's conversations with the monks.

Jesus Christ is God's own—and only—solution for any person on earth to enjoy a relationship with the Creator Almighty God. And it is only because Jesus is uniquely who he is that stories of miracles, faith, commitment, multiplication, and life transformation are possible.

Offended by God's Love

A few years ago, I traveled to Ethiopia with some business leaders. As part of our orientation to the country's history, we went to the Red Terror Martyrs' Memorial Museum in Addis Ababa. We learned about the horrible violence and atrocities committed by the Derg, who ruled the country from 1974 to 1991. Under the leadership of Mengistu Haile Mariam, this military communist government was responsible for more than a million deaths, torturing and killing anyone they thought opposed them. Young people were killed, dragged into the street, and their bodies left in front of their homes. The killers would return the next day to collect payment from the family for the bullets used to kill the family member.

The museum showed instruments of torture and mutilation used against "the opposition." It was impossible to imagine such senseless human cruelty. Pictures plastered the wall of some of the young people and professionals killed by the Derg, which totaled over a million deaths. As we walked through the museum, one of our Ethiopian friends and hosts told us of his own experience under the Derg regime. He had been in prison with his friends, awaiting execution, and on the day of execution, his friends were killed. However, because the authorities could not find his papers, his execution was delayed, and in the end never took place. Now a prominent physician and influential leader in his country, his story added a personal intensity to the museum visit.

As we left the museum, I walked with an Ethiopian friend who told me Colonel Mengistu, leader of the Red Terror, had fled to safe haven in Zimbabwe; the Ethiopian trial for the genocide and his death sentence happened in absentia. My friend also mentioned there were rumors that the Colonel had come to faith in Jesus. After everything I had just seen and heard in the museum, I was incredulous. For the first time, I could understand Jonah's anger in the Old Testament, when Nineveh repented, and God withheld his judgment.[7]

Sometimes we are offended by God's love, that he shows mercy and offers forgiveness to even the worst of sinners. Yet we all have sinned and fallen short of the glory of God.[8] The Apostle Paul reminds us that God showed his love to us, in that "while we were still sinners, Christ died for us" (Romans 5:8). I have heard nothing to confirm the rumors about Mengistu's conversion. But I choose to believe the words of Jesus in his conversation with the Pharisee Nicodemus, "For God so loved the world, that he gave his only son, that whoever believes in him should not perish but have eternal life" (John 3:16).

Have you ever found God's love difficult to comprehend? Maybe you've seen or heard of someone coming to faith in Christ who you didn't believe deserved a second chance. Or perhaps you've seen someone offer forgiveness or mercy in a situation that didn't make sense or seem right.

---

[7]   Jonah 4:1–3, 11.
[8]   Romans 3:23.

In Romans 1:16, Paul says, "For I am not ashamed of the gospel, because it is the power of God that brings salvation to *everyone who believes:* first to the Jew, then to the Gentile" (italics ours). And in Ephesians 3:6, he writes, "This mystery is that through the gospel the Gentiles are heirs together with Israel, members together of one body, and sharers together in the promise in Christ Jesus." God's love and his invitation to a relationship with him is available to each and every person, no matter their religion, background, or sin.

The Strength of Affection

There's something strategic we gain in developing and maintaining personal relationships—especially a personal and intimate relationship with God. Science is beginning to demonstrate that we may not have as much power to control our will as previously imagined. Our human "will" is actually pretty weak.[9] Strength, it turns out, doesn't come from our ability to *will* something into existence. Strength comes from an affectionate connection or relationship. When a mother or father runs into a burning building to rescue their child, they don't sit down and think it over, pump themselves up for it, and then rely on their will power to help them run into the fire. No, they don't even think twice—they're back in that building, because they have a deep emotional connection with the person who needs help.

This same deep affection or intimate connection is what leads people to lay down their comfort and risk their lives in order to share the love of God. They do this quite happily, not because they have a stronger will than others, but because they have a heart connection or a "love attachment" with Jesus and will "run into the fire" if they think they can save one more of their Father's children. If we're going to have God's heart for people and be willing to die to ourselves, it will grow out of a deep personal connection, identity with, and affection for Jesus. To live with a kingdom mindset is more than a decision, or the *will* to do so. It will be rooted in a deep relationship with our God, a willing dependence upon him, and a love that attaches us to and

---

9   Jim Wilder, *Renovated: God, Dallas Willard, and the Church that Transforms* (NAVPress: Shepherd's House, 2020), 76–77.

with him. It is by faith and unwavering trust, not by mere human effort. As we know and feel God's heart for people, we want to be part of inviting them to know the One with whom we are so fully attached.

Perfect Love Casts Out Fear

Fear—especially of people—is ever present in our lives. Turn on any news channel in North America, watch for a few minutes, and you'll hear plenty of reasons for fear, anger, judgment, or frustration with people who are different from you, whether that be politically, economically, spiritually, or in relation to social or moral issues. Have you adopted the world's way of looking at people, or do you have God's heart for your neighbor ... not just the person who lives next to you, but the person you're sharing this planet with? Are you listening to God and viewing people the way he sees them—as human beings made in his image—rather than as potential threats, opponents, or a source of personal danger? When you encounter someone who looks or acts differently than you, what is your gut reaction? Fear? Curiosity? Annoyance? Insecurity? Irritation? Or maybe you don't even have many relationships with people who do not vote, worship, or look like you.

A strong connection and affection with Jesus Christ will influence how we see and respond to others and the situations around us. Love for Jesus gave Jonah and Ali the courage to offer compassion, prayer, and the good news, as they walked into that community where they had every reason to be afraid. A friend of mine helps lead a ministry focused on ministering to Muslim immigrants. He is often surprised at how many Christians are afraid to visit a Muslim family in their neighborhood. We often let fear override the love of Christ. For many Christians, media stereotypes have affected their perception of the average Muslim, yet Muslim families are delighted when someone stops by to welcome them.

What will it take to overcome our feelings and for God's heart for people to permeate and fill our hearts? God's Word raises a high standard. It states very simply, "There is no fear in love. But perfect love drives out fear, because fear has to do with punishment. The one who fears is not made perfect in love" (1 John 4:18). Eugene Peterson in his *Message* paraphrase states it this way: "There is no room in love for fear. Well-formed love banishes fear. Since fear is crippling, a fearful life—fear of death, fear of judgment—is one not yet fully formed in love."

This is the perfect love-without-fear that God wants us to have with him, trusting him with whatever we may encounter, and facing every situation with a joy, based on an eternal love attachment with our Heavenly Father. The joy of knowing God is with us and nothing will change that![10]

In the North American context, we tend to use the words from 1 Corinthians 13 for wedding homilies or meditations. But the Apostle Paul is not writing about romance or marriage. He is writing to the church in Corinth about loving one another within the body of Christ and beyond. Take a few moments to read this passage as though you were reading it for the first time. Are you prepared for the Holy Spirit to plant this kind of love into your heart and life for others, regardless of nationality, religion, or ethnic identity? And how would that affect your thought life, your conversations, and your relationships?

> If I speak in the tongues of men or of angels, but do not have love, I am only a resounding gong or a clanging cymbal. If I have the gift of prophecy and can fathom all mysteries and all knowledge, and if I have a faith that can move mountains, but do not have love, I am nothing. If I give all I possess to the poor and give over my body to hardship that I may boast, but do not have love, I gain nothing.
>
> Love is patient, love is kind. It does not envy, it does not boast, it is not proud. It does not dishonor others, it is not self-seeking, it is not easily angered, it keeps no record of wrongs. Love does not delight in evil but rejoices with the truth. It always protects, always trusts, always hopes, always perseveres.
>
> Love never fails.

1 Corinthians 13:1–8

---

[10] Romans 8:38–39.

God's Heart for People

Hopefully, you want to be a disciple whose heart for people reflects God's heart, but what does this look like in everyday life? It's evident in many ways, but here are a few ways you can tell you've become someone who has the heart of God for the world:

- You are a worshipper of God.
- You are enamored with God and the things he is doing in the world.
- You are filled with a sense of amazement that he's chosen you to be a witness for Christ and an ambassador of his kingdom to those around you.
- When you are put on the spot, the same Spirit that raised Jesus from the dead gives you the right words to say.
- You find yourself filled with grace and mercy for people who in the past would have stirred up feelings of hate and animosity.
- You're alert to spiritual needs, listening to what lies behind others' words or actions to see where they need grace, hope, and salvation.
- You're willing to set aside your comfort to extend friendship and hospitality.
- You see people based on their need for Jesus, not by the labels and categories your culture assigns or your fears give them.

Remember how God led Tet to lead one Buddhist monk to Jesus and then an entire group? Those monks could have brought a lot of trouble into Tet's life, disrupting his ministry, or causing harm to him and his family. But this didn't deter Tet. Why? Because he had God's heart for people. When we see clearly and we understand God's heart for the nations, then there is no other way for us than to pursue the way of kingdom multiplication.

Reflect and Discuss

- What inspired you in this chapter?
- What challenged you?
- What is God inviting you to do in the coming days?
- What obstacles are keeping you from accepting and acting upon this invitation?
- How will you live differently today because of what you have just read?
- What practical actions will you commit to doing soon?
- What questions do you still have?

Additional Study

- **God's Heart for All Nations:** Genesis 12:1–3; Revelation 7:9–11; Psalm 67:1–7.
- **Understanding and Reaching Across Cultures**: 1 Corinthians 9:19–23.
- **World Religions and Cults:** Colossians 2:16–23; Matthew 24:14.
- **The Uniqueness of Jesus Christ:** John 1:1–3; 14:6; Acts 4:12.

9

Anticipating Multiplication

Sejun was an illiterate farmer living in an isolated village on the border of Nepal. He was a Buddhist, and no one in his village had ever heard the name of Jesus. When his wife, Ehani, became deathly ill, Sejun hiked the mountains looking for witch doctors who may be able to help, hoping someone would be able to heal her. But no one could. Soon, Ehani became bedridden, waiting to die. Their home was a place of quiet sadness.

Around this time, two young men from their village left for seasonal work as Sherpas, trekking and helping visitors climb some of the highest Himalayan peaks. One expedition took them into the foothills and to a town close to the Everest base camp. A Christian medical doctor in town found out about the visitors, invited them for a nice meal, and asked if they had ever heard about Jesus the Messiah. As they ate and talked, he shared freely, telling stories of Jesus that amazed these young men. During their conversation, a couple came to the door, seeking the doctor. Their young daughter was very ill. The doctor asked them to place her on a cot, and he went back to the Sherpas to explain the situation.

One Sherpa asked the doctor if his Jesus could heal the little girl in the next room. If all the stories he had told were true, it seemed a small thing to heal the girl. The doctor replied that sometimes God heals with miracles, and sometimes God heals through surgery and medication. "But we can ask Jesus to heal her," he concluded, and the three of them went into the other room with the little girl and her parents. The doctor knelt by the bed, laid his hands on the girl and prayed ... and she was healed!

When the Sherpas saw this, they were convinced, and they decided to become followers of Jesus. Since they were illiterate, the doctor taught them a few simple songs that would help them remember the truth about Jesus. Having encountered something new and amazing, they left with joy in their hearts. They sang the new songs as they traveled on their expeditions and continued singing them when they returned to their village after the expedition season.

Once home, these young Sherpas went to Sejun's house to tell him what they had learned about Jesus and how they had seen the little girl healed.

"Do you think this Jesus could heal my wife?" Sejun asked.

They told him what the doctor had told them—sometimes Jesus heals with miracles, and sometimes he heals with medicine and surgeries. They walked over to her bed and did what they had seen the doctor do, knelt and laid their hands on Ehani, praying for healing in the name of Jesus.

Ehani sat up in her bed, something she had been unable to do for weeks. She was hungry and began eating and regaining her strength. Sejun was beside himself with joy! She was completely healed—without the help of any medicine or witch doctor. Soon after, she conceived and gave birth to a son they named Basta.

After Ehani's healing miracle, Sejun was so amazed he couldn't pull himself away from his wife to go work in the rice fields. But after a few days, he returned to farming, working all morning and then spending the afternoon marveling about what this Jesus had done for him. Having seen God at work so powerfully, Sejun got an idea—he would walk through the village and look for sick people to heal in the name of Jesus. He knew many people had family members who were unwell, and he wanted them to experience what he and Ehani had experienced. So, Sejun worked the fields in the morning, ate lunch at home, and then went out looking for people who were sick. He would tell them all he knew about Jesus (which wasn't much and came from the songs the Sherpas had taught him) and then he prayed for them. They would be healed and subsequently accepted Jesus as their God. It didn't take long before the sick people in Sejun's village were all well, so he started trekking the mountains, visiting neighboring villages, and doing the same thing.

A foreign missionary who lived in the city heard that many people in the mountain villages were being healed in the name of Jesus and coming to faith. The missionary tracked down Sejun—the 5'1" illiterate rice farmer who was preaching the good news and praying for people. The missionary introduced himself to Sejun, took him under his wing, and taught him all about the Bible. The teaching immediately began to impact Sejun. One day, they were studying and came to Ephesians 5:18, "Do not get drunk on wine." "Wait! I didn't know that!" Sejun exclaimed. When he prayed for people and they were healed, the family would often give him a rice brew—the traditional way to thank witch doctors after they healed someone. He would stagger home after enjoying the gift, go to bed, and sleep it off. But from that point on, he never accepted any rewards for his prayers for healing.

Sejun and other Christians in his village were persecuted, beaten, shackled, and warned harshly not to speak to anyone about their faith. Ultimately, this persecution drove them away from their home. Forced to settle in a new town, Sejun vowed he wasn't going to tell anyone about Jesus because he wanted their children to grow up in peace. Shortly after they arrived, however, the mayor knocked on the door, and said he had heard that Sejun was a healer. Sejun couldn't lie, so he reluctantly admitted that yes, he served a God who healed. The mayor said, "Okay, come with me." He took Sejun out to the field where several cows were lying on their side, foaming at the mouth.

"Heal my cows," the mayor insisted.

Sejun had never prayed for animals before—he didn't know if Jesus would heal a cow or not, but he knew the mayor could hurt him if he didn't agree, so he prayed for the first cow. They watched as it shook the froth from its mouth, stood up, and walked away … healed! The mayor then insisted he pray for the next cow. Sejun did, and it, too, was healed. With the mayor's blessing, Sejun was now able to remain in the village, preach the gospel, and participate in even more healing.

Sejun's son was one of the first children from his village to go to school, hiking an hour over the mountains to another village in order to attend. Basta learned to read, and then accompanied Sejun on healing trips, reading Scripture while his father preached and prayed for people. This went on for years, and over time they began to see the miracle of multiplication taking place.

A friend of mine met Basta when he visited their Himalayan region. Through this connection, Basta reached out to Global Disciples and asked for our help—they had more than a hundred churches within a five-day walk from where he and his father lived, but no way to train their people.

We invited Basta to attend a meeting of discipleship-mission directors we had equipped. It was there I met Basta, and we talked about the wonderful things God was doing in his community and surrounding villages. He prayed long into the night about how Global Disciples might be able to support what he was doing. The next morning over breakfast, Basta came back to me and said, "God spoke to me last night."

"Great! What did he say?"

"God told me we are supposed to look to him to provide, not depend on support from the West. So, I won't be asking for any money or seed funds from you."

I knew their resources were limited. "How are you going to collect the money you need to run these training courses?"

"We don't have to collect money," he said. "We'll put baskets by the church, and the rice farmers can contribute rice, and when the baskets are full, we'll fill bags, and when the bags are full, we'll have enough food to start the training."

"Do me a favor," I said. "Let me know the market value of the rice, when you're ready to start."

Basta agreed, and I told him we would like to send a gift toward their startup costs. The people in this church supplied chickens and rice to feed the participants. We considered the value of their gifts of food in kind to be 51 per cent of their training expenses, and we sent a gift for the remaining 49 per cent—$137 for Bibles, mats to sleep on, and some supplies. And their first discipleship-mission training was launched. And more trainings have followed their lead, primarily sustained by the local resources God provides!

On it goes. What began many years ago with two Sherpas and Basta's father—a solitary, illiterate farmer desperate to help his wife—has become an influential disciple-making movement—most of it supported by local resources. And now assisting many groups of churches from various tribes and regions to multiply new fellowships of believers all across Nepal.

God Loves Multiplication

Since the beginning of time, God has made it clear that he loves multiplication. In fact, as Genesis 1 records, every living thing that God created was designed to multiply.

> Then God said, "Let the waters swarm with fish and other life. Let the skies be filled with birds of every kind." So God created great sea creatures and every living thing that scurries and swarms in the water, and every sort of bird—each producing offspring of the same kind. And God saw that it was good. Then God blessed them, saying, "Be fruitful and multiply. Let the fish fill the seas, and let the birds multiply on the earth."
>
> Genesis 1:20–23 NLT

Be fruitful and increase! Multiply! Fill the seas! Increase on the earth! This was God's intention for creation, and his love for multiplication continues as you read further into the Old Testament. God promises Abraham that his descendants will be as numerous as the sands of the sea and the stars of the sky, and that through this multitude of offspring, the entire earth would be blessed, a promise fully realized through Jesus. After the flood in Genesis 8, God told Noah, "Bring out every kind of living creature that is with you—the birds, the animals, and all the creatures that move along the ground—so they can multiply on the earth and be fruitful and increase in number on it" (Genesis 8:17).

156 ORDINARY DISCIPLES, EXTRAORDINARY INFLUENCE

This theme of multiplication is reflected powerfully in the life and ministry of Jesus. He multiplied the supply of wine at the wedding feast in Cana—with unbelievable quantity and superior quality.[1] Jesus multiplied five loaves and two fish to feed five thousand men, women, and children— and there were twelve basketfuls left over![2] And, later, Jesus took seven loaves and a few fish and multiplied them to feed a crowd of over four thousand— with seven basketfuls of leftovers.[3] God loves miracles of multiplication.

Jesus used themes of multiplication in his parables. In the parable of the sower, the seed that fell on good soil multiplied, some thirty, sixty, or one hundred times.[4] Or you may remember the servant who won his master's favor when he multiplied the five bags of gold entrusted to him.[5] Even in foretelling his own crucifixion and declaring the power of dying to ourselves, Jesus reminds us that unless a grain of wheat falls to the ground, it remains only a single seed, but if it dies, it multiplies.[6]

Jesus understood the power of multiplication. And today we are seeing the beauty of this biblical principle on display in movements of Christ in many nations.

Multiplication Movements

There's no way that we will see the knowledge of God's glory cover the earth as the waters cover the sea[7] by only *adding* people to the body of Christ. God's plan is for every disciple of Jesus to be engaged in *multiplying* disciples of Jesus. The story of Sejun and Basta illustrates this so beautifully. As their family spread the good news, more people living among the mountains experienced the love of Jesus. Churches were planted, and those churches planted more churches as even more people came to know Jesus. It was good news, controversial, risky ... but life transforming. Though the new disciples

---

[1]   John 2:6–10.
[2]   Mark 6:35–44.
[3]   Mark 8:1–9.
[4]   Matthew 13:3–23.
[5]   Matthew 25:14–29.
[6]   John 12:24.
[7]   Habakkuk 2:14.

needed to be wise about what they said to who, they couldn't stop talking about Jesus. That's how movements of Christ begin around the world. Movements happen when everyone gets involved in telling their own story about how Jesus touched their lives, in such a way that it grips the hearts of people they know. And their influence multiplies. At a certain stage, there's a tipping point when the news spreads like wildfire.

God invites each one of us to freely share with others how he has touched our lives. Let's ask the Holy Spirit to help us see where God is at work in our world, in our lives, and in our everyday situations, and to share that with others. It makes great everyday conversation and helps to set us up for the multiplication of disciples.

Recently, the multiplication of his kingdom has reached historic proportions. We marvel at Acts 2 and the account of Pentecost, when three thousand people came to faith in Jesus Christ in one day. Today, in this generation, the number of disciples around the world is unprecedented. Even by conservative estimates, about three thousand people *per hour* are coming to faith in Christ. Think about that: three thousand people putting their faith in Christ as Lord and Savior, twenty-four hours a day, seven days a week, 365 days a year. That's more than twenty-six million new believers annually!

That's the power of multiplication!

I've often imagined what it would be like to talk to the Apostle Peter or the other disciples about the day of Pentecost. I'd want to ask about the experience of seeing three thousand people come to faith in Christ after the Holy Spirit was poured out. But the funny thing is that one glorious day in eternity, those first disciples may come looking for us to ask what it was like when three thousand people were being added to the body of Christ *every single hour*! Will they ask you and me what we did to help that become reality? We are living in a time of multiplication, and it's important we do our part by surrendering all to the Lordship of Jesus.

Surrendering to Jesus as Lord of All

As Global Disciples serves multiplication movements around the world, we observe they hold in common one foundational reality: disciples who completely believe in the life-transforming revelation that Jesus is Lord of all creation and Lord of every aspect of their lives and cultures. This requires radical transformation, as new followers of Jesus come to understand that nothing is exempt. As they grow in their understanding of Jesus through Scripture, prayer, and interaction with other Christ-followers, they are seeing what it looks like for all loyalties and attachments in their lives to be redefined and reshaped by Jesus. As this worldview is transformed, it influences their perspective on every aspect of life—whether it be social issues, interpersonal relationships and politics, personal priorities and family life, or cultural and religious practices. And because Jesus makes such an impact on their life, soon their friends and family members who do not know Jesus also realize that they too must choose how they will respond. Often families and peers react negatively or violently even if they are attracted to the changes in the lives of these new believers. When traditional values and cultural customs are challenged by Jesus as Savior and Lord, it usually creates a disturbance in a new believer's primary relationships.

In some situations, miraculous movements of Christ may emerge if enough people are open to hear and learn about the radical and beautiful transformation that Jesus can bring in their lives. There's a tipping point when what was previously viewed as counter-cultural and negative becomes intriguing and attractive. There are usually two factors that bring this about: the convicting and inviting work of the Holy Spirit, and the modeling of a way of life that is infinitely better than what they are currently experiencing.

In the example of Sejun, Ehani, and Basta, God was obviously active by his Holy Spirit in bringing miraculous healings—unlike anything they had ever seen or imagined. This changed their quality of life, enhanced family relationships, and brought joy they had not previously experienced. They saw God doing what witch doctors could never do and doing it freely without sacrifices to idols or any personal obligation. They were simply asked to believe Jesus is God, that he sacrificed his life for us, and was raised from the dead. They saw something different in the lives of those who followed Jesus: joy, satisfaction, kindness, and freedom from the fear of evil spirits. Because of this, many people across their region wanted what they had witnessed in others.

In movements around the world, we have observed a full embrace of the sweeping, all-encompassing claims made by the Apostle Paul to the church in Colossae:

> The Son is the image of the invisible God, the firstborn over all creation. For in him all things were created: things in heaven and on earth, visible and invisible, whether thrones or powers or rulers or authorities; all things have been created through him and for him. He is before all things, and in him all things hold together.
>
> Colossians 1:15–17

With that bold, audacious declaration of the Lordship of Jesus Christ, movements of Christ are being born around the world today—not only among animistic people, but among Buddhist, Hindus, and Muslims.

Characteristics of Multiplication Movements

In North America, where we have so much access and knowledge of the gospel, why aren't we seeing such movements? Could it be that our mind-set of independence and self-reliance creates an unwillingness to embrace the Lordship of Jesus Christ? That holding onto our self-determination, our safety and comfort, raises a barrier to movements and multiplying disciples in our context? We have much to learn from movements of multiplication around the globe. Let's consider three characteristics Global Disciples observes in the movements of Christ we serve.

Engaging in Travailing Prayer

Earlier we talked about *transforming* prayer—prayer that submits to the work of the Spirit to bring change to the lives of those who pray, and those they pray for. It's one of the factors that brought such power and growth to the early church. So, what is *travailing* prayer?

Travailing prayer is an outpouring of longing and grief in the heart of God by the Holy Spirit within us. It's defined in Scripture as "crying out to God."[8] Sometimes it's accompanied by tears, sometimes it's not—but it's always "deep crying out to deep" (Psalm 42:7). At times, it may also include fasting. Travailing prayer identifies with and experiences the grief in God's heart for those who are lost and who resist the good he has for them.

Many times, travailing prayer is birthed out of a burden for those who are for one reason or another ignored or not welcomed into the body of Christ. Early in Basta's adult ministry, he and his wife were called to speak at a prayer and revival gathering. When they arrived, they realized that Christians from high caste Hindu backgrounds would not allow those from the lower castes to join them at the event. Basta shared, "Our hearts were broken. We did not want to be part of a ministry that was separating God's people by class."

A month later, at a Global Disciples training event, Basta made a commitment to fast and pray for three days and three nights. His heart was so broken for the least-reached people across his country and around the world, especially those being held at arms-length by the current churches and those who held to the division of castes. He sought God in travailing prayer, asking for a way to reach them.

During his time of fasting, God gave Basta the acronym PRAY, with each letter providing direction on how to pray for those who have never heard the good news of Jesus.

P: Praise. From a place of brokenness and tears for those without Christ, Basta explained how important it is to give thanks to God, continually bringing to mind the things the Lord has done. As Basta increasingly engaged in this practice, he found himself also praising God for what the Holy Spirit was going to do in the future. This was a new and wonderful practice for him, something he had never understood until he began spending more time with God in prayer. He went from a place of travailing to a place of praise, believing for what the Lord would do in reaching those without Christ.

---

[8] See for example, 1 Samuel 7:8.

R: Repent . When Basta prays, he invites the Holy Spirit to highlight any areas he needs to repent of in his own life. As he prays for someone else, he gives thanks to God for that person. He then acknowledges on their behalf the areas of brokenness and sin in their life that he's aware of, just as Daniel did on behalf of Israel.[9] These are usually things the Holy Spirit prompts Basta to pray for. He does this in the hope that they will be prepared to receive the Lord Jesus.

A: Ask. The Holy Spirit has instructed Basta to be specific and focused in his prayers. He therefore tries to be as specific as possible, and to pray until he sees movement in that area. He continues asking the Holy Spirit to be active in bringing the changes or responses God desires.

Y: Yoke. Basta understands and reminds us that Christ is the one who is actually doing the work, and we simply have the privilege of joining together with him! Jesus said his yoke is light. In all that we ask and pray for, we must ensure that we are pursuing it yoked with Christ, not in our own strength. His yoke is easy if we obey. For example, sometimes when we pray, people will be healed. But we must always remember that God is the one doing the work, and we are simply enjoying the privilege of teaming up with him in his yoke.

Basta and our brothers and sisters in Nepal understand and regularly practice travailing prayer. They sometimes pray all through the day and night. They like to hang the Nepali flag, post a map of their nation, and lay hands on it, seeking God's face and asking him to direct them to people who need to know him. They intercede for people groups across their nation—and in surrounding nations—who are without knowledge or witness of Jesus Christ. And they rejoice and celebrate when God answers their prayers and opens doors.

Without exception, the disciple-making/church-planting movements that Global Disciples has been privileged to come alongside in Africa, Asia,

---

9   Daniel 9:2–19.

and Latin America were all born out of travailing prayer. This requires dedicated, persistent, bold, humble, and Spirit-empowered leaders.

Modeling by Local Leaders

In the multiplication movements we serve, the leaders model the way. They believe that true disciples of Jesus are those who make disciples, who will go on to make disciples. They lead by example, with boldness, humility, and conviction. Their approach to evangelism varies significantly depending on their context, but they are all looking for opportunities to bear witness to Jesus, lead people to Christ, and make disciples. Every leader is expected to be actively engaged as an ambassador of Christ—intentional in introducing their friends and acquaintances to Jesus. It's a key to multiplication!

Whether we're talking about an illiterate farmer and his wife's miraculous healing that led to his dedicated evangelism, or the thousands of other disciple-makers we've had the honor to work with across the globe, the principle is always the same. Major movements that multiply always start with leaders who first submit to Christ, and then model the way. They are leaders who have surrendered their lives fully to Jesus and are willing to sacrifice and pay the cost—whether through persecution, rejection, or simply laying down what they want so that others can find life in Christ. These leaders understand their calling, and like the first disciples of Jesus, view it as an honor to be counted worthy to suffer for the name of their Lord Jesus.[10]

Forming Reproducible, Sustainable, and Contextualized Forms of Church

In multiplying movements, church is more than buildings. In some places where multiplication movements are occurring, house churches or small informal gatherings are the only available options because meeting publicly

---

[10]   Acts 5:41.

or in dedicated worship facilities is not safe or permitted. Other places do not have the financial resources to build larger church buildings. It's always a joy to see movements that have life, vitality, and depth of relationships unencumbered by the weight and responsibility of maintaining properties and costly buildings. During my twenty-five years with Global Disciples, I've visited places where little fellowships meet in houses or former cattle barns, with dirt floors and walls of upright sticks plastered with cow dung. And I've stood under thatched-roof pavilions scattered across a desert where the Holy Spirit was poured out in revival, transforming witch doctors, families, and entire communities for God's glory. I've joined in fellowship under trees, in store fronts, the back room of a salon, and in simple homes. No matter where the meeting place, it is always filled with ordinary disciples united in their passion for Jesus, their love for one another, and their unrestrained longing to see others come to know Jesus as their Lord and Savior.

It requires Holy Spirit creativity to develop and sustain church models that are reproducible and locally sustainable, and it also allows the focus to remain on the people, who are of course the essence of the church. Across the globe, we've seen many delightful examples of God-given innovation and creativity. This should not be surprising; if we have the Spirit of our Creator God living within us, we should be the most creative and innovative of all people. Wherever we may meet, the multiplication of disciples and new fellowships of believers is essential if we are going to reach the world for Christ. Addition alone is simply not adequate to fulfill the task of the Great Commission!

What's Missing in North America?

When we tell our stories from disciple-making movements around the world, we are often asked if something similar could happen here in North America. That's a great question. What do you think? I usually invite people to consider these three characteristics we've just outlined. Do you see these characteristics in your life, in your church, or small group fellowship?

- An extraordinary engagement with travailing prayer and fasting in your life and those in your fellowship.

- Modeling by leaders in witness to Jesus and disciple-making.
- The formation of a multipliable DNA—thinking and talking to-gether about reproducing disciples and other groups.

If you aren't seeing or experiencing these things, don't be discouraged. Multiplication starts small. It takes time and commitment. But it is worth it. Ordinary disciples can and do have extraordinary influence! And we are inviting you to join us on a truly amazing journey.

As Global Disciples, we are not inclined to be critical of any particu-lar model or expression of the body of Christ. Nor do we promote any one type of church development. We have seen many different models and variations work effectively to make and multiply the body around the world. Our basic premise is that as disciples of Jesus Christ, we are called to be disciples who make disciples, who then go on to make dis-ciples. When we fully surrender to the Lordship of Jesus and our focus is on disciple-making, churches will emerge that are appropriate for their context. The Holy Spirit of the living God, within us and among us, cre-atively guides the process.

The greatest barrier to multiplication in the body of Christ may well be a lack of full surrender to the Lordship of Jesus. Before you hear this as critical of the church in North America, let me explain. I'm right there with you in trying to discover what it means to fully surrender to Jesus as Lord of creation and in every aspect of our lives and our loyalties. Earlier I referred to the bold and sweeping declaration of the Apostle Paul in his letter to the Colossians—that in Jesus all things were created and are held together. While most of us may give verbal assent to Paul's claim, we have other ideas about how things actually work and what really holds them together. As a result, over the last few centuries, we have increasingly placed our confidence in other structures and institutions, thus unknow-ingly limiting our surrender to the Lordship of Jesus in certain categories of our lives. Our faith has become a "personal thing," relegated to personal spiritual disciplines, church involvement, and matters of the family and morality. We have lost sight of God's design for his church—those who represent him to the world.

God's Design for the Church

One of the most beautiful and amazing things for us to grasp is God's design and purpose for the church. This is the body of people who represent Jesus to the world. It is the community of those who follow Jesus, who are empowered by the Spirit, and who focus on being God's ambassadors to the world. They are known by their love for one another, a devotion to the Word of God and to prayer, by their joyful sharing of their lives, and by celebrating worship, communion, and baptism.

The church is God's revelation for the world. God designed his church to make known his manifold wisdom to the universe. "His intent was that now, through the church, the manifold wisdom of God should be made known to the rulers and authorities in the heavenly realms" (Ephesians 3:10). His plan of salvation and restoration for the entire world is revealed through his body. God intends to reveal his character, his power, and his love through the church. God's strategy is a corporate strategy; it cannot be accomplished by any one person. But *together*. This is why Jesus said to his disciples, "By this everyone will know that you are my disciples, if you love one another" (John 13:35).

The church is God's strategy to fulfill the Great Commission. The fulfillment of the Great Commission—to make disciples of every people group—requires the multiplication of churches among each and every ethnic group. From the beginning, Jesus' intention was for his disciples to join together and form a community that worships God, serves one another, and reaches their world with his gospel. This community is where discipleship happens, where baptism takes place, and where disciples are taught to obey and follow Jesus. And out of this, disciples will fulfill the Great Commission to "go and make disciples of all nations, baptizing them in the name of the Father and of the Son and of the Holy Spirit, and teaching them to obey everything I have commanded you. And surely I am with you always, to the very end of the age" (Matthew 28:19–20).

We cannot accomplish this mission simply by engaging in evangelism. Yes, we need to share Christ with those who are not believers, but Jesus tells us to make disciples, not converts. In the Book of Acts, when people committed their lives to follow Christ, baptism and discipleship was part of the process.

The fulfillment of the Great Commission requires that disciples are made of all nations.[11] We won't accomplish this by planting a single fellowship of disciples and inviting every new disciple to be part of that one group. God's strategy requires many churches to be planted wherever disciples are made; establishing fellowships of disciples reflects our obedience to the fulfillment of the Great Commission. As we follow his leading, Jesus continues to build his church in and through us.[12]

From the beginning, God created the body of Christ, the church, to multiply.

Created to Multiply

One of the beautiful ways God has created this world is that living things repro-duce after their kind. From microscopic cells to elephants and whales, every organism multiplies to create something that looks and functions like itself. In cells and plants, we might refer to this as *fractal expansion*—the geometry of nature. Cells multiply cells like themselves. Trees multiply the same kind of leaves. The leaf of a fern grows longer by shooting out tiny versions of the same leaf. In the same way, small, reproducible expressions of the body of Christ can naturally spawn similar fellowships. We've seen evidence of this across the globe, and it's why we ensure Global Disciples' training is reproducible.

We believe the greatest promise for multiplication movements here in North America and around the world is through fractal expansion. We have always seen these global movements flowing out of a passion for others to know Christ and an uncompromising surrender to the Lordship of Jesus. The characteristics of those fellowships is described beautifully in Colossians:

> Put on then, as God's chosen ones, holy and beloved, compassionate hearts, kind-ness, humility, meekness, and patience, bearing with one another and, if one

---

[11] Acts 1:8.
[12] See Mathew 16:18; 1 Corinthians 3:6.

has a complaint against another, forgiving each other; as the Lord has forgiven you, so you also must forgive. And above all these put on love, which binds everything together in perfect harmony. And let the peace of Christ rule in your hearts, to which indeed you were called in one body. And be thankful.

Colossians 3:12–15 ESV

This wonderful description continues, and Paul reminds us of the importance of growing in the Word of the Lord, worshipping together, and doing whatever we do in word or deed in the name of Jesus.[13]

Can these characteristics be embraced by the small group or fellowship you are a part of? What would it look like if you were to fast and travail in prayer, and if as a leader (officially or informally) you were to model the way in your life and witness? What if you did your part to encourage others to be reproducing disciples, and to form similar groups or fellowships?

Multiplication always starts small, allowing us to work out the kinks and learn as we grow. Could you help to launch a small movement of multiplying disciples and Jesus worshippers?

The diagram below shows what fractal expansion might look like.

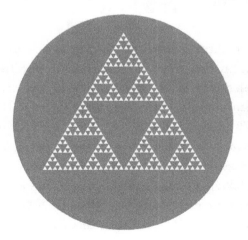

---

[13] Colossians 3:16–17.

If every triangle represents a fellowship of believers and that group multiplies other fellowships like it by making disciples who make disciples, who then go on to make disciples, you can see there's no limit to the growth potential. So, for every fellowship, whether a small group or a small church, it's worth asking the following questions:

- Is it reproducible?
- Are the standards or best practices clearly defined?
- Is it locally sustainable?
- Are the leaders in each group modeling the way and equipping other leaders?
- Is there a desire to multiply?
- Are the members of each fellowship hungry for Jesus and honoring of one another?
- Is the vision for multiplication shared often and freely?
- Are the members all accountable in their disciple-making initiatives/ relationships?

What Part Will You Play?

Every follower of Christ is called to take part in this great ingathering of people from every nation, tribe, and language. The directive of Jesus to his disciples as he left this earth was intended for every one of us as disciples— go and make disciples of all peoples. It's a job for all of us who are part of the global body of Christ.

The world population reached two billion people around 1930. It took another thirty years to reach three billion people, but only fourteen years to add the next billion. In 2022, the global population reached 7.9 billion people and experts project another two billion by 2050.[14] With over seven billion people in our world, completing this Great Commission is only

---

[14] Worldometer, (n.d.), Current world population, www.worldometers.info/world-population/. [Retrieved September 21, 2021]

possible by multiplying disciples. We will never reach the world for Christ by adding a few new believers to our church each year or each month. Filling a few chairs with new attendees from another church will not come close to addressing the needs of the lost in our world.

Addition alone will not get the job done.

How are you going to help spread the gospel to those who haven't yet heard?

What role will you play in multiplication?

What are you going to do about it?

Reflect and Discuss

- What inspired you in this chapter?
- What challenged you?
- What is God inviting you to do in the coming days?
- What obstacles are keeping you from accepting and acting upon this invitation?
- How will you live differently today because of what you have just read?
- What practical actions will you commit to doing soon?
- What questions do you still have?

Additional Study

God's Design for the Church: 1 Corinthians 12:27; Matthew 16:18.
God's Desire for Multiplication: Genesis 1:28; 9:7; Acts 6:7; 9:31.
Challenges to Multiplying Fellowships of Disciples: Acts 2:42–47.
Practical Lessons From the New Testament: Acts 13:2; Luke 10:1–7.

PART FOUR
ABOVE AND BEYOND

Partner with the King. Step out in obedience: recognize God's unique calling upon your life, moving beyond the obstacles and challenges with Holy Spirit power and accountability.

"Instead, speaking the truth in love, we will grow to become in every respect the mature body of him who is the head, that is, Christ. From him the whole body, joined and held together by every supporting ligament, grows and builds itself up in love, as each part does its work."

Ephesians 4:15–16

10

What Are You Going to Do About It?

B orn and raised a good Muslim in Chad, Ronel came to faith in Jesus Christ and began reaching others with the gospel. Before long, he had planted over two dozen churches. As time passed, he realized he was caught up in administrative work and problem-solving, rather than the evangelism and church planting he was gifted to do. He had a big decision to make.

He found a trusted church denomination and entrusted the twenty-six churches into their care, agreeing that he would partner with them as an evangelist and church planter. For years he was effective in teaching and encouraging the pastors of those churches while working to plant new churches as well.

When Ronel heard Global Disciples was interested in serving churches in Chad, he went to the denomination's leaders and convinced them to initiate a Global Disciple Training program, equipping young leaders to be disciple-makers who go out, make disciples, and plant churches among

Chad's least-reached peoples. Ronel saw an opportunity for multiplication, and he convinced those leaders this was the best way to go. And he stepped in as the first training program director.

I sat at the breakfast table across from Ronel at a Global Disciples event in 2017. Every year, we host regional equipping events where we bring together all the program directors we serve in a region. I was in Cameroon attending the event for our West Africa programs, and it was the first time Ronel and I met. As we chatted and got acquainted, I asked him how the new discipleship training was going.

He smiled. "It's going very well, but you have a problem. I'm the chairman of our Evangelical Churches Fellowship in Chad, made up of nineteen denominations. Our group is the only one with a Global Disciple training program, and all the other groups want to start their own training. So, what are you going to do about it?"

I grinned back. "Maybe the real question is, what are *you* going to do about it? If we're going to meet that kind of need, we're going to need a facilitator to represent us. Are you available?"

The following day Ronel came back to me. "I called my wife after I talked with you yesterday, and then I called the leader of our denomination. They're both supportive of me giving half time to work as a facilitator with Global Disciples in Chad."

A few months later, Ronel participated in a staff orientation for our new facilitators, and he approached me in line for lunch. We had a good time catching up, and then he said, "I'm not sure that investing half time as the Chad facilitator is going to be adequate to meet the demand."

I smiled, recalling our earlier conversation. "So, what are you going to do about it?"

Ronel laughed. "I thought that might be your question. Well, I talked with my wife and the head of our denomination again—and I talked with my children and with other leaders in our congregation. If you and the leaders of Global Disciples would agree, I'm glad to serve full-time representing and working with Global Disciples in Chad."

Ronel quickly became a leader within our Global Disciples community simply through his spiritual giftings, passion, persistence, and determination.

He was a big, husky guy, built like a rugby player—just his presence and his booming voice were impactful. When he spoke, people listened. When he taught, people paid attention.

Within three years, Ronel helped groups of churches in Chad to launch twenty-one new training programs and three more in neighboring Niger, a country that is over 98 percent Muslim.[1] Two years after starting programs in Chad, he traveled to the border of Libya to meet with Libyan church leaders and discuss using the Global Disciples approach to equip their people to be disciples who go and make disciples among least-reached people groups in Libya—a country that is about 96 per cent Muslim[2] and torn apart by the chaos of a civil war.

I am confident that you or I probably won't be going to Libya anytime soon to be witnesses of the Prince of Peace, but Ronel's team can and will, as we pray and help them to develop reproducible, locally sustainable, disciple-making patterns that offer hope in what often seems like a hopeless situation.

It all comes back to how Ronel responded to the question, "What are you going to do about it?"

So.

I ask you.

What are you going to do about it?

Ultimately, the influence your life has for the kingdom of God will be determined by how you answer that question.

Your Own Answer

As Global Disciples we want to challenge people to do their part. For a few years, we had fun chanting at our annual equipping events:

---

[1] U.S. Department of State, "Niger – United States Department of State," *U.S. Department of State,* December 1, 2020, www.state.gov/reports/2019-report-on-international-religious-freedom/niger/. [Retrieved September 20, 2021.]

[2] U.S. Department of State, "Libya – United States Department of State," *U.S. Department of State,* December 1, 2020, www.state.gov/reports/2019-report-on-international-religious-freedom/libya/. [Retrieved September 20, 2021.]

I do my part
Yes, I do
I do my part
How about YOU?

It was a joy to hear people from all around the world calling this out in different languages and accents—and to see them return to their communities, doing what each had been called to do.

"What are you going to do about it?"

This question to Ronel has become a rallying cry within Global Disciples. At the heart of the question is a calling to see the world as God sees it, to see people as God sees them. And then to respond as Jesus would.

When we read or watch the news, when we listen to the radio or a favorite podcast, this question is so important: What would happen if we saw current events from God's perspective? If all the conflicting groups and political parties and worldviews could see each other as God sees them? What would happen if we chose to love people across race or culture or origin because Jesus loves them? He asked us to love others as we love ourselves, yet we struggle to do that.

This question gets to the heart of who we are as disciples of Jesus. It reminds us to consider what God would want in any given situation, how Jesus would respond, and then to take our direction from that.

But it's easy to think our answer lies in how someone else is living their life. As a new believer in my teenage years, I watched how Christians I respected were living their lives: how they dressed, how they walked, how they spoke. I joined a Fellowship of Christian Athletes huddle, and as a freshman, I remember one of the senior guys in the group who was a superb athlete. I tried to match his stride and his swagger when I walked. *If I could be like him,* I thought, *I'd have a real impact for Jesus.*

When I got involved in youth ministry years later, I attended seminars and workshops presented by nationally famous youth-leader trainers. I tried to mimic some of their styles and patterns of presentation as I delivered training in my region. Then a friend came up to me after one of those presentations. "That was great content," he said. "It would have been even stronger if you would have just been yourself in the delivery." Ouch!

We look to others in the body of Christ to inspire us by who they are, how they relate, the way they communicate, where or how they serve the Lord—and many other admirable things.

Maybe you hear Ronel's story and think, *Oh, that's what I need to do! Something radical and bold for Jesus!* That's great inspiration, but is it really what God has in mind *for you*?

Ronel was uniquely gifted and perfectly placed to do what God called him to do. His background as a Muslim gave him a personal understanding of what it meant to leave Islam for Jesus Christ. His spiritual giftings meant he was bold and able to bring others into partnership, to lead and motivate the body and serve in his setting. You and I are created by the same Father God, but uniquely gifted by the Spirit and perfectly placed to be effective, influential disciples, reflecting the Father's glory in whatever setting he calls us into. It may be something radical for you, your family, and others—or it may be living out the calling of an ordinary disciple, one with influence, in your corner of the world.

The reality is that God is asking you and me to answer that question for ourselves, with the guidance of the Holy Spirit. The uniqueness of our callings is beautifully addressed by the Apostle Paul in Romans 12, 1 Corinthians 12, and Ephesians 4.[3] These are not exhaustive lists of spiritual gifts, but they invite us to celebrate, enjoy, and benefit from the many gifts and callings within the body of Christ. Which ones describe gifts God has given you?

The Apostle Paul reminds us we have different gifts as God determines. And he encourages us to make the most of the gifts we have. If your gift is prophesying, then prophesy with faith. If it's serving, then serve; if it is teaching, then teach; if it is to encourage, then give encouragement. If your gift is giving, then give generously; if it is to lead, do it diligently; if it is to show mercy, do it cheerfully. Your love must be sincere, Paul reminds us. Maintain a proper perspective by hating what is evil and clinging to what is good. And he wraps up this list of gifts by reminding us to be devoted to one another in love and to honor others above yourselves.[4]

We're reminded repeatedly that all these gifts of the Holy Spirit are given by God for the common good. One may have the gift of wisdom or a message

---

[3] Romans 12:6–8; 1 Corinthians 12:7–11; Ephesians 4:11–16.
[4] Romans 12:10.

of knowledge—then share that with other disciples who need it. Another may have faith, or gifts of healing or of miraculous powers—then use this gift to bring hope and life to those whose faith is faltering or who need healing. It all comes by the same Spirit. Some may have the gift of prophecy and others the gift of distinguishing between spirits. The body of believers needs them to speak truth, to discern what is at work. Some will have the gift of speaking in different kinds of tongues and others the interpretation of tongues. And the Apostle Paul keeps reminding us that all these are the work of one and the same Spirit—who gives these gifts as he determines.

We love how the words of Ephesians 4:11–16 lift out primary functions of church leadership. All the gifts listed in other places are for all believers within the body of Christ, as the Holy Spirit determines. But these five are key to providing direction and balance in leading the church:

> So Christ himself gave the apostles, the prophets, the evangelists, the pastors and teachers, to equip his people for works of service, so that the body of Christ may be built up until we all reach unity in the faith and in the knowledge of the Son of God and become mature, attaining to the whole measure of the fullness of Christ.
>
> Then we will no longer be infants, tossed back and forth by the waves, and blown here and there by every wind of teaching and by the cunning and craftiness of people in their deceitful scheming. Instead, speaking the truth in love, we will grow to become in every respect the mature body of him who is the head, that is, Christ. From him the whole body, joined and held together by every supporting ligament, grows and builds itself up in love, as each part does its work.

In Alan Hirsch and Tim Catchim's excellent book *The Permanent Revolution*, you can find a full and rich treatment of how these fivefold gifts complement one another and empower the church to be who God has called the body of Christ to be. [5] As you look through these lists of the gifts, consider which

---

[5]   Alan Hirsch and Tim Catchim, *The Permanent Revolution: Apostolic Imagination and Practice for the 21st Century Church*, (San Francisco: Jossey-Bass, 2012).

ones you see operating in your fellowship of disciples. Or maybe some are absent. If so, what are they? It's interesting to consider how our natural, God-given abilities often interface with these spiritual gifts.

These passages all weave in a reminder of the beautiful impact when various spiritual gifts are exercised with love. In fact, the focus of gifts in 1 Corinthians 12 is followed by a whole chapter on how essential love is for the body to benefit from these gifts. In loving and honoring one another, we are becoming in every respect more like Jesus, joined and held together, growing and being built up.

"As each part does its work."

As we each do the work apportioned to us, the body of Christ—the entire body—grows, multiplies, and is built up!

An Urgent Need Right Now

Remember Basta, the disciple from Nepal? Basta was recently asked why he does what he does to reach people with the good news of Jesus.

Basta said he imagines each lost person on earth as if they were one of his two daughters: "How far would I go to make sure my daughters heard the good news? What lengths would I go to to make sure my daughters were saved? If every lost person was one of my own daughters, at what point would I stop trying to share the gospel with her?"

When you begin to understand even a fraction of the love God has for each lost son and daughter created in his image, then our skin color, nationality, tribal affiliations, and even differences in personality fade. There are no differences between us that will keep us from answering the call God places on our lives.

A Daily Infusion of Love

Phil was my neighbor and not a pleasant guy to interact with. He always seemed to be complaining about something: the kids with the skateboards on our street, the guy who did a lousy job fixing his roof, the newspaper's delivery time, the doctors who didn't know how to treat his many physical issues ... and the litany rolled on. I could often hear his loud, high-pitched voice even from inside our house across the street. I wanted to be a good neighbor, but sometimes Phil really got under my skin.

As a young man, Phil had abused his body in many ways including through alcohol, and now he was paying the price. He was on kidney dialysis and had significant heart issues, which were common topics in his complaints. I often prayed for Phil, for his salvation, and for the Spirit to infuse the love and compassion of Jesus in me—because I couldn't muster it up on my own!

One Christmas as I made my rounds with holiday goodies for the neighbors—sugarless in Phil's case—I found him sitting in his recliner with his feet propped up, and a cast up to his knee on one leg. He had stepped in a hole in their yard and broken his ankle. He told me. "I'm just tired of all this crap. I'm ready to just end it all!"

I asked Phil if I could pray for him. "Whatever," he said. I took a knee next to his recliner, laid my hand on his arm, and began to pray that Jesus would show Phil God's love for him and that he would keep running into people who reminded him of the love of Jesus. Then I prayed that God would heal his ankle quickly, just as one more reminder of his love.

As I was praying, I heard Phil's wife coming out of the kitchen. I looked up and saw her mouth drop open as she mouthed the words, "You're praying?"

Phil's ankle healed more quickly than anticipated and, despite all his health challenges, he was a bit more positive in the months that followed. Then one fall day, as I raked our leaves, I noticed that none of the leaves had been touched in Phil's front yard. So, I went over and began raking their leaves.

A few minutes later, there it was—the loud voice from the front porch. "Hey, what're you doing? Am I an embarrassment to the neighborhood?"

"Hi, Phil," I said.

"Put that rake down and come over here," Phil demanded. I joined him as he took a seat on the porch steps. "You'll never believe what happened to me," he said. "In fact, sometimes it's hard for me to believe myself."

Phil's wife is a schoolteacher and when the parents of one of her students passed away, he went to the funeral with her. He said it was strange—he had not been in a church since his mother carried him in as a baby. But the church had a good band, and his wife convinced him to go see what a weekend service was like.

Phil explained he planned to only go for the band and slip out when the music finished, but he got stuck with people on either side, and with his balance difficulties, he didn't want to make a big scene. The pastor stood up to talk and explained that the main pastor was traveling. Phil said to me, "Can you believe it? The only time I go to church, and I get the second-string guy! That's my life."

Then the speaker announced that his topic was anger. "I was so upset," Phil told me. "I just wanted to get out of there. I thought, I don't have an issue with anger, I just want out—but all these damn people have me trapped in!" Phil's voice dropped a few decibels, finally sounding like a conversation. He said, "As the guy was talking, even the second-string guy, I had tears running down my cheeks. It was crazy. But when the thing was over, I decided to go talk with the guy. And he led me into a relationship with Jesus."

"Wow, Phil. That's great!" I replied

"It's crazy, that's what it is," Phil said with a smile. "If you would've told me this would happen to me a couple weeks ago, I would've told you you're full of sh*t." He raised his hand toward the sky and said, "And God, you know that's true."

"Ever since you prayed that magic prayer over me when my ankle was broken, I kept running into people all over the place—at the store, the gas station, the dialysis center, the hospital—everywhere people were talking to me about Jesus. It was strange, man, really strange. But it finally got through my thick head that there's a God who loves me. And it's changed my life."

Rarely have I seen someone's life change so radically and quickly. Phil got involved with a men's Bible study. He led his next-door neighbor to the Lord—another man I had been praying for. Phil's health didn't get any easier in the following years—he was hoping for a kidney transplant, but the doctors didn't think his heart was up to it. But Phil's conversation had changed. He always wanted to talk with me about Jesus—and about the people at the dialysis center he was telling about Jesus.

One day, I saw an ambulance in front of their house. I ran over and found the EMT trying unsuccessfully to revive him. His wife asked them to stop. Phil didn't want any heroics. He was ready to be with Jesus.

I was privileged to speak at Phil's funeral, along with others who talked of his transformed life and his love for Jesus. There were folks present who had come to know Jesus through Phil. Others attended who didn't know Jesus yet, but I doubt there was anyone present who had not heard about Jesus from Phil. Ordinary disciples like Phil have an extraordinary influence on the lives of those around them.

When I think about Phil and the people in so many of the stories we tell, I think about what Jesus said in Simon's house in the Gospel of Luke. A sinful woman from the town slipped in, wet Jesus' feet with her tears, wiped them with her hair, kissed them and poured perfume on them. Simon and his friends were critical. *Didn't Jesus know who this woman was?*

Jesus responded, "Therefore, I tell you, her many sins have been forgiven—as her great love has shown. But whoever has been forgiven little loves little" (Luke 7:47).

Could it be that as the North American body of Christ, we have lost sight of just how much we've been forgiven? And therefore, we love ... but only a little. Phil knew how much Jesus had forgiven him and what Jesus had saved him from, and he wanted everyone else to know Jesus could save and forgive them, too. Have you really grasped how much Jesus has forgiven you? Has it led to a deeper love and gratitude for his grace? And is it growing love and compassion for others?

May God by his Holy Spirit daily open our eyes to the reality of our condition and infuse into our lives the love and compassion of Jesus that compels us to love others beyond what is reasonable or understandable to those who haven't fully surrendered their lives to Christ, who are not empowered by the Holy Spirit or walking in intimacy with Jesus.[6]

Is someone you know lost and in need of Jesus ... maybe someone like Phil?

---

[6]   2 Corinthians 5:13–21.

Your Near-Culture Opportunities

Every day our paths cross with people who need Jesus. Ordinary people just like you or me, who carry hurt and pain and sin, and whether or not they express it, they are looking for someone to carry that for them. Who will reach them? Probably someone who knows their language, understands their culture, has kids in the same school, or rides the bus to work with them each day.

In mission terms, we talk about *near-culture workers*. A disciple of Jesus who shares the same or a similar culture to a person or people group in need of the gospel is better able to reach them than someone without that pedigree or experience. You and I are the near-culture workers, perfectly placed by God, to connect with and share the good news with people who don't yet know Jesus here in North America.

Is it challenging? Yes, at times.

Building relationships takes time and energy—and sometimes a lot of patience and prayer, as Phil taught me. Compassion, kindness, a willingness to help, hospitality, prayer, and so much more, are all ways we can show God's love to our local neighbor or coworker. You can lean on the Holy Spirit to prompt you to speak up and give the words you need as you share truth and love and the amazing message of the gospel.

Conversations about Jesus as the one way to salvation and eternal life don't always sit well in our pluralistic culture. And in recent years, we've seen more open criticism and outright antagonism to views and expressions of Christianity. The world is watching closely, and so, as disciples of Jesus, it's crucial that how we act and what we say in any context—privately, publicly, or on social media—aligns with what we say we believe. But genuine expressions of love, personal interest in others, authentic compassion, and conversation about who Jesus is to you will almost always open doors. You are uniquely gifted by God, equipped by the Spirit, and perfectly placed to reach those around you, whoever they may be.

The Whole World on Your Doorstep

As Global Disciples, our primary focus has been on equipping disciples within their own context to share good news with the least-reached ethnic groups in their nations—people like Ronel in Chad. But for North American disciples, we need to not only be aware of our near-culture opportunities but also the least-reached people God has brought into our cities, and who now live in our neighborhoods. People from places where it is challenging—even illegal—to share the gospel are now making their homes in communities and neighborhoods like ours. However, sharing the good news of Jesus is legal and usually not an issue here.

Let's take Somalia, as an example. It is an intensely Muslim nation and very closed to Western workers. Global Disciples partners with near-culture workers from the region to reach Somalis, because for you or me to go to Somalia as a missionary is virtually impossible. However, more than eighty thousand Somali people now live in Toronto, Canada, over seventy thousand in Minneapolis, MN, and more than forty-five thousand in Columbus, OH.[7]

Or take the Buddhist country of Bhutan, where it is illegal to share the gospel and meet to worship Jesus. Today, more than twenty-four thousand Bhutanese live in the US, with most of them arriving only in the last ten years.[8] I remember when the small congregation we attended a decade ago sponsored the first Bhutanese refugees to live in our state of Pennsylvania.

The numbers are much larger from other countries where witness to Jesus is restricted. As of 2018, about 2.455 million foreign-born Chinese were living in the US.[9] Another 2.7 million people born in India were living in the US,[10] and Iran has 385,000 foreign-born Iranians living in the US.[11] India and China represent the largest foreign-born populations in Canada as well, with over 668,000 and 649,000 respectively.[12]

---

[7]   Global Gates, "Gateway Cities," June 4, 2021, https://globalgates.info/gateway-cities/.

[8]   Philip Connor and Jens Manuel Krogstad, "Key Facts About the World's Refugees," *Pew Research Center*, October 5, 2016, www.pewresearch.org/fact-tank/2016/10/05/key-facts-about-the-worlds-refugees/.

[9]   Carlos Echeverria-Estrada and Jeanne Batalova, "Chinese Immigrants in the United States," *Migration Policy Institute*, January 15, 2020, www.migrationpolicy.org/article/chinese-immigrants-united-states-2018. [Retrieved September 20, 2021.]

[10]   Mary Hanna and Jeanne Batalova, "Indian Immigrants in the United States," *Migration Policy Institute*, October 16, 2020, www.migrationpolicy.org/article/indian-immigrants-united-states-2019. [Retrieved September 20, 2021.]

[11]   Tianjian Lai and Jeanne Batalova, "Immigrants from Iran in the United States," *Migration Policy Institute*, July 15, 2021, www.migrationpolicy.org/article/iranian-immigrants-united-states-2021. [Retrieved September 20, 2021.]

[12]   Statista Research Department, "Top 10 Countries of Birth for Foreign-born People Canada 2016," *Statista*,

What a strategic opportunity this gives us to be ambassadors for Christ to least-reached people in our own backyards! Let's look at these ethnic groups that are on the move and entering our neighborhoods.

Refugees: In 2013, the number of people forced to flee their homes across the world exceeded fifty million for the first time since the Second World War. In 2020, there were 82.4 million people worldwide who were forcibly displaced from their homes as a result of persecution, conflict, violence, human rights violations, or events that seriously disturb public order.[13]

Many refugees in our countries have come from places like Syria, Yemen, and Pakistan—where few of them have ever met a Christian or had a believing friend. Half the world's refugees are children, many traveling alone or in a group with a desperate quest for sanctuary and often falling into the clutches of human traffickers.[14]

Immigrants: More people than ever are living outside their country of origin. The foreign-born population in the US reached 44.8 million in 2018, up from 31 million in 2000. About 21 percent of Canada's population is foreign-born, with China, India, and Pakistan contributing the most immigrants.[15] All the while, back in their homelands, China and India each have more people unreached with the gospel than the combined total populations of the United States and Canada.[16]

International Students: There are tremendous opportunities for global mission among the massive movements of students between countries. In 2019, the number of international students in the US reached an all-time high of 1,095,299.[17] In 2019, the number of international students in Canada

July 6, 2021, www.statista.com/statistics/556078/top-10-countries-of-birth-for-foreign-born-canadian-citizens/. [Retrieved September 20, 2021.]

[13] UNHCR, "Global Trends: Forced Displacement in 2020," *UNHCR Flagship Reports*, June 18, 2021, www.unhcr.org/flagship-reports/globaltrend. [Retrieved September 20, 2021.]

[14] Jeanne Batalova, Kira Monin and Tianjian Lai, "Refugees and Asylees in the United States," *Migration Policy Institute*, May 13, 2021, www.migrationpolicy.org/article/refugees-and-asylees-united-states-2021#refugee-arrivals-countries-origin. [Retrieved September 20, 2021.]

[15] Statistics Canada, "Canada's Population Estimates: Age and Sex," *The Daily*, July 1, 2021, https://www150.statcan.gc.ca/n1/daily-quotidien/210929/dq210929d-eng.htm. [Retrieved December 4, 2021.]

[16] Joshua Project, "Global Statistics," *Joshua Project*, www.joshuaproject.net/people_groups/statistics. [Retrieved September 20, 2021.]

[17] Melanie Hanson, "College Enrollment and Student Demographic Statistics," *Education Data Initiative*, August 7, 2021, https://educationdata.org/college-enrollment-statistics#international. [Retrieved September 20, 2021.]

reached 642,000.[18] The US enrolled more than a million foreign students in higher education programs in 2019, about 5.5 percent of the total US student body.[19] The highest international student populations by their nation of origin were:

- China, with 369,548 students
- India, with 202,014 students
- South Korea, with 52,250 students
- Saudi Arabia, with 37,080 students[20]

It has been estimated that between 75 to 80 percent of all international students in the US never get invited into someone's home.[21] Whether or not the percentages are correct, it's sobering when we realize that more than half of these students come from what we consider least-reached nations.[22] And many will return to their home nations to become leaders in business, government, education, and technology, with the potential to influence their people in significant ways.

Embracing Opportunities for Influence

On a whiteboard in my office I have written, "Where fear sees crisis, faith sees opportunities." We live in a time of opportunities to speak the truth of Jesus and demonstrate his love to our friends, family members, peers, and neighbors—no matter where in the world they come from. We continue to invite the Holy Spirit to impart—to plant—into our lives a love and compassion that causes us to honor others above

---

[18] Kareem El-Assal, "642,000 International Students: Canada Now Ranks 3rd Globally in Foreign Student Attraction," *CIC News*, February 20, 2020, https://www.cicnews.com/2020/02/642000-international-students-canada-now-ranks-3rd-globally-in-foreign-student-attraction-0213763.html#gs.hu3k0m. [Retrieved September 20, 2021.]

[19] Hanson, "Student Statistics."

[20] Ibid.

[21] Craig Thompson, "International Students, Hospitality, and Squishy Statistics," *Clearing Customs*, August 18, 2019, https://clearingcustoms.net/2019/08/18/international-students-hospitality-and-squishy-statistics/. [Retrieved September 20, 2021.]

[22] Hanson, "Student Statistics."

ourselves.[23] As ordinary disciples of Jesus, it will give us extraordinary influence in the lives of those with whom we interact. Let's consider the opportunities before us.

- What if every congregation or fellowship of believers with access to immigrants or international guests would equip their people to understand the cultures of their new neighbors, to serve them in practical ways, and give witness to Christ through their lives and conversations? People are usually most open to the gospel in times of transition.

- Would you be willing to pray with fellow disciples of Christ and keep your eyes open for a "person of peace"? This would be a person in or connected with the ethnic group that you can relate to or build a relationship with. Pray for a person of influence who is open to the gospel, can be discipled, and will be effective in leading others of their group to Christ. As Global Disciples, we have repeatedly seen the effectiveness of this near-culture person of peace, as one who can be the bridge to the rest of the group.

- Build a friendship with an international student, invite them to your home, learn about their culture and their understanding of God, and share your own. Most colleges and universities have an international student office to help make a connection. If you have a college student in your family, encourage them to build relationships too—and to invite an international student home with them.

- Tools like Discovery Bible Studies, can show you ways to build friendships, stimulate helpful discussions, and satisfy the curiosity your new neighbors from other nations may have about who Jesus is and what it means to follow him.[24] You can also use it with your own near-culture relationships—in a neighborhood or workplace group, for example.

---

[23] Romans 12:10.
[24] See www.dbsguide.org/.

The Responsibility of a Disciple

We seldom find ways to talk about how to balance the joy of the treasure we have discovered in Jesus with the responsibility of being a disciple who makes disciples.

In Luke 12:42–48, Jesus used a parable to show us there is a clear expectation not to fritter away our time on earth but to go about our Father's business. It underscores that big question, "What are you going to do about it?"

> The Lord answered, "Who then is the faithful and wise manager, whom the master puts in charge of his servants to give them their food allowance at the proper time? It will be good for that servant whom the master finds doing so when he returns. Truly I tell you, he will put him in charge of all his possessions. But suppose the servant says to himself, 'My master is taking a long time in coming,' and he then begins to beat the other servants, both men and women, and to eat and drink and get drunk. The master of that servant will come on a day when he does not expect him and at an hour he is not aware of. He will cut him to pieces and assign him a place with the unbelievers.
>
> "The servant who knows the master's will and does not get ready or does not do what the master wants will be beaten with many blows. But the one who does not know and does things deserving punishment will be beaten with few blows. From everyone who has been given much, much will be demanded; and from the one who has been entrusted with much, much more will be asked."

I like to think of the joy the servant must have felt when the Master entrusted him with his estate while he was away. But it came with significant responsibility.

When I was fifteen, I spent my summer working for a neighbor on his farm. When he decided to visit his son in Colorado for a few weeks, he put me in charge of milking his small dairy herd, and other farm operations. I was honored—and a little nervous. The barley would be harvested while he was away and there were lots of regular chores. It went surprisingly well. I was milking the cows when he returned home. He walked into the barn, looked around and said, "Well, things look better around here than when I left." Then he walked over to me, reached out and shook my hand, "Thank you! Good job."

That was a long time ago, but I still remember that great feeling—to know I had done well with the responsibility entrusted to me!

The servant in the parable seemed to miss the joy and understanding of the privilege that comes with being trusted with responsibility. He was not dedicated to performing well the tasks expected of him, and he treated the servants he oversaw harshly. So, he received no congratulations or expressions of thanks when the master returned.

As citizens in God's kingdom, each of us has been entrusted with a responsibility beyond anything we can handle on our own. That's why it's so important that we learn to rely on the power of the Holy Spirit each day. When we're not sure what to do next, the Holy Spirit guides us. And in many decisions, we also have brothers and sisters in Christ to help make sure we're hearing the Holy Spirit well.

The truly amazing thing is that while our Master is away, he has placed his Holy Spirit within us as our advocate and teacher—and to remind us of the Jesus way to respond.[25] Jesus is the Vine, we are the branches. Our source of life and strength, along with our capacity to produce the desired results (fruit) is dependent on him. In the parable of Luke 12, the key is in the final verse: If we have been given much, much will be expected of us.

Is that a heavy burden to carry? No, not if we are yoked with Jesus as we were reminded in the previous chapter.[26] And not if we understand the privilege of being entrusted with something of such tremendous value, that when handled carefully brings so much joy, satisfaction, and fulfillment to us and to those with whom we share it!

God never gives us something to do that he doesn't empower us by his Spirit to do. When we being to grasp that, then caring for and sharing that treasure is such a glad privilege!

---

[25]   John 14:26.
[26]   Matthew 11:28–30.

A Thorough Self-Examination

If you're going to answer the big question and move forward, you must be prepared to take a hard look at your life. Consider this an inventory of the unique talents, skills, and gifts God has entrusted to you to help build up and grow the body of Christ in this generation.

The following four areas of examination can help you figure out what you are going to do.

Examine Your Relationships

When Ronel decided to expand his mission to include North Sudan and Libya, it wasn't a random decision on his part. He didn't pin a world map to the wall and throw darts at it. No, he had relationships in those regions, and those relationships led him in that direction.

Think about the relationships you already have in your life—the friends, the relatives, the business acquaintances, or classmates. What about the churches you've gone to, the pastors you know? All these relationships can help point you to the thing you're going to do. Take a moment and list them out, then pray over the list and try to discern what God might be leading you to do based on the people he's placed in your life. How does God want to open doors to increase your influence?

Examine Your Gifts and Skills

Have you ever sat down and made a list of your skills, strengths, and spiritual gifts? God's first calling to your life might very well revolve around the things you are good at and that you already love to do.

Reflect on the skills you've developed on the job, in avenues of service in your church, and other unique experiences God has built into your life.

Earlier we considered the lists of spiritual gifts in 1 Corinthians 12, Romans 12, and Ephesians 4. Which of these have you seen in your life? Are you quick to give mercy? To serve faithfully? To act in faith or speak truth with love? It might be that you need to sit with a trusted friend and ask them to help you discern your gifts—sometimes it's hard to evaluate ourselves, and we don't notice what another spiritually-tuned person does. Perhaps someone you serve with in your fellowship can offer that insight or counsel because they've worked with you.

Whatever you discover your gifts to be, I want you to focus on their main purpose. Spiritual gifts are given to each of us *so we can help each other*, for the *common good.*[27]

For the common good.

If you're not using your gifts in a way that benefits the common good of the kingdom of God, then knowing and using your gifts is probably the first step in answering the question, "What are you going to do about it?"

Examine Your Opportunities

There is mission abroad and there is mission at home, and as the body of Christ, we can participate in both without neglecting one or emphasizing the other. We often expect that the call from God to use our talents will involve a radical change of lifestyle, location, or vocation. We think the only thing God might ask us to do would be something that will throw a massive wrinkle into our lives.

Sometimes we need to ask God to open our eyes to the opportunities within our reach, like the ethnic groups of unreached or least-reached people in your own city, as we just considered. It might be a service opportunity at an organization down the street that really needs you to be salt and light for the people they assist. What about your local business association? A school board or booster club? Or a community garden?

Perhaps the opportunities are simple—a meal for the colleague with a new baby or raking your neighbor's leaves as he deals with illness. It may mean befriending a Muslim family from your child's school or offering hospitality in a crisis. Look at your community and filter what you see through the places or activities where you can meet people from many walks of life

---

[27] 1 Corinthians 12:7.

and create an opportunity to build relationships, living out and speaking the gospel of Jesus.

Examine Your Resources

We tend to think of our resources in financial terms—our money and how and where we give it or invest it. But money isn't everything, and poverty isn't merely a lack of money. If you think you are struggling financially or have little to give, perhaps there are other resources you have been entrusted with. What will you do with the home you live in? The business or farm you own? How will you use these things to reach people with the gospel and influence others for the kingdom? Maybe you have a wealth of experience in a field that you can use to train and equip others—passing along a legacy of skill and influence.

One resource we all have in equal measure—time. We each have twenty-four hours in a day; what we do with it can be enormously influential for the kingdom. What are you doing to invest it wisely?

Earlier in chapter three, we touched on the small business training in our Global Disciples model. It's used with church planters and disciple-makers to develop sustainability and identity among least-reached people. The key question we ask is "What's in your hands?" As a church planter in a least-reached area considers what God has put in his or her hands—a skill like mechanics, an asset like a pair of goats, or even an experience—he or she is amazed to see how God can do mighty things through even just a little.

In considering our resources, we want to be wise and careful, but we also need to beware of greed. I rarely hear people confess to being greedy, and even less do I hear this sin being called out as a problem, but in our culture, greed is such a common issue. We have much, we want more, and we hold tightly to what we can grasp. Yet we're called to be generous, not greedy. We need more teaching on generosity because it's such a profound antidote to greed. Generosity is not solely about money—it's about time, relationships, resources, opportunities, and love. Be generous in all things.

In every level of this self-examination, it's important to engage with the Holy Spirit in order to discern our spiritual gifts, understand our relationships, and have eyes that see our resources clearly. What is the Holy Spirit calling you to do? We each need to ask the Holy Spirit to show us the next steps.

Remember, you have something to offer. God created you with your own unique abilities; he gave you individual gifts, and placed you in a specific context, all of which allow you to contribute to the kingdom of God in unique ways. Examining these four areas will go a long way in helping you identify what you have to offer.

"What are you going to do about it?"

When I first asked Ronel that question, neither of us had any idea what was ahead. We saw a beginning, something new that God was about to do in Chad, and Ronel had the vision to say yes and pursue the opportunity.

Imagine what God is waiting to do through you as you answer that question in your life. Imagine the lives waiting to be changed! It may be an entire group of people, or a neighbor you see each day. But each one is just waiting to be brought into the kingdom, if you'll only answer the question and begin doing the good work prepared for you by God.[28]

Reflect and Discuss

- What inspired you in this chapter?
- What challenged you?
- What is God inviting you to do in the coming days?
- What obstacles are keeping you from accepting and acting upon this invitation?
- How will you live differently today because of what you have just read?
- What practical actions will you commit to doing soon?
- What questions do you still have?

---

[28] Ephesians 2:10.

Additional Study

One Body, Many Parts: Romans 12:3–8; 1 Corinthians 12:13–31; Ephesians 4:1–16.

11

Being a Global
Disciple of Jesus

hroughout this book I (Tefera) have shared bits and pieces of my story. In this last chapter, as we commission you to go out and live as a global disciple[1] of Jesus, I'd like to tell you more, because you will see how every principle we have shared throughout the book has been a part of my discipleship journey.

I was born in Ethiopia in May 1964 and raised in an Orthodox Christian background, very dedicated to all the laws of the Orthodox church. In 1974, the Ethiopian communist military killed the king, overthrew the central government, and formed a dictatorship which lasted until 1991. From 1974 to 1982, the government's ill-treatment of the people turned many to the church. However, when I turned fourteen, I became an atheist after reading

---

[1] We describe a "global disciple" as a whole-hearted disciple of Jesus who lives with a global perspective to advance the kingdom of God.

two books on communism. *This is it,* I thought to myself. *I have found the truth. There is no god.*

Through high school, I became increasingly committed to communist teaching—I even became the leader of our district's communist youth movement. But when I went to university in October of 1982, away from my family and friends, I experienced a deep loneliness that I couldn't shake. I didn't know where to turn.

I was looking for peace. And I was introduced to a friend who asked me to go with him to a nearby Protestant church. My understanding of church was limited to the Orthodox church of my childhood, and no memory of that brought me peace. In our family, the teachings of the church were nothing more than superstition; the Bible was just a book you put under your mattress to protect you from evil spirits.

Jesus found me in October 1982. This was about the time the government became sick and tired of the evangelical churches and confiscated all church properties, buildings, accounts, followed by anything else a church owned. They also expelled all white or Western missionaries from the country.

There I was, eighteen years old, looking for peace, entering a type of church I had never been in before. The people were singing worship songs I vaguely recognized from my childhood, and inside I could feel myself crying out. Then I heard preaching from the Bible, followed by an altar call. I was the first to raise my hand and gave my life to follow Christ on that day. This was the beginning of a new life. I surrendered all my worries to Jesus and felt complete peace and joy.

In my loneliness, Jesus found me.

The church leaders gave me a copy of the New Testament, and I read it in one month! At first, I couldn't understand the stories of Jesus, and especially why people were beating and killing an innocent man of God. But when I read it a second time, the Holy Spirit opened my eyes.

This is for you, the Holy Spirit spoke to me, so I rededicated my life and started to worship the Lord with understanding. I decided I wanted to be baptized as an adult, but the church I attended wouldn't do it. Since I had been baptized as a child in the Orthodox church, they said I could not be baptized again.

But I couldn't shake the idea, so I went to another church. After listening to the preacher, I went up to the pastor and asked him to be baptized.

"I read the Bible, and it told me I needed to be baptized!"

"You should come back on Saturdays," he said with a smile. "There is a teaching that I give to people like you."

I was eager for that first Saturday, and I went to learn what they could teach me. Week after week, the pastor pressed on, teaching us from the Word of God, especially on the person and work of the Holy Spirit. However, when the pastor asked me if I was ready to be baptized, I said no, because I wanted to learn more about water baptism before I was willing to take that step. I had some doubts about it, because of the other church's unwillingness to baptize me.

I went back to the campus that afternoon and talked with the leader of the University Christian Students Fellowship, who connected me with an underground house church. In that underground church, they taught me and five other friends what it means to be a disciple of Christ, including teaching on water baptism and communion. They baptized me along with my friends, all on the same day, in a bathtub in a home.

It was one of the turning points in my life, a declaration that Jesus is the Lord of my life—no more me, but Jesus living in me. I became free from alcohol and drugs. I realized that dying to self and relying on Jesus changes everything for the better. But this is not without cost.

I remember the day when ten of us, leaders in the university Christian students fellowship, were blacklisted. Our names were posted on a wall at the university for a public shaming. Yet we were all happy and joyful to have the privilege "on behalf of Christ not only to believe in him, but also to suffer for him" (Philippians 1:29). Did we like the pain and suffering? Absolutely not. But our joy sprang from an intimate relationship with Jesus. We did not serve or suffer alone, but in union with Christ. What an honor to be part of his salvation story! Adopted by our Heavenly Abba, embraced as brothers and sisters by Jesus, and strengthened by the Holy Spirit, we were delighted to be children of God.

Through the University Christian Students Fellowship, I was able to minister to other students, even though I didn't have a deep knowledge of the Word of God. I became one of the leaders of the Bible study material production team. I simply read the Bible, reflected on it, and shared what I learned as I led my small group.

I graduated from the university with a degree that equipped me to teach mathematics and a "degree" in discipleship that came from immersion in a vibrant Christian community that formed me to be a disciple-maker. Going out two by two, we shared the gospel with other students. We met in house fellowships. In all-night meetings, we fasted and prayed for each other to be filled with the Holy Spirit.

After my graduation, I was sent to northwest Ethiopia as a schoolteacher and paid by the communist government. Math was crucial to anyone seeking higher education. Since I taught math, I was an important person in the lives of my students. When the smart students came to me for extra help, I would answer their questions, but I would also share the love of Christ with them. They started coming to faith! As I discipled them, someone would mention they had a sick family member, so I'd travel to villages a few hours away on foot and pray for people, and God would heal them. Then a fellowship of believers would emerge as a result.

We were able to plant twenty-seven fellowships over eleven years. I was teaching mathematics half a day and then leading small groups and discipling people in my remaining half-time and in the evenings.

I finished my first year of teaching in June 1987, and during that first summer, I was sent to plant a church in another region. I thought I would come back after the summer break and resume my job as a teacher—but when I returned, my apartment was empty. All my belongings had been taken away.

Another disciple who lodged in my rented house told me that the local authorities came, collected my things, and took them to the prison. If I wanted my things, I'd have to go to the jail and get them. When I arrived, they seemed surprised to see me.

"We were looking for you," they said. "You have been preaching Christianity, so you're now going to spend time here in prison."

As they went through my things, they read my transcript, my diploma, and some spiritual materials, including a postcard that said, "The virgin will conceive and give birth." The communist leader who controlled the district gave me a strange look.

"You had a good grade in biology," he said, looking over my transcript. "So, how can you believe a virgin gave birth?

They kept me in the jail for about ten days. The students brought me meals, and I shared my food and the gospel with other prisoners. Eventually, my students protested loudly—they needed me to be released, so that I could teach them math. There was no other math teacher in the school to replace me, and math was important to their future.

So, I was released.

A few months later, a new principal was appointed to my school. His wife—who was a math teacher—joined him. As a result, I was transferred to another school in need of a math teacher, about fifteen miles away. We had established a fellowship in the community I was leaving, so I trained those I had discipled the previous year to lead the group. God had already prepared us to multiply.

Before I arrived at the new school, however, some of the parents had heard that a preaching Christ-follower was coming, so they began warning their children to not be persuaded to believe in my preaching! Yet by the grace of God, we managed to plant another fellowship in this new town. I kept teaching mathematics and sharing the love of Jesus with my students and coworkers. Once more, I was sent to prison for sharing the gospel, this time for two weeks, with eight other disciples.

Nothing stopped me from sharing the love of Christ. However, I had a problem that God brought to light when I was thinking of getting married and establishing my own family. He had to deal with my prejudices and teach me to see people as Jesus sees them. You see, I was from one tribe but serving as a schoolteacher among a different tribe. The one thing I was sure about was that I was not going to marry one of them!

When my spiritual mentor pressed me about this issue, I said, "No way. I can't marry someone from this tribe."

His first response was, "If you do not love these people, then stop serving."

Well, that changed my perspective. And eventually, I met and married my wife who is from that tribe! Next to my salvation, I am most thankful for my wife, my marriage, and the four wonderful children God has blessed us with, who also love and follow Jesus. I thank God for godly mentors, who helped me to become who I am today by challenging me to depend on the Author and Finisher of our faith, Jesus, the true Vine.

Where Do Your Loyalties Lie?

During those years under communism, when the church went underground in Ethiopia, we were completely dependent on the Lord. We had no formal structure and were entirely led by local Ethiopian believers. Those conditions actually helped multiply the body of Christ! In one instance, a church building was taken over by the government, but all the people who had attended in that building began their own home fellowships, starting as many as fifty or sixty worshipping communities. It was like the seed that fell on the good soil and produced a hundred-fold, sixty-fold and thirty-fold.[2]

In the denomination I belonged to, the church went underground in 1982 with about five thousand members. When we were free to come back together in 1992 and restructured, there were over fifty thousand believers—in less than ten years! When they closed the church buildings, every home became a church, and every believer became a disciple-maker. Think what would happen if each one of us took seriously the commission to make disciples, who will go on to make disciples.

Everything came down to a question of allegiance: Were we going to remain loyal to our corrupt government, or would we accept that our allegiance, our loyalty, our responsibility was to Christ and his body, the church? For us, it was an easy question to answer.

Our allegiance was with Christ. Everything we did, every choice we made, was for him.

What about you? Where is your primary loyalty? Is it to being a citizen of the US or Canada, or to political ideals or parties? Maybe your loyalty is wrapped up in your job or profession, pursuing a dream, better education,

---

[2]   Matthew 13:8.

or more money. It may be tied to your family, or a church culture that is focused on maintaining its comfort and the status quo, rather than extending the kingdom of God until everyone has an opportunity to choose and follow Jesus.

Or is your allegiance to the Vine? Remember Jesus' words in John 15:1–5 (italics ours):

> "I am the true vine, and my Father is the gardener. He cuts off every branch in me that bears no fruit, while every branch that does bear fruit he prunes so that it will be even more fruitful. You are already clean because of the word I have spoken to you. *Remain in me, as I also remain in you.* No branch can bear fruit by itself; it must remain in the vine. *Neither can you bear fruit unless you remain in me.*
>
> "I am the vine; you are the branches. If you remain in me and I in you, you will bear much fruit; apart from me you can do nothing."

When Jesus says, "Remain in me," in effect he's putting two options in front of us: You can remain in him, or you can depart from him. You can't do anything meaningful on your own, he explains, and if you remain in him, you'll bear much fruit.

But if we're going to do this, if we're going to commit our lives to the call of Christ, if we're going to become vessels of multiplication, our allegiance must be completely to him. And why would our allegiance be anywhere else, when our true citizenship is in the kingdom of God?

Jesus calls us, "Follow me."

Following him requires dedication and wholehearted commitment. Out of loving obedience we die to ourselves, renounce certain lifestyles and habits, and give up many things. But there are also many privileges that come with becoming a follower of Christ. We receive the blessings of eternal life and the gifts of the Holy Spirit. We get to live an abundant life overflowing with joy and hope!

The history of the church is a beautiful, passionate story of flawed people who dedicated their lives to sharing the good news of the kingdom of Jesus Christ no matter the consequences. They pursued intimacy with Christ above all other things. They set the foundation for a church that would multiply exponentially over the coming millennia.

What will we do with this heritage that has been given to us?

Will we renounce old allegiances and take up a new allegiance to Christ the King and his kingdom? Will we make an unbreakable promise to put him above all other things in our lives, and will we share this passion with others within our reach?

The door is open before you, a door that leads into an invigorating, exciting, meaningful life in which you have influence and take part in the beautiful work God has prepared for you.

You have been given the opportunity to grow deeper in him as a disciple of Jesus so that you might have extraordinary influence in this generation.

It comes back to that question.

What are you going to do about it?

A Commitment to Live as a Global Disciple of Jesus

Living as a disciple of Jesus begins with a serious decision to put your faith in Jesus Christ for salvation and eternal life. But it also requires daily, moment-by-moment choices determined by our primary allegiance and loyalty to Christ.

At the end of each Global Disciples training, we invite the participants to sign a pledge. This pledge is not a commitment to the organization we call Global Disciples but rather a commitment to "live as a global disciple of Jesus Christ." We see a "global disciple" as a whole-hearted disciple of Jesus who lives with a global perspective to advance the kingdom of God.

In our twenty-five-year history, a version of the pledge has been signed by tens of thousands of disciple-makers around the world. We encourage everyone who signs it to seek accountability in the five key commitments of the pledge and to live them out in community with fellow disciples. Each commitment helps us to make the decision again every day, bringing us back to Jesus, reminding us that our primary loyalty must be to him.

This is the pledge:

I am a global disciple of Jesus.

My allegiance is to Jesus Christ. He is the Living Word of God, as revealed by the Holy Spirit and through the Bible.

I want to do my part so everyone has the opportunity to hear the good news of Jesus and to choose if they will believe and follow him. My desire is to see each person experience the transforming love of Jesus, live in the fullness of the Spirit, and enjoy God forever.

As a participant in a local expression of the global body of Christ, I am united in heart and purpose with sisters and brothers of many nations, ethnic groups, languages, and churches to glorify God and to make him known.

I believe my part as a global disciple of Jesus Christ is to:

- Pursue intimacy with God as my Creator, Provider and Father, through Jesus my Savior, Lord and Friend.
- Love others as Jesus loves them, relating and serving as witnesses in word and deed, loving even enemies.
- Pray diligently for people who do not yet know Christ, especially those unreached with the good news of Jesus.
- Live generously as a steward of all God has entrusted to me, being an ambassador of our generous God.
- Rely on the Holy Spirit and the Word of God to lead, guide and empower me to live, love and serve for God's glory.

God is longing for a restored relationship with every person he has created in his image and likeness. He sent his own son, Jesus, to redeem and restore all creation. The death and resurrection of Jesus marks the tipping point in human history: evil has been defeated, and a new world is coming. It is imperative that people from every tribe and every language have an opportunity to hear the gospel, which comes by knowing and trusting Jesus as Savior and Lord.

How will this happen?

It is only possible when disciples of Jesus take their responsibility seriously to go and make disciples. When we become obedient and do our part, the healing of our broken world will take place from the inside out as the love of Jesus brings reconciliation to individuals, then families, communities, and the world.

Jesus spent three years with a core group of a dozen people, teaching them to love as he loved, to live as he lived, and to serve as he served. God is on a 24/7/365 mission to redeem the broken world through ordinary disciples who make disciples and plant churches ... until the whole world has an opportunity to hear the gospel.

We are all called to do our part as disciples of Jesus so that Christ's redeeming love will touch the lives of our neighbors and bring healing in our world. This is not only the work of a professional pastor or evangelist, but of every disciple from every nation and many vocations doing their part to share the love of Christ with neighbors and coworkers.

If you are willing to do your part, we encourage you to make this personal commitment to live as a global disciple of Jesus by pursuing intimacy with him daily; loving people as he loves them; praying persistently, especially for those who do not know Jesus; living generously; and relying on the truth of the Word of God and the power of the Holy Spirit.

Extraordinary Influence

Remember our brother Ronel, the man who took the gospel into least-reached places in North Africa? The man who inspired us to ask, "What are you going to do about it?"

In three years with Global Disciples, Ronel's influence had a significant impact for Christ in Chad and Niger, and he then followed God's leading to make inroads in Sudan. He expanded our vision and grew a team of leaders—ordinary disciples who are passionate for Jesus and have extraordinary influence in the region.

In April 2019—a year after he joined our Global Disciples staff—Ronel was planning to join our annual staff gathering in Kenya. But he suffered from diabetes and became ill during a church service. Ronel was taken to a local hospital, and we kept in touch with his doctors from our meeting in Kenya. They said Ronel was doing well and should be out of the hospital in a day or two.

Then late one morning, he had trouble breathing. He needed oxygen, but the hospital had run out of oxygen tanks, so they put him in a car to take him to another hospital across town where he could get the care he needed.

Ronel died on the way.

The call came at lunchtime informing us that he was gone.

Our whole Global Disciples family was devastated.

We often think back to the first times we met Ronel. Tefera met him in 2016 at the first directors training we held in Cameroon, where we hoped to launch multiplication into the surrounding regions. Ronel showed up from Chad, and Tefera immediately recognized Ronel's heart for those who haven't heard of Christ. One day he led a moving and sincere devotion, and Tefera knew right away—*this guy gets it.*

I met Ronel the next year. When we talked about mission, I could see that this was his life. This was what he was all about.

This was where he belonged.

Even today, it brings tears to my eyes to think that he is gone. He had such a heart for those far from Christ. What an inspiration!

Ronel's legacy will continue for a long time in the lives of those he introduced, directly and indirectly, to Christ. And his question continues to echo in our ears.

Where there is a sense of urgency, things get done. Where there is no sense of urgency, an organization, a project, or a church will tend to stall.

Did you know that more than fifty thousand people die every day who have never heard the good news of Jesus in a way they could understand and respond to?[3] That's fifty thousand people every single day! We can't address this desperate need by relying on anything less than the power of the Holy Spirit as we step out in obedience to however God is calling us to connect with our neighbors who don't yet know him.

I go back to the question that started it all. What was it about the work we did as Global Disciples that enabled us to partner with the Holy Spirit and see so many people come to faith in Jesus?

---

[3] Worldometer, (n.d.), *Current world population*, www.worldometers.info/world-population/. [Retrieved September 21, 2021]; Todd M. Johnson and Gina A. Zurlo, eds., *World Christian Database* (Leiden, Boston: Brill, 2021).

I'm not sure that I could have articulated it at the time, but now I know.

It's simple obedience to the call of Jesus to live as his disciple, making disciples as we practice and teach others.

We seek to do this in the way of Jesus—teaching, reflecting, and applying. We keep Jesus as the center of our life and teaching. We open ourselves to the Holy Spirit's leading, making the Word of God our curriculum and building accountability with other disciples so that iron sharpens iron.

All these components that we practice and teach must be permeated with prayer and blended gently with a moment-by-moment attentiveness to the Holy Spirit. Combine and practice these in your life for a few months, a year, a lifetime, allowing God to keep it warm and active in your life, even as you pour it out into the lives of others.

When we respond to his call to engage in these biblical essentials, becoming a disciple and living our life with God by dying to ourselves, developing a kingdom mindset, aligning our life with the Word of God, we gain new perspectives. And as we deepen our intimacy with Christ, and our relationships with others, the Holy Spirit can bring about real change through us and enable us to see all that is in store for us, as we do our part, responding to that question, "What am I going to do about it?" Then we can and will experience healthy, God-inspired multiplication.

What if Ronel hadn't asked himself, "What am I going to do about it?" If he hadn't joined Global Disciples or taken the gospel to Libya and other difficult-to-reach African areas like northern Sudan, how many people would not have heard the good news? How many Christ-followers and churches would not even exist?

Ronel's decision to consider the question and to answer it with action not only opened new regions in Chad to the gospel, but opened doors to an entire region of North Africa.

What if he had simply sat back and waited, or kept doing what he had been doing?

Ronel accomplished what he did by the power of the Holy Spirit in only three short years with Global Disciples. Jesus started a worldwide movement with twelve primary disciples in the same amount of time.

While you have breath on this earth, you can have extraordinary influence, but you need a sense of urgency and a willingness to follow Christ, no matter the cost.

We've all been given a path forward with the nine essential components laid out throughout this book, a way that will lead us to have extraordinary influence when we respond in love and obedience to God's calling. In his teaching, Jesus clearly mentioned that the thief (Satan) came to steal, kill and destroy, but he (Jesus) came to give us abundant life.[4] When we die to ourselves and surrender all to the Lordship of Jesus, we begin to experience that fullness. Jesus modeled what it means to live our life to its fullest—living his entire earthly life for the glory of the Father.[5] As we continue to abide in Jesus and walk in step with the Spirit, we find satisfaction and meaning in life. There is no greater satisfaction than to hear Jesus say at the end of our earthly life, "Well done, good and faithful servant" (Matthew 25:21).

Only one thing remains, and it comes to each one of us, as it did to Ronel, in the form of a question. And the way you choose to answer that question could be the difference between life and death for someone.

What are you going to do about it?

---

[4] John 10:10.
[5] John 17:4.

Appendix A

The Essential Components

The Global Disciples' model for training and multiplying disciples is framed around the following essential components.[1] We see them as foundational to multiplying Christ-like disciples who know him and love him, growing together, and representing him as witnesses and ambassadors in this world.

Discipleship is not limited to personal enrichment; it encompasses loving and serving God and people. There may be resistance to surrendering all, but for those who have died to self and live under the Lordship of Jesus, there is real joy and freedom in living an authentic life that glorifies the Lord and attracts people, as Jesus did.

---

[1]   In our Global Disciples training model, we focus on these components in the following order:

Intimacy with God; Right Relationships; Holy Spirit Empowerment; Biblical Truth; Dying to Self and the Lordship of Jesus; The Kingdom and the Church; Evangelism and Compassion; World Mission; and Multiplying Churches

Chapter 1 Essential Component:
Dying to Self and the Lordship of Jesus:
Surrendering All and Receiving Abundant Life

- The Cost of Discipleship (Luke 9:57–62; 14:25–33; John 12:24–25; Acts 4:2–3)
- Dying to Self (Philippians 3:10–14; Romans 6:5–14; John 12:24–25; Galatians 2:20)
- Whole Life Stewardship and Fullness of Life (1 Peter 4:10–11; 2 Corinthians. 9:6–15; Psalm 24:1; John 10:10)
- The Lordship of Christ and Obedience (Philippians 2:5–11; Romans 10:9; John 14:15–21)

Chapter 2 Essential Component:
The Kingdom and the Church:
Participating in God's Redeeming Work

- The Kingdom of God and Our Citizenship (1 Peter 2:9–12; James 4:1–4; Matthew 3:2; 4:17, 23; Luke 4:5–6)
- Our Place and Identity in Christ (Romans 8:37–39; John 1:12; 2 Corinthians 1:21–22; 5:17–20)
- Fellowship and Accountability (Psalm 133:1–3; Hebrews 10:24–25; Acts 2:42–47)
- Functions within The Body (Romans 12:3–8; 1 Corinthians 12:22–27; Ephesians 4:1–16)

Chapter 3 Essential Component:
Biblical Truth:
Understanding, Receiving, and Communicating the Word of God

- The Authority and Power of Scripture (2 Timothy 3:16–17; John 17:17; Isaiah 55:8–11; Hebrews 4:12–13)

- Biblical Interpretation and Application of the Word (2 Timothy 2:15; Acts 8:30–33; 2 Peter 1:19–21)
- The Practice of Bible Study (Joshua 1:6–9; Psalm 1)
- The Centrality of Jesus Christ (Luke 24:25–27; John 1:1–3; 5:39–40; Colossians 1:15–20, 28–29; Hebrews 1:1–3)

Chapter 4 Essential Component:
Intimacy with God:
Knowing and Loving God

- Solitude: Time Alone with God (Mark 1:35; 6:31, 45–46; Luke 4:42)
- Prayer and Fasting (Matthew 6:5–18; Philippians 4:6–7; Isaiah 58:6–8)
- Worship and Confession (John 4:24; Romans 10:9–10; 1 John 1:5–10; James 5:16)
- Meditating on Scripture and Listening to God (Joshua 1:8; John 10:14–15, 27)

Chapter 5 Essential Component:
Holy Spirit Empowerment:
Receiving and Walking by the Spirit

- The Divine Person of the Holy Spirit (Acts 5:3–4; 1 Corinthians 3:16; 6:19–20; John 14:17; 15:26; 16:8–15)
- Gifts and Ministry of the Holy Spirit (1 Corinthians 12:4–11; Romans 12:4–7; Ephesians 4:11–13)
- The Fruit of the Holy Spirit in Daily Living (Galatians 5:22–26; Ephesians 5:8–11; 2 Corinthians 3:18)
- The Role of the Holy Spirit in Spiritual Battle (Ephesians 6:10–18; 2 Corinthians 10:3–6)

Chapter 6 Essential Component:
Evangelism and Compassion:
Seeing as He Sees and Responding as He Would

- Sharing the Gospel and Witnessing (John 4:28–2; Mark 5:18–20; Romans 1:16; Acts 1:8; 1 Corinthians 2:1–5)
- Compassion for Those in Need (Matthew 9:35–38; 25:31–46; Luke 4:18–19)
- Evangelism and Making Disciples (Matthew 28:19–20; Mark 16:15–16)
- Christ's Commission (Matthew 22:37–39; 28:18–20; Mark 16:15–18)

Chapter 7 Essential Component:
Right Relationships:
Experiencing and Imparting Healing, Wholeness, and Peace

- Right Relationship with God (Genesis 3:1–8; John 3:16–18; Romans 5:6–10; 1 John 1:9)
- Forgiveness and Inner Healing (Matthew 5:23–24; 6:12–15; 18:21–35)
- Christ-like Relationships with One Another (John 13:34–35; Colossians 3:12–17; Ephesians 4:29–5:7)
- Being Ambassadors of Reconciliation (2 Corinthians 5:18–21)

Chapter 8 Essential Component:
World Mission:
Reaching Least-Reached Peoples to the End of the Earth

- God's Heart for all Nations (Genesis 3:8; 12:1–3; Luke 4:24–30; Revelation 7:9–11)

- Understanding and Reaching Across Cultures (Matthew 9:9–13; John 1:1–14; Acts 16:6–10)
- World Religions and Cults (Matthew 24:14; Colossians 2:16–23; Acts 19:26–27; 2 Corinthians 11:1–5)
- The Uniqueness of Jesus Christ (John 1:1–3; 14:6; Acts 4:12)

Chapter 9 Essential Component:
Multiplying Churches:
Disciples and Fellowships Multiplying Themselves

- God's Design for the Body of Christ (1 Corinthians 12:27; Matthew 16:18; Ephesians 3:10)
- God's Desire for Multiplication (Genesis 1:28; 9:7; Acts 6:7; 9:31)
- Challenges to Multiplying Fellowships of Disciples (Acts 2:42–47; 16:6–10; Mark 1:38–39; 1 Corinthians 9:19–23)
- Practical Lessons from the New Testament Fellowship of Disciples (Acts 13:2; Luke 10:1–7; 1 Corinthians 9:19–23; Matthew 28:19; 2 Timothy 2:2; Romans 10:13–17)

Appendix B

Listening to God

Steve and Evy Klassen are the founders and executive directors of MARK Centre, a retreat and training center in Abbotsford, British Columbia, Canada. They have had a profound impact on the lives of our Global Disciples team as they taught and modeled healthy patterns and disciplines of listening to God. You can find their books at www.markcentre.org/steveklassen/bookstore/.

Their book, *Your Ears Will Hear: A Journal for Listening to God*, provides an inspiring and refreshing guide to knowing God's voice and cooperating with him. It invites readers on a journey of listening to God speak through his Word and by his Spirit. As the Klassens write:

> Four truths undergird this book:
> God speaks today.
> Our ears can and will hear.
> What God speaks transforms us.
> As people listen to God it inspires others.
> As we have given ourselves to embracing and multiplying a lifestyle of listening to God, we have witnessed these four truths at work again and again; God speaks to people, they listen and hear, and as they believe and receive what

he is saying, their lives are changed. Then the miracle of multiplication goes to work; the words they hear inspire others around them. People who listen to God and allow his word to transform them are an inspiration wherever they go.

The parable of the Sower and the Seed (Mark 4:1–20) describes this process as clearly as any in the New Testament text we are aware of, which explains why Jesus said emphatically to his disciples, "Don't you understand this parable? How then will you understand any parable?" In the telling and the explanation of the parable the words "listen" or "hear" (same word in the Greek) occur eight times. Jesus calls his disciples to a life of listening. What will they listen for? In the explanation of the parable is something Jesus calls "the word" or "the message."

The link Jesus makes between the seed and "the word" opens up our understanding and expectation for how a lifestyle of listening to God can transform us. The words we hear will be like seeds in our hearts and minds. It may start small, but it will grow into something beautiful. As we listen to God's words it has the potential for amazing impact. Just as seeds have life packed into them, so do the words that God speaks into our hearts…

As you listen to God and allow his word to transform you, you will come to know his character more intimately. Just as friendships deepen through being together and speaking and listening to each other, your relationship with your Creator deepens as you hear God's voice. One of the reasons God speaks is because he wants to be known. As you listen there are different aspects of God's character that are going to become real to you over time.[1]

Another resource for learning to listen to God is the daily blog, "Listening to the Word" from Randy and Marjorie Friesen (listeningtotheword.blogspot. com). It's also available on the YouVersion Bible app as the one-year plan, "Listening to the Word." Each entry includes a highlighted passage from the reading, a brief reflection, and a prayer. Randy is the Global Disciples vice president for leadership development.

---

[1]   Steve and Evy Klassen, *Your Ears Will Hear: A Journal for Listening to God* (Abbottsford: Mark Center, 2011) 6–7.

Appendix C

Jesus is the Only Way: The Uniqueness of Christ

Jesus is the only way. If God's heart is for all people, and the stories of the Bible are to make God known, how will we make him known in our generation?

We live in a postmodern world that believes there is no absolute truth; that truth is relative. In seminary, I (Tefera) remember a heated debate about whether all religions lead to God or not. One of my friends said, "Yes, all religions lead to God. But except for one—the way of Jesus—the rest lead to God's judgment." I responded with AMEN!

How can we present the uniqueness of Jesus Christ? For us, as disciples of Jesus Christ, the Word of God is our guide in our journey and ministry. And in God's Word, the uniqueness of Jesus Christ is evident. We must be familiar with this truth and ready to speak this to those who are asking:

- The God of the Bible is the only God who manifested himself through his own son, Jesus Christ (John 3:16)
- Jesus is different from all false gods (Jeremiah 10:6; Deuteronomy 6:4; 1 Corinthians 8:46).
- Jesus is not one of many ways to God—he is *the only way*. No one

can come to God except through Jesus Christ (John 14:6; Acts 4:12)

- Jesus is the only One who has been conceived by the Holy Spirit and born of a virgin (Isaiah 7:14; Matthew 1:18–25; Luke 1:26–38)
- Jesus is the only One who is eternal (Colossians 1:17; John 1:1–3; 8:57)
- Jesus is the only One who is God incarnate, God in human flesh (John 1:1–18; Hebrews 1:1–3; 2:14–18; Philippians 2:5–11; 1 Timothy 2:5–6)
- Jesus is the only One who is the visible image of the invisible God, who is fully God and fully man (Colossians 1:15–20; 2:9)
- Jesus is the only One who lived a sinless life that qualified him to become the Savior (2 Corinthians 5:21; Hebrews 4:15; 7:23–28)
- Jesus is the only One who forgives sin (Mark 2:5–7)
- Jesus is the only One who has conquered death (1 Corinthians 15:3–8)
- Jesus is the only One who will come back to judge the world (2 Timothy 4:1; Revelation 19:11)

The Lausanne Movement have some helpful statements to describe the uniqueness of Jesus Christ:

> We affirm that there is only one Savior and only one gospel . . . Jesus Christ, being Himself the only God-man, who gave Himself as the only ransom for sinners, is the only mediator between God and people.[1]
>
> We are called to proclaim Christ in an increasingly pluralistic world. . . . In the first century too there were "many gods and many lords." Yet the apostles boldly affirmed the uniqueness, indispensability and centrality of Christ. We must do the same. . . .
>
> We nevertheless are determined to bear a positive and uncompromising witness to the uniqueness of our Lord, in His life, death, and

---

[1]   Lausanne Movement, Lausanne Covenant – section 2, The Uniqueness and Universality of Christ, 1974. https://lausanne.org/content/covenant/lausanne-covenant#cov.

resurrection, in all aspects of our evangelistic work including inter-faith dialogue.[2]

To understand the uniqueness of Christ, we must also look at the living, triune God who has revealed himself in the Bible to all of humanity. The Scriptures of the Old and New Testaments tell us clearly that God is eternally one and, as the living and sovereign One, he differs fundamentally from all false gods (Deuteronomy 6:4f; Psalm 115:3–7; Isaiah 44:6; Jeremiah 10:6; 1 Corinthians 8:4–6).

In his tri-personal nature as Father, Son, and Holy Spirit, God is one perfect and complete community of love in himself who has fulfilled his re-demptive plan in the person of his only begotten Son, Jesus (Genesis 1:1f; John 1:1f; 15:26; 1 John 4:9; 2 Corinthians 13:14).

God created humankind in his own image (Genesis 1:27). He is the Creator, Redeemer, Sustainer, and Renewer, the origin and ultimate pur-pose and goal of every human being.

God the Father has spoken to us through Jesus Christ the Son as his special revelation of salvation (Hebrews 1:2). By the initiation of the Father (John 1:1–2; 3:16), through his incarnation by the Holy Spirit, and by his atoning death, Christ reconciled humanity to God and redeemed us from the destructive powers of sin, death, and the Devil (2 Corinthians 5:19; Ephesians 1:7f; Hebrews 2:14f).

The uniqueness of Jesus Christ, the only Son of God, demands a re-sponse. The necessity of personal belief, of placing one's faith in this unique One, is at the heart of the Christian gospel. Christ fulfills and completes all the aspirations of humanity. He comes as the Second Adam to restore sinful humanity and a broken world.

When people come to know Christ, they discover meaning and pur-pose, and their full identity is regained. While a decision to accept the free offer of salvation is crucial to evangelism, it must also affirm that this unique Savior offers not merely salvation as a work, but he also offers himself in a

---

[2]   Lausanne Movement, Manila Manifesto, Section 1 *The Whole Gospel*, clause 3, *The Uniqueness of Jesus Christ*, 1989. https://lausanne.org/content/manifesto/the-manila-manifesto.

transformational way. The whole purpose of the Christian life is to become like Jesus.

By Christ's bodily resurrection and ascension to heaven, God the Father has confirmed him as the only mediator between himself and humanity, and he has appointed him the universal Lord over all powers and authorities as well as Judge of the world (Matthew 28:18; Acts 10:36–42; 1 Timothy 2:5f). Therefore, eternal salvation or eternal damnation is determined by either turning to him in faith or by rejecting him (John 3:16; Mark 16:16).

Jesus is the only answer to our sinful human condition. Since the Fall in Genesis 3, humanity has been sentenced to eternal death: life without God (Luke 19:10; Ephesians 2:12). But Jesus has died for us, to reconcile us to God (2 Corinthians 5:19; Ephesians 1:7; Hebrews 2:14). That is the glorious truth we share with the world!

Appendix D

What's in Your Hand?

"What's in your hand?" This question is the core of Global Disciples' small business training, as we encourage a church planter or disciple-maker to look at the skills, assets, abilities, and experience God has put into his/her life that can be used to develop a business for ministry and sustainability. However, this question goes beyond business: What has God given to you or woven into your life so that you can build up and multiply the kingdom?

These key areas may help you discern "what's in your hand" for kingdom use and expansion. Ask the Holy Spirit to guide your heart as you consider these questions.

1. **Examine your relationships**. God has a purpose in the many different relationships he's brought to your life.
   a. Who are your friends?

   b. What is your circle of influence?

    c. Who connects with or shares your heart for others? Who gets excited with you?

    d. Who can connect you with the areas of influence, witness, or service you're interested in?

    e. What connections do you have to people or settings where the gospel of Jesus is needed?

    f. Who in your circles or networks can you disciple? Or who can help disciple you?

2. **Examine your gifts and skills.** God built into you a unique mix of things that bring value to your part of his mission.

    a. What are your skills? List what you do well with your hands, your mind, your heart; the physical, intellectual, experiential tools you are good at using.

    b. What are your strengths? This is where you excel or feel confident, creative, or fulfilled.[1] For example, you may have skills in motor repair, and one of your strengths is problem-solving.

    c. What are your spiritual gifts? See 1 Corinthians 12, Romans 12, and Ephesians 4. Spiritual gifts are given to benefit and build up the kingdom. How are you using your gifts in your local context?

---

[1] The Clifton Strengths Finder is an excellent tool for uncovering your strengths and how to use them effectively in all areas of life. https://www.gallup.com/cliftonstrengths/en/252137/home.aspx.

If you're uncertain about your gifts, ask a friend or pastor what they have observed in you, or they may have tools to help you discern and apply that gift.[2]

3. **Examine your opportunities.** These are openings from God to give you room to exercise your gifts or apply them to building kingdom influence. Ask God to alert you to these opportunities and give you the courage to step into them.
   a. Where do you interact with people the most?

   b. Do you have a network, business, or school association where you can be salt and light?

   c. Do you see a local and/or global need that could use your strengths, skills, and gifts as a disciple of Jesus?

   d. Is there something from your business or experience that could benefit others in the kingdom locally or in another part of the world?

4. **Examine your resources.** We all have resources that extend beyond our bank accounts.
   a. Finances: Consider your income, investments, property, business, home, equipment, etc. How can you use those to fulfill your kingdom work? Are you investing in what God is doing in your community, your church, and around the world? Can you help meet specific needs, using what God has entrusted to you?

---

[2] *Discover Your Spiritual Gifts* by C. Peter Maxwell (Bloomington: Chosen Books, 2012) is a widely used guide to spiritual gifts and includes questionnaires to help you discover and use those gifts.

b. Experience or Expertise: God is building experience—or expertise—into your life every day. How are you using that experience to build up other disciples? To reach those without Jesus? To meet needs? What can you pass along as a mentor or influencer?

c. Time: God gives us each twenty-four hours in a day. How are you investing your time? What percentage is focused on living as a disciple? Is there something you feel the Spirit calling you to, but you don't feel you "have the time"? What needs to change?

Remember, you have something to offer. God created you; he put these gifts in your hands and placed you perfectly to be part of fulfilling his purposes and mission in this world. This self-examination is just a beginning, an exercise to start engaging with Jesus in the work of his kingdom.

Appendix E

I Am a Global Disciple

Living as a disciple of Jesus begins with the decision to put your faith in Jesus Christ for salvation and eternal life. It also requires daily, moment-by-moment choices determined by your primary allegiance and loyalty to Christ. We invite you to consider making this pledge—not as a commitment to any organization, church, or group, but as a visible, concrete way of saying, "I want to live as a disciple of Jesus with a global perspective to advance the kingdom of God." Keep this pledge for your reference or share it with a friend or a discipleship group for greater accountability. You can also fill it out online at www.globaldisciples.org.

I am a global disciple of Jesus.

My allegiance is to Jesus Christ. He is the Living Word of God, as revealed by the Holy Spirit and through the Bible.

I want to do my part so everyone has the opportunity to hear the good news of Jesus and to choose if they will believe and follow him. My desire is to see each person experience the transforming love of Jesus, live in the fullness of the Spirit, and enjoy God forever.

As a participant in a local expression of the global body of Christ, I am united in heart and purpose with sisters and brothers of many nations, ethnic groups, languages, and churches to glorify God and to make him known.

To live as a global disciple of Jesus Christ, I make a commitment to:

- ***Pursue intimacy with God*** *as my Creator, Provider and Father, through Jesus my Savior, Lord and Friend.*
- ***Love others as Jesus loves them****, relating and serving as witnesses in word and deed, loving even enemies.*
- ***Pray diligently*** *for people who do not yet know Christ, especially those unreached with the good news.*
- ***Live generously*** *as a steward of all God has entrusted to me, being an ambassador of our generous Master.*
- ***Rely on the Holy Spirit and the Bible*** *to lead, guide, and empower me to live, love, and serve for God's glory.*

Name _____

Date _____

We recognize this is your personal commitment with God, but if you would like to let us know, please contact us online or by mail at Global Disciples, 315 W James St, Suite 202 Lancaster, PA 17603 USA. We will not make your personal info available to any person or entity beyond Global Disciples.

Acknowledgments

Writing a book is not a solo act. As the authors, we would like to gratefully acknowledge the many who have contributed their time, ideas, and energy to putting this into your hands.

Thank you, Shawn Smucker and Wendy Nagle, for helping us pull together stories and concepts, assisting in blending our voices, and giving shape and direction to the initial manuscript.

We deeply appreciate the work of Anna Robinson, Liz Andrasi Deere, and the 100 Movements Publishing editorial team in refining and fine-tuning this book with excellence; and Barbara Gerhart, our Global Disciples editor, for encouragement, wise counsel, and tireless labor in navigating changes and shepherding this project with us.

Kimberly Lapham and Sarah Kelley as our executive assistants made it possible for us to maintain our schedules, manage our workloads, and still get this book written. You've both been amazing.

Thank you, Sherry Lee and Barb Martin, with our Global Disciples marketing and communications team, for your expertise in communications and graphics, which have enhanced this book and its distribution.

And our Global Disciples executive team from four countries around the world have encouraged, supported, and blessed this endeavor—and the time we invested in writing. This is really your book as well, for it tells the stories we have experienced together.

We are deeply grateful for the thousands of church leaders, program directors, disciple-makers, church planters, and colaborers in the Great Commission who shared their stories and inspired us with their committed example to live as ordinary disciples with extraordinary influence. They are our heroes.

This book would never have been possible without the loving support, sacrifices, and patience of our wonderful wives, Marie and Hannah, and our families. They have been incredible sources of love, grace, and encouragement as we pursue our common calling, and together pursue loving the Lord with all our hearts, souls, minds, and strength. We are honored to be on this journey with you!

Recommended Resources

Global Mission

Brian Fickert and Steve Corbett, *When Helping Hurts: How to Alleviate Poverty Without Hurting the Poor or Yourself* (Chicago, IL: Moody Publishers, 2009).

Russell T. Hitt, *Jungle Pilot: The Story of Nate Saint, Martyred Missionary to Ecuador* (Grand Rapids, MI: Discovery House, 2016).

Steve Saint, *End of the Spear* (Carol Stream, IL: Tyndale House Publishers, 2005).

Fasting and Prayer

Bill Bright, *7 Basic Steps to Successful Fasting and Prayer* (New Life Publications, 1995).

Bill Bright, *The Transforming Power of Prayer and Fasting* (New Life Publications, 1997).

John Eckhardt, *Fasting for Breakthrough and Deliverance* (Lake Mary, FL: Charisma House, 2016).

Cindy Jacobs, *The Power of Persistent Prayer: Praying with Greater Purpose and Passion* (Bloomington: Bethany House, 2010).

John Piper, *A Hunger for God: Desiring God through Fasting and Prayer* (Wheaton, IL: Crossway, 2013).

Spiritual Gifts

Alan Hirsh and Tim Catchim, *The Permanent Revolution: Apostolic Imagination and Practice for the 21st Century Church* (San Francisco: Jossey-Bass, 2012).

Using Bible Study in Reaching Others

Use this guide as you meet to study the Bible: Discovery Bible Study, www.dbsguide.org.

Least-Reached People Groups

- **alliancefortheunreached.org**

An alliance of organizations focused on catalyzing a movement that unites churches, organizations, and individuals around the cause of reaching every unreached people group on earth with the gospel of Jesus Christ. Actively promotes Pentecost Sunday as the International Day for the Unreached.

- **athirdofus.com**

Take steps to bring awareness and help to the third of the world that needs access to the good news. (It is part of the Alliance for the Unreached.)

- **joshuaproject.net**

Functions as a wiki for accessible information on people groups, evangelization status, languages, etc.

- **mnnonline.org**

Provides current news and reports on the work of the global church, and those involved in mission, compassion, and supporting kingdom efforts.

- **operationworld.org**

Combines statistical data with a primary focus on prayer for the nations and people groups, and includes resources for personal, family, and corporate use.

- **worldchristiandatabase.org**

Provides comprehensive statistical information on world religions, Christian denominations, and people groups. (Subscription required.)

The following resources are available through **Global Disciples.org**

- "The Least-reached in Our Backyard"—Bonnie (from chapter two of this book) tells her story and offers insight into engaging least-reached people within North American settings.
- *Near-culture Ministry*—eBook from Galen Burkholder focused on the near-culture worker, the effectiveness and value of this strategy for reaching least-reached people.
- Global Stories—our blog packed with transformative stories from Global Disciples' partners and activity (similar to those in this book).
- Prayer resources—several resources are available to help you pray for the least-reached, and for the work of Global Disciples. If you're interested in developing an intercessors group to pray as part of our 24/7/365 prayer coverage, please contact pray@globaldisciples.org.

About the Authors

Tefera's identity is protected for security reasons.

Coauthors Galen Burkholder and Brother Tefera have invested their lives in equipping people to be influential, mission-minded disciples of Jesus Christ. Despite their radically different backgrounds, Galen and Tefera share a common passion to see disciples of Jesus engaged in making disciples who make disciples, until the knowledge of God's glory covers the earth as the waters cover the sea (Habakkuk 2:14).

Galen was captain of the Fellowship of Christian Athletes for his high school in eastern Pennsylvania and started in youth ministry in college. He invested seventeen years in youth and young adult ministry, discipleship-mission training, and sending teams cross-culturally before launching Global Disciples in 1996.

Growing up in Ethiopia, Brother Tefera embraced atheism and chaired the Young Communists Party in high school, before coming to faith in Christ at university. His math degree earned him a teaching position in an unreached area of northern Ethiopia. While teaching high school math, he helped to plant twenty-seven new fellowships of believers in eleven years and was imprisoned for his faith three times.

Both Galen and Tefera have graduate degrees in evangelism and church planting.

Since 2007, Galen and Tefera have worked side by side as leaders in Global Disciples. With the Global Disciples team, they serve over 1,450 clusters of churches in sixty-two countries and have helped launch more than 2,000 training programs. In the past decade, these training programs have seen over 400,000 new believers added to the kingdom, most of whom now worship in 19,000 new fellowships, planted mainly among people least-reached with the gospel.

Global Disciples:
Equipping People to Reach
Their Nations

A third of our world has
not yet heard the Good News of Jesus.

But we live in a time where many of those
are within reach of a local church

Through our simple
and effective strategy of training and coaching

Believers share the Gospel in their own nations and cultures

To multiply disciples and locally sustainable fellowships

As Global Disciples, we believe that every person should have an opportunity to hear and respond to the Gospel of Jesus Christ. That is why we exist. It's our vision and our passion.

So, we partner with clusters of local churches to develop practical training they can support through their own resources to equip near-culture workers. Our approach or model focuses on three phases of training that together activate and support the multiplication of disciples and new churches.

- **Discipleship-mission training** equips a disciple to go and make disciples and plant a church.

- **Small business training** provides the church planter with a means of support, and to have a presence or gain access to a community unreached with the Gospel.

- **Leadership training** equips the church planter so that a new fellowship grows and matures spiritually under Christlike leaders and mentors.

All training programs are owned and operated by a local church cluster. Global Disciples provides a percentage of training expenses as seed funds for the first three years but by year four, local resources fully support the training.

Global Disciples integrates prayer and worship coaching with our training model, to develop intercessory teams and worship leaders for trainings, outreach, and new fellowships.

The Global Disciples model is based on reproducing trainers who can train others. This equips the church in Africa, Asia, and Latin America to accelerate multiplication, reduces a reliance on North American trainers, and expands ownership of the vision to reach the least-reached with the Gospel of Jesus Christ.

In response to requests from church leaders in Africa and Asia to train their people in making disciples, Global Disciples launched this sustainable, reproducible discipleship training in 1996. Since then, we have grown from five training programs in three nations to over two thousand training programs in more than sixty countries.

Global Disciples activity is led and managed by continental staff close to the action; about 80 percent of our team lives and works in their home context outside North America. They are assisted by nine national foundations, comprised of business and professional leaders who are committed to promote, provide, and pray for Global Disciples in their countries. The North American team supports and promotes Global Disciples by building relationships with individuals, business leaders, and churches, inviting them to pray, give, and become advocates.

Get to know us at **globaldisciples.org**

CPSIA information can be obtained
at www.ICGtesting.com
Printed in the USA
JSHW022119130123
36248JS00002B/9

9 781955 142106